FERTILE GROUND IN MIDDLE LEVEL GENERAL MUSIC

Fertile Ground in Middle Level General Music guides music educators to inspire their middle level students (grades 5–8) to engage more deeply in the general music classroom, where students are given the opportunity to "try on" a range of roles: musician, composer, listener, and critic. The book outlines the Fertile Ground Framework, a teacher's aide for curricular decision-making that unites the middle level concept with the National Core Arts Standards while emphasizing the developmental needs and cultural identities of students. This resource-rich book provides teachers with an array of adaptable classroom support tools, including:

- Lesson sequences
- Activity ideas
- Teacher resources and worksheets
- "Do-Now" exercises

Featuring the real-world perspectives of thirteen music educators, *Fertile Ground in Middle Level General Music* is both practical and theoretical, presenting methods for creating rich, inspiring learning environments in middle level general music classrooms of all shapes and sizes, and highlighting the unacknowledged strengths that already exist therein. Focused on the aim of motivating students to pursue lifelong music learning, this book helps instructors find joy and excitement in teaching a wide array of musical topics to diverse groups of middle level music students.

Stephanie Cronenberg is Assistant Professor of Music and Director of Clinical Experience and Practice at Mason Gross School of the Arts at Rutgers, The State University of New Jersey.

FERTILE GROUND IN MIDDLE LEVEL GENERAL MUSIC

Stephanie Cronenberg

NEW YORK AND LONDON

First published 2022
by Routledge
605 Third Avenue, New York, NY 10158

and by Routledge
2 Park Square, Milton Park, Abingdon, Oxon, OX14 4RN

Routledge is an imprint of the Taylor & Francis Group, an informa business

Library of Congress Cataloging-in-Publication Data
Names: Cronenberg, Stephanie, author.
Title: Fertile ground in middle level general music / Stephanie Cronenberg.
Description: New York : Routledge, 2021. | Includes bibliographical references and index.
Identifiers: LCCN 2021020134 (print) | LCCN 2021020135 (ebook) | ISBN 9780367643805 (hardback) | ISBN 9780367643775 (paperback) | ISBN 9781003124245 (ebook)
Subjects: LCSH: Music--Instruction and study. | Music--Instruction and study--Outlines, syllabi, etc. | Education, Elementary.
Classification: LCC MT1.C85 F47 2021 (print) | LCC MT1.C85 (ebook) | DDC 780.71--dc23
LC record available at https://lccn.loc.gov/2021020134
LC ebook record available at https://lccn.loc.gov/2021020135

ISBN: 978-0-367-64380-5 (hbk)
ISBN: 978-0-367-64377-5 (pbk)
ISBN: 978-1-003-12424-5 (ebk)

DOI: 10.4324/9781003124245

Typeset in Interstate
by KnowledgeWorks Global Ltd.

For you who have chosen this book with the hope of making change within your middle level general music class, I hope this book inspires your journey.

CONTENTS

PREFACE

The writing of a book is an unusual and prolonged journey. While this project began in 2018 and much of the text was drafted in 2019, the editing and refinement of this text was interrupted in 2020 by twin events that cataclysmically shifted education in the United States and across the world: the COVID-19 pandemic and the ongoing social justice and racial reckoning in the United States. As a result, music teachers have been forced to confront their assumptions about what counts as music learning, their preconceived notions about how music is taught, and whether the music curriculum at their school equitably serves all students. I could not ignore the impact of the events of 2020 on myself as a teacher, on the middle level music teachers with whom I worked, on my preservice students preparing to enter the profession, or on my writing of this book. The lesson plan sequences featured in Chapter 5 and 6 were developed prior to 2020 and based on the curriculum materials each teacher chose to share during the interview process. I hope that these lesson plans, newly contextualized within more recent events, are valuable to middle level general music teachers long afterward. As I write this, music education is shifting and evolving to accommodate virtual and hybrid learning as well as conversations about equity, social justice, and the inclusion of all students and all musical forms of knowing in the music classroom. These are not new conversations in music education, but they ring with a new urgency. My hope is that music teachers across the United States and beyond are able to pause, to confront their own limitations and implicit biases, to reconsider, and to reimagine what it means to cultivate a fertile ground for music learning both within and beyond middle level general music.

Stephanie Cronenberg
New Brunswick, New Jersey
February 2021

ACKNOWLEDGEMENTS

This book would not be possible without the music teacher participants who were willing to share their successes and challenges with me and with those who read this book. Thank you to Abby, Alexis, Danielle, Eric, Hannah, Holly, Jackie, Jessica, Katie, Lindsey, Nicole, Robert, and Tyler. You have helped shape this book into what it has become.

In addition to the music teacher-participants featured in this book, I would like to thank other middle level music teachers with whom I have worked. Thank you to Kristin, Jackeline, and Kiera who were willing and eager to improve their practice in middle level general music by trying out some of the materials featured in this book, and in doing so challenged me to clarify my ideas. In addition, thank you to Beth, Michael, Rachel, and Sarah whose stories of teaching middle level general music first catalyzed this project many years in the making.

My thanks go out to all of my past and present students at both the middle and undergraduate levels. To my middle level general music students, thank you for allowing me to work alongside you as you developed your musicianship and sought answers to your musical questions. To my undergraduate music education students, past and present, your questions, concerns, and desires for knowledge are why I wrote this book. Thank you for continually asking the tough questions and pushing me to think about what it means to be a music educator in an ever-changing educational climate.

The Fertile Ground Framework presented here is the result of conversations and feedback from many music educators who asked questions or initiated conversations at conferences and other professional events. Thank you also to the anonymous reviewers who pushed my thinking and challenged me to refine the Framework and consequently the shape of this book. I would also like to thank the team at Routledge for believing in this project and helping me see it through to fruition. This book was funded, in part, by a grant from the Rutgers University Research Council.

Several people contributed to the final stages of this book when I most needed inspiration. First, to Liv Headley who completed the graphic design for the Framework figures featured throughout this book. Their graphic design skills reenergized this project when it needed it most. I am eternally grateful to Liv for transforming my original idea into something both communicative and visually pleasing. Second, to Catherine Lugg and Marcia Gail Headley who, with fresh eyes, read the manuscript in its entirety and provided helpful recommendations and encouragement as this book neared the finish line.

Finally, and perhaps most importantly, a project of this nature is not possible without those who love and support you. While my close friends and extended family regularly asked about the progress of the book, it is my husband Mark Keitges to whom I am most grateful. Mark is an extraordinary editor without whom this book would be far longer and less clear. Not only has he put up with me on days when I could not form a coherent thought on any other topic, but he now knows more about middle level general music than any non-music teacher ought to know. Thank you, Mark for your continued love and support in all of my endeavors.

Introduction

Finding Fertile Ground

I wanted to be a high school band director; my own high school band director was retiring right after I finished my Master's and I applied for his job and didn't get it, which ended up being the best thing that's probably happened to my career.

—Eric

I always thought I'd be elementary, and then I got [a] job in high school. I did the musical theatre, I did everything, and I improved vastly at piano because—you had to. I thought I'd be doing high school for the rest of my life.... So, I'm very happy that I got laid off, because I feel like middle school is definitely, 100% the place where I belong.

—Nicole

I think it's because of my own immaturity, I don't think that I've ever quite grown up ... I just knew right away that I wanted to work with middle school kids; I knew it during my practicum work. Middle school's where it's at. I just knew.

—Robert

What is your journey to teaching middle level (5th–8th grade) general music? Perhaps you see similarities between your story and those of Eric, Nicole, or Robert, or perhaps not. Everyone's journey as a music educator is unique. If you have questions about teaching middle level general music as a preservice, early career, or experienced teacher, this book is for you. Whether you selected this book because you are hoping to challenge yourself in teaching that you love, learn more about the middle level concept you have heard mentioned in faculty meetings, or prepare yourself for a teaching assignment that is new and daunting, I hope you will find the joy in middle level general music that I, and the teachers featured in this book, have found.

This book is both a theoretical *and* practical resource for the teaching of 5th–8th grade general music. The theoretical framework I put forward, the Fertile Ground Framework, seeks to unite the fields of music education and middle level education. This Framework is one *possibility* for thinking about middle level general music. It is certainly not the *only* Framework that might

DOI: 10.4324/9781003124245-1

be used. In uniting music education and middle level education, I am informed by democratic principles of teaching and learning articulated in the middle level concept, particularly from *This We Believe: Keys to Educating Young Adolescents* (NMSA, 2010; see also Bishop & Harrison, 2021). The Fertile Ground Framework should provide you with a visual tool and the language to talk to your principal and colleagues about the importance of general music to the young adolescents in your school.

While a theoretical framework for middle level general music is important, equally important is the practical application of the framework into the classroom. As teachers, sometimes we just want to know how to make tomorrow better! Throughout the book, I share real-life stories and perspectives—my own and those of 13 music teachers—to illuminate the Fertile Ground Framework. Lesson plans, activity ideas, worksheets, and other resources based upon the practices of the teachers interviewed for this book are included throughout, and may be used, reused, and modified (with attribution) as best fits your classroom. I share these teaching resources not to endorse them as "the best" resources available for middle level general music, but rather to illustrate aspects of the theoretical framework and to provide inspiration for your own classroom. Each teaching circumstance is different. What may prove successful in one classroom community may completely flop in another classroom. Varied perspectives are important because students and learning communities across the United States and beyond each have their own unique needs.

In my work and research as a music educator, I have regularly heard the term "dumping ground" used to refer to certain classes, particularly general music (Cronenberg, 2020a). Perhaps you have also heard this term used. Its use within schools and the field of music education is prevalent and demonstrates deficit thinking (Delpit, 1995; Valencia, 1997) about students and learning. A "dumping ground" attitude does not affirm the teachers or the students in middle level general music classes and often places unnecessary barriers between music teachers and their administrators, colleagues, and students. Yes, there are challenges to teaching middle level general music (some of which will be discussed later), but deficit thinking hinders educators and their students. Just because students cannot always choose to enroll in our general music class does not mean that they are "dumped" into our classroom as a last resort, are lacking in some fundamental way, or possess no desire to be musically inspired. This attitude sets up a negative relationship between ourselves and our students before we even meet them. Students who enroll in general music (required or otherwise) are being given a gift—the gift to try on a musician-, composer-, arranger-, listener-, and/or critic-identity—and to see if any of these identities inspires them to future musical learning. The title of this book, *Fertile Ground in Middle Level General Music,* pointedly inverts the phrase "dumping ground," language I seek to eradicate from the field.

As music educators, it is important that we face the challenges of middle level general music with a positive outlook. We need to critically examine the curriculum and pedagogy currently used and to consider changes that will meet students' developmental needs, improve learning outcomes, and increase engagement. Middle level general music, whether called music exploratory, music technology, or by some other name, deserves attention and teachers willing to reframe their expectations, their attitudes toward their students, and their view of themselves as music educators. Middle level general music is not about flashy concerts, winning contests, or producing high level performances. Middle level general music is, however, about inspiring all students to engage more deeply with music. Bringing the ideas of the middle level concept into music education discourse provides one avenue for creating a fertile ground in middle school general music and for extolling the unacknowledged "fertile grounds" that already exist in music classrooms of all shapes and sizes. My hope is that this book will inspire music educators to find their own joy, excitement, and wonder in teaching a wide array of musical topics, concepts, and skills to students who possess varied and diverse musical interests, knowledge, and abilities.

A Few Important Terms

As we begin our journey, it is important that we share a common vocabulary. Throughout this book, I will use a few terms from middle level education that may be unfamiliar.

In this book, the term **middle level** refers to any and all learning that occurs during fifth, sixth, seventh, or eighth grade. Middle level might refer to the students, the school, or the learning environment. The more common term "middle school" is misleading because it most commonly denotes a specific kind of school building serving students in grades six through eight. Rather, the term middle level encompasses the fifth, sixth, seventh, and eighth grades (in the United States, students who are typically between the ages of 10 and 15), regardless of the school building they attend.[1] While many middle level students attend traditional middle schools, many others attend schools also serving elementary or high school students (McEwin & Greene, 2011). My use of the term middle level over middle school is intended to include *you*, the music educator who teaches students at this age, wherever you may teach. If you do not teach in a named middle school, you may not regularly use the term middle school, but your fifth, sixth, seventh, and/or eighth grade students are still middle level learners.

The phrase **young adolescent** refers to any young person between the ages of 10 and 15. Broadly defined, adolescence is the period from puberty through independence, whenever true independence might arrive. Using this definition, many (but certainly not all) undergraduate students might still be classified as adolescents due to their financial dependence on their parents/guardians. It is important to distinguish the young adolescent or middle level learner from the older adolescent as young adolescents have specific developmental traits and fewer freedoms than adolescents old enough to drive or vote. The term young adolescent is sometimes used interchangeably with the term early adolescent (Mee & Haverback, 2016), but for the sake of clarity, I will use young adolescent throughout this text unless I am quoting another author.

The **middle level concept** is a common term used in middle level education. It refers to the philosophical foundation of the middle level movement which began in the 1960s.[2] The foundational premise of the middle level concept is the importance of designing education for young adolescents around their specific developmental needs (Brazee, 2005). According to John Lounsbury, one of the founders of middle level education, "the concept's ideals and recommendations are direct reflections of its two prime foundations, the nature and needs of young adolescents and the accepted principles of learning, both undergirded by a commitment to our democratic way of life" (2009, p. 32).

The influential position paper ***This We Believe: Keys to Educating Young Adolescents*** (hereafter *This We Believe*)[3] is the most prominent expression of the middle level concept (NMSA, 2010). This document, like many of the guiding documents in music education, has been revised several times by leaders in middle level education. The version used most prominently in this book is the 2010 version. An updated version, entitled *The Successful Middle School: This We Believe*, was published in 2021, just as I finished writing this book (Bishop & Harrison, 2021). Where appropriate, I have integrated the 2021 version, as much of what is stated therein parallels my argument here. Primarily designed for the practitioner or school administrator, *This We Believe*'s exposition of the middle level concept assists school leaders in focusing their institution's philosophical frameworks and curricular structures and addressing young adolescents' developmental needs and multi-faceted identities within a democratic framework.

Finally, I define **middle level general music,** here and elsewhere (Cronenberg, 2020b), as *developmentally appropriate music learning for all young adolescents, music learning that inspires students to continue learning (formally or informally) in music*. Middle level general music, particularly those courses that are required by schools and districts, may indeed be a student's final experience within a music classroom (Burton, 2012; Giebelhausen, 2015; McAnally, 2016). It is important that middle level general music shows young adolescents that they can be intelligent and capable performers, creators, and/or consumers of music, regardless of whether they continue formal music learning. Many middle level students will continue their musical journeys outside of the formal classroom in garage bands, on their mobile devices, in their communities, as online creators, or in some other form yet unimagined. Our goal should be to captivate and inspire students so that they choose to continue learning music as they see fit, armed with tools to better understand the music with which they choose to engage.

Can you imagine a middle level general music classroom derived from these definitions? What would the music classroom look like? How would it sound? How would it differ from what you remember about your own music learning experiences? This book will not offer one singular answer to these questions. It will, however, ask you to think about how you might make positive changes in your classroom in order to be better attuned and responsive to the interests, needs, identities, and developmental evolution of the middle level learners in your school community, and inspire the students with whom you work to continue their life-long music learning experiences.

Voices from the Field

The 13 music teacher-participants featured in this text helped to shape this book through the stories of experience they shared with me over two years. These teachers were selected based on their responses to a survey I conducted as part of my dissertation research (Cronenberg, 2016). At the time when they completed the survey, they indicated a willingness to be contacted for future research and their responses to the survey suggested success and confidence in teaching middle level general music. Prior to summer 2018, I had not spoken to any of the teachers who I interviewed for this book. I initially interviewed 24 teachers and selected 13 based on the rapport established and the unique perspective each provides. In sharing their stories here, I do not intend to imply that each teacher is the perfect model to follow or even that I agree with their perspectives. Drawing on John Dewey's theory of experience, Barrett and Stauffer describe experience as "shap[ing] who we are, how we know, and the meanings we make of our worlds" (2012, p. 4). *Your* experience as a reader adds a layer of interpretation to all that I present here. Each reader will have his/her own opinion of each of these teachers' perspectives, and this is how it should be. Throughout this text, I provide you with an interpretive space (Gadamer, Weinsheimer, & Marshall, 2004) to read, reflect, and draw your own conclusions about the perspectives, experiences, and approaches of each teacher. How does what is shared here resonate (or not) with your own experience? What might your story of experience add to this conversation?

Beginning in summer 2018 and extending through late 2019, I interviewed each teacher three times using Seidman's (2013) three-interview model derived from phenomenological research. Following Seidman's model, the first interview focused on the teacher's journey to arrive at teaching middle level general music. The second interview focused on the teacher's current practice during which teachers were asked to review a series of middle level curriculum and pedagogy terms, to select the terms that they felt most represented their general music practice, and to discuss these terms along with a curricular unit or lesson sequence they had chosen to share. Finally, the third interview asked the music teacher to make meaning of his/her practice through reflection and provide feedback on early drafts of this text and the lesson-related materials presented herein. Because the third interview occurred over a year after the first two interviews and because they were being asked to review several documents, teachers were given the option to respond in writing rather than through an oral interview. Four teachers chose to respond in writing and one teacher chose not to respond. All other teachers were interviewed via Skype or phone in alignment with the previous interviews. All interviews were recorded and transcribed. Analysis was cyclical and occurred after each interview as well as across the three interviews.

My story as a music teacher stands alongside those of the teachers featured in this book. Currently, I am an assistant professor of music focused on music education at the Mason Gross School of the Arts at Rutgers, The State University of New Jersey. While I attended a traditional Bachelor of Music Education preservice program, my background as a music educator is less than traditional. For a total of seven years, I taught fourth through eighth grade general music at two different independent (private) all girls schools (one economically advantaged and the other with far fewer resources) in two different states and regions of the United States. In between these two schools, I worked for four years at a choral non-profit organization that provided music education experiences to students and professional development to teachers in the District of Columbia's public schools. I acknowledge this here because it is important for readers to know my background and to know that the participants featured in this book were selected to provide perspectives and experiences different from my own.

Middle level general music is taught in schools of all forms (religious private, independent, charter, and public) in the United States and taught by teachers with varied backgrounds, experiences, and musical specialties. My goal is to show a spectrum of possibilities for middle level general music within the theoretical framework put forward in this book. For this reason, my own experiences are balanced with those of the teacher-participants, ten of whom obtained certification by the traditional bachelor's degree route, while three obtained certification by alternative means. Just over half of the participants hold master's degrees, many because it is required for promotion in their state. Of the 13 participants, 11 work in public schools, 1 in a charter, and 1 in a religious private school. Seven of the participants identify as vocalists, five identify as instrumentalists, and one identifies as both. All 13 teachers taught some combination of 5th–8th grade general music during 2017–2018 and 11 did so during 2018–2019. These teachers range in teaching experience from 5 years to over 20 years and they teach in the following US regions: New England, Mid-Atlantic, Midwest, Southwest, and West. I hope that you as the reader find at least one voice, one participant's experience, that resonates.

Throughout my career, my focus and interest has remained on general music, specifically at the middle level. I have always found young adolescents energetic, engaging, spontaneous, hilarious, eager to learn, and fun. I love challenging them to think deeply and listening to their passions. It is my love of this age group and of general music that sustains me in this work.

Two short stories help to illustrate moments when I experienced clarity regarding my interest in middle level general music:

Story One: In my junior year as a music education major, I remember a meeting with a member of the faculty to discuss my upcoming student teaching placement. He told me that he had arranged a band placement for me (my primary instrument was bassoon) and I immediately felt a sense of dread. I remember looking at him and saying, "I want to teach general music, particularly middle school. I don't want to teach band." I am not sure why we had never had this conversation prior to this moment, but it certainly took him by surprise. Thankfully, he was able to change my placement and I experienced both elementary and middle school general music during student teaching.

Story Two: In my first teaching position, I was teaching fourth through seventh grade general music at a school that served grades 3-12. I easily gravitated toward the 5th-7th grade classes as I felt most comfortable interacting with the older students. At that school, I was assigned to attend the elementary level (3rd-6th grade) faculty meetings, but one day I attended the meeting for middle level teachers (at our school, 7th-8th). Suddenly, I felt comfortable in a way I had not in the elementary meetings. The things that were discussed in this meeting and the way in which the teachers communicated and cared about students resonated deeply with me. Of course, elementary teachers do this too, but the discourse and mood seemed different to me as a young teacher. Perhaps this was due in part to the people in the room, but I think that is important—there is something indescribably unique about teachers who love teaching middle level students. I knew that this was where I belonged.

The music teacher-participants featured in this book each have their own stories of their journeys to the middle level and general music. This introduction began with short excerpts from Eric's, Nicole's, and Robert's experiences, and teachers share their perspectives throughout this book. My hope is that you are able to put your own experiences next to theirs and add a new voice to the conversation about middle level general music. Your voice matters as much as theirs. Regardless of how we arrive at a teaching assignment involving middle level general music, I hope that we can all agree that young adolescents offer something special to the experience of teaching. I hope the passion that I, and the teachers featured here, share for working with middle level students rings true throughout.

Briefly, I introduce you to the middle level music teachers who, through their participation in interviews, helped to shape this book. Quotes and curriculum materials from the 13 teacher-participants are used throughout this text to highlight important points and to demonstrate the different ways teachers are successful in teaching middle level general music. Further details regarding their school communities, student population, and general music curricula can be found in the Appendix. Pseudonyms are used to allow teacher-participants to describe their experiences freely without fear of harming their careers, thus their specific schools and states are not named. Teachers are listed alphabetically by pseudonym and what follows describes their 2017-2018 responsibilities.

Abby teaches middle school choir and general music at a 6–8 affluent suburban school in the Midwest.

Alexis teaches seventh and eighth grade general music, a high school music appreciation course, and non-auditioned middle school and high school choirs in a small Midwestern farming community in which grades K-12 are all housed under one roof.

Danielle teaches kindergarten through eighth grade general music along with choral and instrumental ensembles at a K-8 charter school in the Northeast.

Eric teaches general music at a 5–8 school in a small suburban district in the Northeast while concurrently pursuing his doctorate.

Hannah teaches general music, choir, and a musical theatre class at a 7–9 school in an affluent school district, the largest in her Western state.

Holly teaches seventh grade general music and a before-school choir at both 7–8 grade schools in a medium-sized district in the Midwest.

Jackie teaches general music and band at a K-8 arts-focused school while serving as the district fine arts coordinator in her small suburban K-8 school district in the Southwest.

Jessica teaches general music and orchestra at a 6–8 school in a large, diverse, suburban district in a Mid-Atlantic urban center.

Katie teaches general music, drama, and choir at a 6–8 school in a large suburban school district in New England.

Lindsey teaches choir and sixth through eighth grade general music in a small 6–8 grade school in a preK-8 suburban district outside a major urban center in the Midwest.

Nicole teaches sixth through eighth grade general music and choir at a 5–8 school in a small rural district in a Mid-Atlantic state.

Robert teaches a combined seventh and eighth grade advanced general music class, along with band, orchestra, and choir, at a 6–8 arts-focused school in a college town in a Western state.

Tyler teaches second through eighth grade general music, as well as band and choir, at a preK-8 Catholic academy in a major Mid-Atlantic urban center.

Notes

1 Within education, there is a debate regarding the best learning community for middle level learners. Some scholars maintain that academic rigor and achievement is lowered when students move from an elementary building to a middle school building. However, the research is mixed (see Carolan & Chesky, 2012; Rockoff & Lockwood, 2010).

2 For those interested in the historical evolution of the term "middle level," please see Valentine, Clark, and Clark's (2016) entry in the second edition of the *Encyclopedia of Middle Grades Education*.

3 First published in 1982, *This We Believe* was originally a professional guidelines position paper for the then fledgling National Middle School Association (now called AMLE) founded in 1973 (NMSA, 2010). Much like the national standards and other music education position documents produced by the National Association for Music Education (NA*f*ME), this document serves as a "touchstone" statement of precepts for the middle level education community.

1 The Fertile Ground Framework

> The moment of disquiet, the instance of unsettling, and the recognition of certainties troubled may be the very times and spaces where insight takes root—the places of fertile ground.
>
> (Barrett & Stauffer, 2009, p. 2)

This journey to find fertile ground in your middle level general music classes begins by recognizing the fertile grounds that already exist. Where have you seen fertile ground develop in your own practice? Do you see it in the student who struggles and later succeeds? Is it in the process and products of group projects? Or in the student who returns years later to say thank you? How about in the principal who visits the classroom and suddenly realizes the impact you have on students? Or the delight on a student's face when you share a common musical interest? Regardless of the struggles you may face, fertile ground already exists within your own practice.

Looking for existing fertile ground may also help you to see more clearly where fertile ground is possible, but not yet cultivated. In gardening, weeds must die before the ground is ready for seeds to take root. The same might be said for teaching. Ineffective practices, curricula, or attitudes may need to be altered or removed before fertile ground can emerge.

The fertile ground in middle level general music for which I advocate may require an unsettling, a shift in thinking, and a deep reconsideration of those aspects of music education you consider most important. Randall Everett Allsup, music education faculty at Columbia University's Teachers College, argues "that music teachers in public schools are endowed with an obligation to alter—to (re)form, to (re)musick—the quality and character of their musical forms to ensure that student life and learning is enlarged, deepened, and enriched" (2016, p. 23). It is through this lens that we begin to cultivate fertile ground.

Whether you work in a public, private, or charter school, engaging students by deepening and expanding their understandings of themselves, others, and their place in the world through musics ought to be a high priority. Allsup's (2016) charge asks all of us as music teachers to think beyond our own experiences with music(s), our own definitions of music learning, and our existing conceptualizations of a music teacher's role within the classroom—to imagine something new, something beyond the conservatory or ensemble model, something specific to our own contexts, something student-centered, something democratic.

DOI: 10.4324/9781003124245-2

Democratic Grounding

The present moment in education within the United States, with its focus on standardized learning and testing, often prevents administrators and teachers from cultivating democratic learning communities in which all students' identities are welcomed and their learning needs addressed (Elliott, 2016; Michelli & Jacobowitz, 2016; Wall & Wall, 2016). While a standardized education has the guise of an equal education, the reality is that standardized education is one-size-fits-all, not an education that democratically meets the needs of all. The emphasis in standardized education on all students meeting or exceeding specific standards often results in students with specific learning needs being excluded from music learning due to required courses labeled generically as "remediation" or "tutoring." These reasons, among others, are why Allsup (2016) and other music education scholars (see DeLorenzo, 2016; Woodford, 2005) call for music educators to rethink music education democratically.

The idea of integrating democratic principles into education is not new. Educational philosopher John Dewey (1916) wrote thoughtfully on this subject in his book *Democracy and Education*. Yet, as Paul Woodford (2005) points out, democratizing music education has faced many challenges, including the emphasis on auditioned ensembles, the primacy of Western classical music, and the authority of the conductor. Although the quest for democratic music education is imperfect, I believe that ideas from democratic education may aid music teachers in the cultivation of fertile ground for middle level general music.

As stated in the Introduction, I define *middle level general music* as developmentally appropriate music learning for all young adolescents, music learning that inspires students to continue learning (formally or informally) in music. While there is no single definition of general music in the music education literature (Haldeman, 1988), most definitions have coalesced around two democratic characteristics: the inclusion of comprehensive and diverse musical experiences, and the teaching of all students (Abril, 2016). As music educators, we must ensure that a democratically grounded middle level general music class meets the varied needs of all learners and provides a variety of music learning experiences that cultivate a desire for future music learning.

There are six democratic principles that I believe are worthy of being incorporated into all thinking about middle level general music.[1] Through the use of these six principles, teachers will be able to facilitate a general music experience that inspires young adolescents to continue music learning in the future, thus meeting my definition of middle level general music. Our responsibility as educators is to allow these six democratic principles to guide our choices, always remembering that our goal is to inspire these students toward their own future musical identities.

Democratic Principle #1: Educating the Whole Student

The basic tenet of the middle level concept is that learning environments for young adolescents are responsive to their developmental needs and multifaceted identities. While you can never know everything about your students, developing knowledge of your specific students as whole persons helps you reach your students musically, connect their learning to their lives, and provide a firm democratic foundation upon which to construct a learning environment. When learning environments for young adolescents educate the whole student, they are positive and engaging places to learn and grow.

Democratic Principle #2: Integrating Students' Perspectives

As young adolescents mature and develop the ability to think abstractly and be reflective, they need and desire a personal connection to their learning. Since it is essential that students are actively and purposefully engaged in music learning, middle level educators should integrate students' perspectives into the classroom. This shift in thinking places more responsibility for learning on the students and requires a change in the teacher–student relationship within the classroom.

Democratic Principle #3: Helping Students Connect

Students should understand how learning in one classroom within the school connects to other areas of their lives within and beyond the school. Connections should be made both through cross-curricular or integrated music learning and learning designed to be relevant to students' own lives. While young adolescents are ready to begin making these connections for themselves as they develop musical independence, they need teachers to model this connection-making process.

Democratic Principle #4: Encouraging Growth

In order to cultivate, within young adolescents, a desire to continue learning musically, it is vital we scaffold learning experiences so that students begin to take more responsibility for their own learning. This encouragement of growth helps challenge students in their musical knowledge and skills, but in a safe and protected environment where they can experiment and test their own limits through activities that encourage both exploration and challenge. In addition, evaluative feedback through authentic and intentional assessment extends this principle by furthering students' independence as music learners.

Democratic Principle #5: Including Comprehensive and Diverse Musical Experiences

General music is democratic because a wide variety of musical knowledge, content, skills, and genres can and should be included in a general music classroom (Hedden, 2002). Music education researcher Carlos Abril argues that "if the musical experiences in school music are singular and rigid, they fall outside of the concept of general music" (2016, p. 15). Comprehensive and diverse musical content should allow students to experience the four artistic processes articulated in the 2014 US National Core Arts Standards: performing, responding, creating, and connecting (SEADAE, 2014a). Whether you choose to cover American rock, Caribbean drumming, Cantonese opera, and/or Western classical music in your general music class, comprehensive and diverse musical content is a longstanding principle of general music in the United States (MENC, 1994). This book provides some *possibilities* for comprehensive and diverse music learning, but these examples are limited and are *not* the *only* content that might be covered.

Democratic Principle #6: Teaching All Students

General music is democratic because no student, in principle, is excluded from enrollment or participation. This sets general music apart from auditioned ensembles or music courses that require a set of prerequisite skills. General music is for everyone—the student who has taken 10 years of private piano lessons to the student who recently transferred from a school that did not offer music in the curriculum (Hoffman, 1981). While inclusion of all students is a foundational democratic principle of general music, a music classroom of this nature critically requires curricular and pedagogical differentiation. In educating all students, it is equally important to include and motivate students with cognitive, physical, or emotional exceptionality as it is to motivate and challenge those who remain unchallenged perhaps because the planned musical content is too rudimentary.

A Framework for Middle *Level* General Music

Drawing on the six democratic principles outlined earlier, in this section I present my Framework (see Figure 1.1) for middle *level* general music. In the introduction to their 1996 book *Strategies for Middle-Level General Music*, June Hinckley and Suzanne Shull suggest that "general music teachers at the middle level provide the all-important bridge between required general music instruction for all elementary students and traditionally elective music study for high school students" (p. 1). While I agree with Hinckley and Shull's statement, I believe middle level general music provides a bridge between elementary general music and whatever form(s) of formal or informal learning students might choose both during and beyond high school. For me, this is an important distinction. Middle *level* general music inspires students to continue learning and

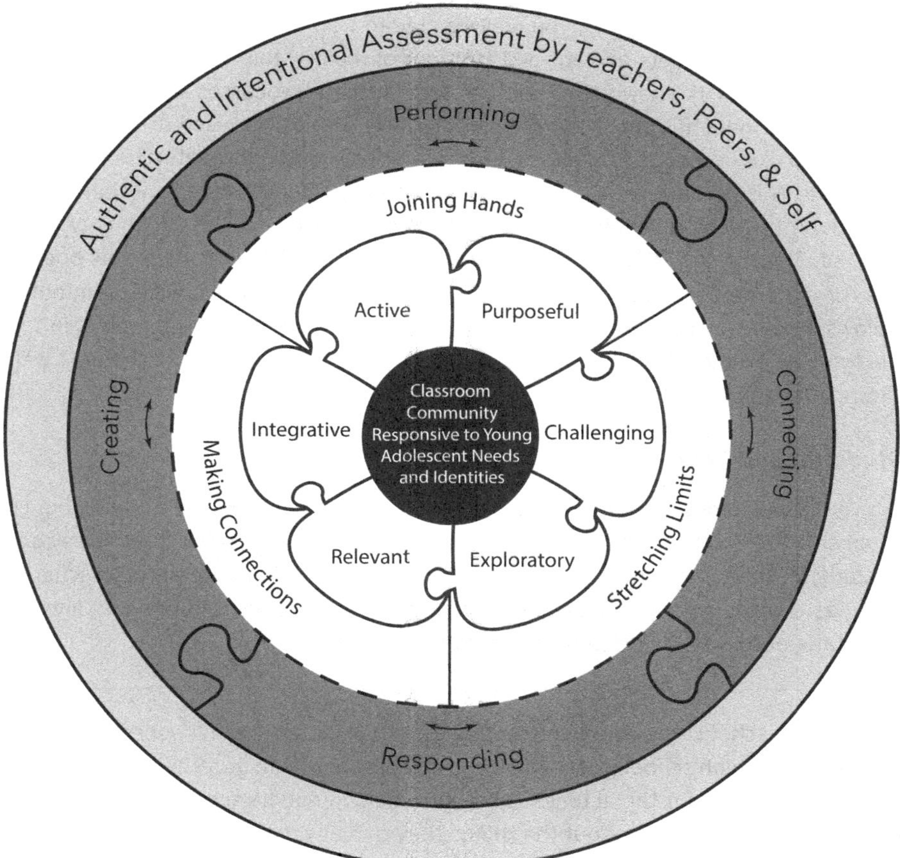

Figure 1.1 The Fertile Ground Framework

engaging in music, both during their formal education and throughout their lifetime. Middle level general music is not only ensemble preparation, though certainly some students will be inspired to join school or non-school ensembles as a result of their participation in middle level general music. In order to meet this goal of inspiring ongoing student learning, we must construct general music classroom communities that are developmentally appropriate and accessible to *all* young adolescents. The Fertile Ground Framework is *one* possibility for constructing such a middle level general music learning community, not the *only* possibility. Notwithstanding, I do hope that this Framework leads you to think differently about finding and cultivating fertile grounds within your own classroom.

In my work with practicing music teachers, one challenge faced by most who teach middle level general music is the absence of tools to guide decision-making. To my knowledge, no framework that unites music education and middle level education currently exists to guide middle level general music curricular and pedagogical decisions.[2] My hope is that you find the Fertile Ground Framework, and its foundation in democratic principles, useful for your own work. I do not intend for every music teacher to use the Framework in the same manner, but I hope that my discussion of the Framework and the curricular examples provided by the teacher-participants in this book will germinate new ideas. In addition, I believe that a distinct advantage of the Framework is that it provides you with language to discuss with administrators and colleagues about why middle level general music is important to the mission and purpose(s) of your wider school community. Using the Framework in these ways, you may be able to transform not only your general music classroom, but also the understandings and attitudes of those within your school community.

The Fertile Ground Framework brings the four artistic processes (creating, performing, responding, and connecting) of the National Core Arts Standards (used in the United States) together with six key concepts expressed throughout the middle level literature, including the 2010 version of *This We Believe*. The Framework diagram presented here is designed to provide a visualization of how to think about and enact general music through the lens of the middle level concept. The Framework diagram also helps to organize the sections of this book. As you progress through the book, you move from the center of the Framework diagram outward. In what follows, I briefly explain the Framework and how it overlays onto the chapters in the book. Then I provide an example lesson sequence to illustrate its use. Subsequent chapters will examine various components of the Framework in more depth.

The Students and Their Classroom Environment

At the core of the Framework, represented by the center of the flower, is a classroom community responsive to young adolescents' needs and identities. Based on the interviews conducted for this study, classroom community, particularly the relationship between the teacher and the students, has evolved into an important unifying element of successful middle level general music. As Katie observed, this idea is central to her practice:

> For me, middle school is all about connecting with the kids, and I don't necessarily know if that's true at the high school level, I think you can probably be a good high school teacher and just be like all about the actual subject. But man, in middle school if you're not connecting with the actual kids about the things they actually do, you're [in trouble].
>
> –Katie

While other teachers used different language, the essence is the same: successful middle level teachers create a motivating, positive, and safe classroom environment specifically designed to support young adolescents wherever they are on their journey of development. Placed in the center of the Framework, all curricular and pedagogical decisions emerge from and are dependent on this classroom community that requires continual cultivation. This part of the model will be discussed in Part 1, Chapters 2 and 3.

Middle Level Pedagogical Essentials

White petals encircle the core of the Framework in the shape of a flower. There are six individual petals, one for each of the six aspects of middle level curriculum and pedagogy identified in *This We Believe* (NMSA, 2010). Here, the petals are paired to highlight how active, purposeful, integrative, relevant, challenging, and exploratory instruction can be fit together to produce middle level general music that joins hands, makes connections, and stretches limits. The petals are drawn as similarly shaped puzzle pieces to indicate that the order in which the petals are connected is interchangeable. In Part 2, Chapters 4–6, I will discuss the paired petals of the model in detail. In what follows, I briefly define the three pairs of concepts within the context of middle level general music.

Joining Hands

Middle level general music that strives to be hands-joined is both active and purposeful.

- **Active:** Students and teachers are actively engaged and participating in music learning, physically and cognitively. Active learning includes hands-on and minds-on collaborative, and/or student-directed, music learning.
- **Purposeful:** Students and teachers both understand the goal of the learning activity *and* are working together to achieve that goal. Students understand why they are asked to do something in the classroom or they work with their teacher to decide for themselves how best to meet the learning goal.

Making Connections

Middle level general music that strives to make connections is both integrative and relevant.

- **Integrative:** Music learning occurs in connection with other subjects and life beyond school. Teachers help students understand these connections, and students are asked to use knowledge and skills from other subjects within the music classroom.
- **Relevant:** Students understand the connection between what they are learning in music class and their own lives and experiences. Teachers identify and help students to answer their own questions or guide students in pursuit of their own interests and ideas about music.

Stretching Limits

Middle level general music that strives to stretch students' limits is both challenging and exploratory.

- **Challenging:** The learning tasks set for students stretch their abilities to create and perform music as well as their abilities to respond to music and make connections between music and other areas of their lives. Students are asked to master complex tasks and conquer multi-step projects. They are also asked to take ownership, responsibility, and leadership at various times.

- **Exploratory:** Music learning enables students to try new musical skills, learn about new topics, listen to new genres, produce new musical sounds on instruments, their bodies, and through technology, thus diversifying their understanding of the world of music. Students are allowed to try out new things and test the boundaries of their musical knowledge and skills with confidence that the teacher will support them when they struggle or fail.

The Four Artistic Processes

A shaded, rotating ring surrounds the paired petals. This ring is made up of four pieces representing the four artistic processes found in the 2014 US National Core Arts Standards (Standards). As you may know (if you teach in the United States), the National Core Arts Standards identify four artistic processes shared across all art forms. In music, these artistic processes are creating, performing, responding, and connecting. The Standards document labeled "Music" specifically articulates general music learning standards through grade eight (SEADAE, 2014c). These are the standards that will be used in the lessons and other materials throughout this book and are available online at nationalartsstandards.org (select "Music" from the "Standards at a Glance" menu to download the pdf). If you teach outside of the United States, please feel free to replace the Standards identified throughout this book with those used in your country. Likewise, teachers within the United States are welcome to replace the Standards identified here with your state's standards. The four artistic processes that shape the National Core Arts Standards and this book are broad aspects of music learning and can easily be adapted to your local expectations. Grade level Standards are associated with each resource in this book, but teachers need not feel bound to the grade level specified here.

Dynamically Combining the Artistic Processes and Pedagogical Essentials

The four pieces of the rotating ring are drawn as similarly shaped puzzle pieces to indicate that the order in which they are connected is interchangeable. The arrows in the diagram indicate that the shaded ring can rotate around the flower petals. The flexibility of the model allows the artistic processes to be aligned with any of the pedagogical essentials represented in the flower (and vice versa). In Part 2, Chapters 4-6, I will discuss the flexibility of the model in more detail and provide examples of lesson sequences and activities designed to focus on particular pedagogical essentials and artistic processes.

As with any puzzle, the strongest middle level general music occurs when all pieces are united through a learning sequence or unit. However, uniting all ten pieces may only be possible across the entire breadth of your general music course (rather than within one unit). Consider your entire middle level general music course, whether 12 days or 12 weeks in length. How might you integrate all puzzle pieces into the class you already teach? Which of the pieces do you already do well? Which pieces have you never considered? Which pieces are a struggle for you? What is the first step you might take to bring one or two new puzzle pieces into your classroom?

Assessment

The outer ring, which holds the model together, represents the authentic and intentional assessment necessary to create a cohesive middle level general music lesson, unit, or course. The use of intentional and authentic assessments, including teacher, peer, and self-evaluation, are emphasized as important in both the US National Core Arts Standards and *This We Believe.*

Assessment of student learning and growth is perhaps the place where these documents are in closest alignment. When students understand how and why they are being evaluated, assessment becomes more than data collection for report card grades or "student growth objectives;" it becomes authentic and intentional assessment to help students grow and guide teachers in enabling this growth. Authentic and intentional assessment in a variety of forms is key to shaping successful middle level general music. This aspect of the model will be discussed in more detail in Part 3, Chapter 7 and the Conclusion.

Flexibly Using the Framework

As a planning tool, the Fertile Ground Framework is flexible. It is meant to be used as a tool to help you evaluate where your middle level general music class is unbalanced or what changes might be made to make your class more successful. The Framework is not meant to be a fixed or directive tool that requires you to use all aspects at all times. While this book is linear, the Framework is not.

There are a variety of ways in which the Fertile Ground Framework might be used flexibly. Not only can the puzzle pieces move, be reordered, or be variously combined, but you might choose to read the Framework diagram from outside-in or inside-out, depending on whether you are respectively planning a unit or lesson or reconsidering your entire class. Outside-in planning using the Fertile Ground Framework could be used in conjunction with the "backward design" approach to planning advocated for in the Understanding by Design Framework (Wiggins & McTighe, 2005) used by many school districts. Alternatively, planning from the inside-out focuses more globally on course or school-year planning because you begin a semester or rotation period by getting to know your students, both their needs, interests, and desires as young adolescents and their musical skills, abilities, and aptitudes.

The Fertile Ground Framework also assumes that you have or are developing the skills necessary to be an improvisatory and reflective practitioner. As an improvisatory and reflective practitioner, I assume that my lesson plan designed using the Framework will change based on the responses I receive from my students, and that I will need to adjust in the middle of a lesson accordingly. I also assume that a beloved lesson plan or unit may need adjustments from year to year as I reflect on my own practice and get to know the students assigned to a particular class.

Keeping young adolescents at the center of the curriculum and pedagogy requires continual reflection on your teaching practice and a willingness to change in order to meet their needs. Are the various components of the Framework balancing in a way that is leading to successful and quality music learning for all students in the general music class? If not, changes can and should be made, both in the moment and in future planning. My hope is that the Fertile Ground Framework provides you with a tool to guide your reflection and self-improvement so that you can better serve the young adolescents in your charge.

Creating Music: The Framework in Action

Throughout this book, lessons sequences, activity ideas, and Do-Nows are presented as both possibilities for classroom implementation and as illustrations of components of the Framework in Figure 1.1. For each example provided, I identify the teacher or teachers who shared the particular example so that readers can consider the lesson sequence or other resource within the context of the teacher's described teaching circumstances. While modified for presentation in this book, the teacher(s) named on each resource have approved the write-up presented here as representing what they have tested and refined within their own classrooms. These resources are shared for the purposes of illustrating important components of the Framework and should be used for *inspiration* within your own classroom. While you might choose to implement these lesson sequences as presented here, I strongly encourage you to make modifications to fit your own circumstances. Just because a lesson worked for one teacher in his/her circumstances does not mean that it is the "best of the best" and/or that it will work for you. These lesson sequences are shared here to help you better understand how the Framework might be interpreted and used in your work. You may choose to apply the Fertile Ground Framework to lessons and units that already exist in your curriculum and/or use and modify those presented herein.

Lesson sequence 1.1 is presented to introduce the layout used throughout the text to both convey details of the lesson sequence and highlight the lesson's connections to the Fertile Ground Framework. The top of the lesson sequence includes basic information about the lesson: recommended grade level(s), approximate number of class days, essential question, materials, objectives, standards, and assessments. Then, the main steps of the lesson sequence are outlined in a level of detail appropriate for an inexperienced music teacher including a breakdown by each class day and suggestions for learning extensions. Finally, the lesson sequence ends with a Framework commentary. The Framework commentary begins with a modified Framework diagram that highlights the components featured in the lesson. This diagram is followed by brief descriptions that elucidate the pedagogical essentials, the artistic processes, and the authentic and intentional assessment components of the Framework featured in the lesson sequence.

Throughout this book, teacher resources are provided to help you implement the learning experiences described herein. The teacher resources that take the form of worksheets are meant not only to help explain the learning described, but also save you time as a teacher. Throughout this text, I advocate for adaptation of existing resources for your specific classroom circumstances and thus all worksheet teacher resources may be used or modified (with attribution).

When new lesson sequences are introduced in this book, I will pause briefly to highlight work in music education related to the artistic process from the US National Core Arts Standards that is most relevant to the lesson. These sections focused on the four artistic processes from the Standards are not meant to provide a comprehensive discussion of the particular artistic process, but rather to provide a brief introduction to the literature in music education, provide some perspective about the artistic process as it relates to middle level general music, and point interested readers to additional resources. Here, I will briefly discuss the artistic process of creating which is featured in the example lesson sequence below.

Artistic Process: Creating

Music education researchers have found that music teachers often avoid addressing the creating standards in their general music classrooms (Louk, 2002). Some teachers suggest that this avoidance of the creating standards is because of a lack of personal experience with composition, improvisation, or arranging while other teachers suggest that limited classroom time and access to appropriate compositional resources such as technology are contributing factors

(Kennedy, 2002; Menard & Rosen, 2016; Strand, 2006). Those music teachers who specialize in jazz or composition have a distinct advantage over their colleagues due to personal experience and preparation in composition and improvisation. Regardless of your own level of experience in composition, I hope that you will agree with music education researcher Maud Hickey (2012) who argues for why students need experience in musical composition:

> Music instruction in schools sometimes includes too much focus on grammar and little room for creativity. If we want children to read better, we should have them write stories; if we want children to become poets, we should ask them to write poetry. Similarly, if we want our students to be fulfilled and creative musicians, then they must be given many chances to compose—without the rules of "grammar" impeding their way. We simply need to let them compose and improvise. Creative activities will open the door to a much deeper understanding of all of the concepts, the "rules" that should be taught in music education. (p. 15)

The importance of the artistic process of creating in helping students develop their total musicianship cannot be overlooked. Music is one of the creative arts, and yet the field's emphasis on concerts and contests means that performing "correctly" and at a "high level of quality" often takes priority over students experiencing creativity in music class.

Drawing on research on composition, music education researcher Jackie Wiggins (2007) suggests that teachers developing composition assignments "need to recognize, honor, and validate (a) the holistic nature of the composition process, (b) the intentional and cognitive nature of the conception and generation of musical ideas, and (c) the need for personal agency within the sociocultural and musical contexts" (p. 466). Composition projects, whether notated in traditional Western notation, notated with invented notation, or un-notated, require a process-oriented way of thinking about music education. Students need time to be creative, to explore, and to develop their ideas independently or with classmates, while applying their existing musical knowledge to the compositional task. Once students have had this creative and imaginative time, teachers can guide them to improve their compositions through elements of music theory appropriate to the students and/or the compositional task. It is in the process that learning occurs, not necessarily in the presentation of the finished product.[3]

Hickey (2012) suggests that a "compositional prompt" can serve as inspiration for a composition assignment. Using the compositional prompt as inspiration, students might then learn about form, musical elements, or what Hickey calls "big elements" (such as unity/variety, tension/release, and balance). The inclusion of and order in which students learn about these "grammatical" aspects of the compositional process will depend on the particular compositional project being conducted.

Hickey's model for a composition curriculum could easily be used alongside the four process components of the general music creating standards, specified in the US National Core Arts Standards: (1) imagining, (2) planning and making, (3) evaluating and refining, and (4) presenting (SEADAE, 2014c). Any compositional prompt will require students to imagine before planning and making, while learning about form, musical elements, and/or big elements might require students to evaluate and refine their initial work to make musical improvements. The composition process is cyclical. In any given compositional activity, students might move through each of these four process components and return to any as needed to complete the assignment.

Composition activities enable students with years of musical knowledge to employ pre-existing skills in a new forum while simultaneously allowing those with limited musical knowledge and skills to contribute at their own level (Menard, 2013). Creation activities also require students to employ performance and responding skills, so while composition projects may take some class time, remember that students are simultaneously advancing their skills in performing and listening. Thus, music creation activities allow students to employ varied musical skills and are naturally differentiated for classrooms with a wide range of musical abilities.[4]

Lesson: Color Poem Composition

To briefly show how each component of the Fertile Ground Framework might be used in a lesson sequence, I present a composition activity I used in my seventh grade general music class (see Lesson Sequence 1.1 and Teacher Resource 1.1). The composition project presented here uses Hickey's (2012) idea of a "compositional prompt" to inspire musical creation. The compositional prompt is a book of poems called *Hailstones and Halibut Bones* by Mary O'Neill (1990).[5] Each poem focuses on a particular color (red, green, black, etc.) and includes vivid illustrations using the color of focus. The purpose of the color poems is to serve as lyrical and musical inspiration for the students' compositions. Without access to this book, it is hard to imagine the imagery that these poems conjure. Here are a few stanza examples:

- "White is a marshmallow/and vanilla ice cream/and the part you can't remember/In a dream." (O'Neill, 1990, "What is White?")
- "And in the fall/When leaves are turning/Orange is the smell/Of a bonfire burning ..." (O'Neill, 1990, "What is Orange?")
- "The sound of black is/'Boom! Boom! Boom!'/Echoing in/An empty room." (O'Neill, 1990, "What is Black?")

Your school or local public library may have a copy of *Hailstones and Halibut Bones* for you to use or you can purchase it fairly easily online. The artwork in the 1990 edition is more vibrant than in the original edition, so use it if you can. My middle level students were inspired by the poetic language and artwork in this book. Their discussions of how to recreate the poem musically were energetic and enthusiastic. Please be mindful of students with visual impairments or those with a form of color-blindness. These students will need special support, a modification to the assignment, or perhaps an alternative activity. A similar composition activity might be done with other poetic resources, works of visual art, or children's books specifically selected to evoke musical moods.

As will be discussed in the next two chapters, projects like this group composition project are only possible because of the classroom community developed with your students. It is critical that you know your students' needs and cultural identities, develop relationships, and collaboratively agree upon classroom norms in order for student-centered pedagogical strategies to succeed. When conducting this lesson sequence, I observe students working but only step in when asked or when a group is struggling to work productively. This cultivation of student independence is possible because the classroom norms are well established and every student feels safe to experiment musically.

Lesson Sequence 1.1
Color Poem Composition

Basic Lesson Information

Grade Level:

- 7th

Approximate Number of 45-Minute Periods:

- 4-6

Essential Question:

- How can a color be conveyed musically?

Materials:

- *Hailstones and Halibut Bones* by Mary O'Neill
- Classroom instruments
- Teacher Resource 1.1
- Markers/crayons
- Poster-sized paper

Primary National Core Arts Standard:

- MU:CR2.1.7.a: "Select, organize, develop, and document personal musical ideas for arrangements, songs, and compositions within AB, ABA, or theme and variation forms that demonstrate unity and variety and convey expressive intent" (SEADAE, 2014c, p. 2).

Objective:

- Given classroom instruments and a color poem, the students will be able to work together as a group to create and document a composition with a beginning, middle, and end (or other form specified) that conveys the poem's mood.

Formative Assessment(s)/Check-ins:

- Completion of brainstorming questions on Teacher Resource 1.1
- Daily teacher check-ins

Summative Assessment(s):

- Performance of composition for the class
- Group composition notation

Lesson Sequence

Day 1:

- Introduce the new project by showing students the illustrations in *Hailstones and Halibut Bones* and occasionally reading stanzas aloud.
- Read the students the final poem, "The Colors Live" which describes the expressive potential of colors.
- Discuss the poem's meaning and ask them what they think lines like "and colors sing" and "each has a taste/and each has a smell" mean (O'Neill, 1990, "The Colors Live").
- Ask them whether they associate specific colors with specific sounds, tastes, or smells.
- Ask the students if they have ever heard of the term "synesthesia." Depending on the time of year, students may have learned about this in science class. If not, define synesthesia as an involuntary association between one sense and another and explain that this is a unique condition and only some people experience.
- Have the students pair and share to tell their neighbor their favorite color, two items they associate with their favorite color, and what they think their favorite color sounds like.

- Introduce the composition project to the students.
    - o Tell the students that they will be working in groups to analyze one of the color poems and to create their own musical composition using at least some of the words of the poem.
    - o Allow students to choose any instruments including those they might bring from home.
    - o Emphasize that every student is required to participate musically either with their voices, body percussion, or on an instrument.
- Provide students with Teacher Resource 1.1.
- Write the color poem options on the board and have students self-select the color group they want to join.
- Some groups will work organically and will not find Teacher Resource 1.1 useful. Alternatively, some groups will work systematically through the worksheet questions before proceeding. Be flexible regarding collecting the worksheet depending on what you see is happening in your classroom during the first lesson. Take the lead from your students and potentially respond differently to each group based on their needs.

Day 2-4

- Begin the second class period by reviewing the project.
- Provide the students with large pieces of paper/poster board and markers/crayons.
- Ask the students to use the paper and markers to document their composition.
    - o Students do not need to use standard notation, but they need to document their composition so that they can remember it for the next class.
    - o Students can invent notation that helps them remember, so long as they can explain it to someone else.
    - o Ask that any words from the poem that are used as lyrics are also written on the paper at the appropriate place in the composition.
    - o Encourage the students to decorate their paper with drawings/decorations related to their chosen color.
- Allow class time for students to work on their projects as a group.
- As class proceeds, check-in with each group to see if they need help, guidance, or suggestions. Try not to steer students' compositions; rather, provide helpful hints or suggestions such as: "have you tried ..." or "what about ..."
- As needed, ask groups to perform their "draft" compositions for you in order to assess their progress and provide any help that might be needed.

Day 5 (and 6 if necessary)

- Based on progress in the previous class, you will likely know when your students are ready or nearly ready to share their compositions. When this occurs, begin class by reminding the students that they will present their compositions to the class.
- Plan or have the students select the order in which the groups will present their compositions.
- Remind students of respectful audience behavior and classroom norms regarding listening to other's work.
- Ask those performing to present their composition and then share/explain their notation with the class.
- Ask those listening to write down one compliment and one comment for improvement for each group. After the group performance, call on various students to provide feedback.
- Wrap-up the presentations by thanking the students for their hard work and leading a discussion about what they learned during the project.

Possible Extensions or Additions:

- Work collaboratively with the class on Day 2 or 3 to develop a rubric that will be used to evaluate the group compositions.
- Have the students use the collaboratively created rubric or another tool to evaluate the performances given by the other groups.

- Add in a day in which each group shares their "rough draft" with the class and receives peer feedback from members of the other groups.
- Develop a self-evaluation or reflection tool for groups or individual students to complete at the conclusion of the project. Group reflection can be useful if the emphasis is on the process of creation and on the final musical performance. Individual reflection or self-evaluation can be useful if you want students to think about how they contributed to the overall group success or to think about what they individually learned about themselves as musicians.

Framework Commentary

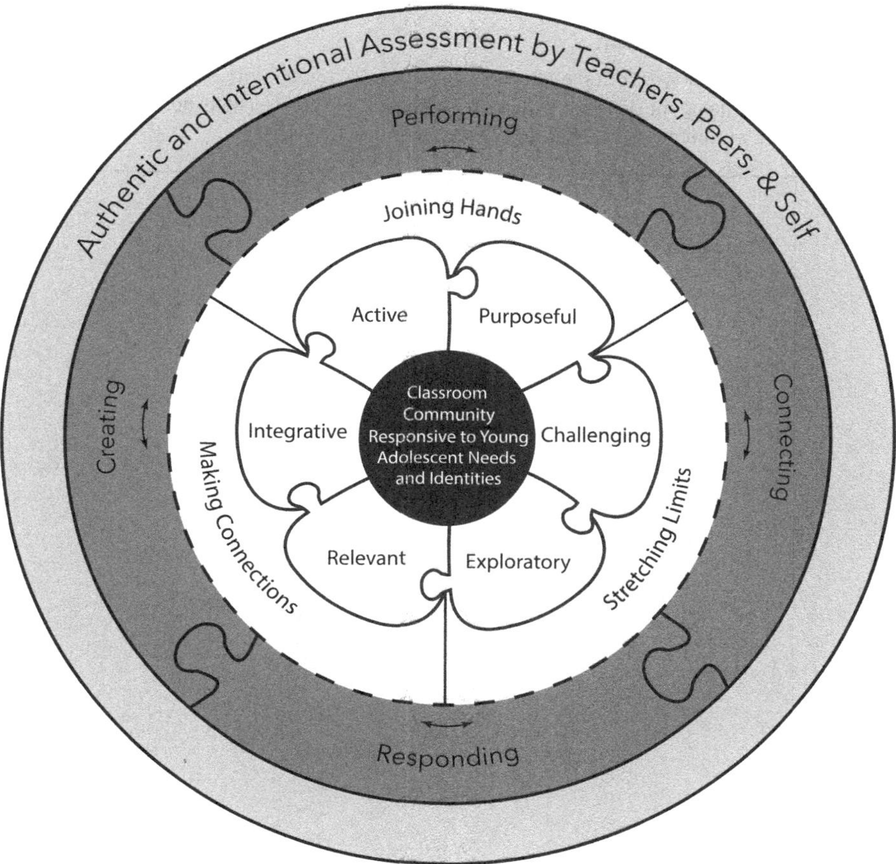

Making Connections

The opening class discussion and the subsequent poetic analysis help students make *integrated* connections between music learning and language arts, science, and visual art. The choices students make in this lesson, from selecting their color-group to the musical instruments used in the composition help make music learning *relevant* to the students' own experiences outside of music.

Joining Hands

Throughout the composition process, all students are *actively* involved, working collaboratively with their peers, and taking on various leadership roles. The continual cycle of composition, performance testing, and revision is an active process that requires independent and collaborative decision-making in order to achieve a specific learning *purpose*. For those struggling with self-direction, Teacher Resource 1.1 guides their decisions.

Stretching Limits

The task of collaborating to create a new composition is *challenging* for most middle level students both because of the requirement to collaborate and the struggle to create the sounds they imagine. In order to develop their compositions, students must *explore* in order to experiment with sounds, test out possibilities, develop new notation systems, and create multiple drafts prior to finalizing their composition.

Artistic Processes

While the primary focus of this lesson sequence is *creating*, the students are *performing* and *responding* throughout the lesson sequence, both during the creation process and in the final presentations to the class.

Authentic & Intentional Assessment

The performance of compositions for an audience is an authentic and intentional form of assessment that mimics the work of practicing musicians. In addition, the assessment extensions described earlier enable students to take more autonomy over assessing themselves and their peers.

Teacher Resource 1.1

Color Poem Composition Planning Worksheet

Begin your color composition by working with your group to brainstorm answers to the questions below:

- What does your selected color make you think about?
- When you think of your color, do any particular sounds come to mind?
- What does the text of your poem mean?
- What kind of mood do you think the writer was attempting to convey?
- How might you convey that mood musically?
- Does your poem have a rhyme scheme?
- How might you emphasize the rhyme scheme musically?
- Does your poem have a form/poetic structure?
- How might you use the form/poetic structure musically?
- If your color poem was conveyed musically, what would it sound like?
- What instruments would best help to convey your color?

Reminders:

After you answer the questions, spend some time improvising different musical ideas related to your color. Be sure to share instruments with the other members of the class.

Composition Requirements:

- Introduction
- Conclusion
- At least four independent parts. These parts should fit together and be played at the same time, but there can be rests.
- Include the text of the poem (sung, chanted, or rapped)—these are your lyrics.

Notation Requirements:

- Using any kind of notation (standard, graphical, or invented), notate your entire composition on one of the large sheets of paper.
- Include your lyrics where they belong in the song—be sure to indicate how to say or sing your lyrics.
- Other people in class should be able to read your notation and play your composition.
- Decorate your notation as appropriate to your color poem.

Wrap-Up: The Fertile Ground Framework

In this chapter, I discussed the need for a theoretical framework to guide middle level general music and presented the Fertile Ground Framework as one possibility to fulfill this need. This Framework is grounded in six principles of democratic education that guide discussion throughout this book: (1) educating the whole student, (2) making connections, (3) integrating students' perspectives, (4) encouraging student growth, (5) including diverse and comprehensive musical forms, and (6) teaching all students. Through these six principles and the Fertile Ground Framework, general music and middle level education are united. The Fertile Ground Framework is a flexible tool designed to allow you to use it as best suits your needs as a teacher and the specific students with whom you work. Based on what you know now, how might the Fertile Ground Framework help you to improve your work in middle level general music? In what ways might you begin using the Framework to guide your current practice? Which part of the Framework is most confusing or most clear to you?

Notes

1 In another publication, I discussed five democratic principles for middle level general music; the fourth principle described here was not included in that publication (Cronenberg, 2020b).
2 See Regelski's (2004) book *Teaching General Music in Grades 4-8: A Musicianship Approach* for a different approach to middle level general music.
3 A simple composition exercise Lindsey and Stephanie have done involves asking students to write AAB lyrics for the 12-bar blues to be sung or chanted over the chord progression.
4 An excellent example of differentiation in middle level general music composition is found in Elizabeth Menard's (2013) article in *Music Educators Journal*.
5 Lesson ideas I use in my practice were often introduced to me by another teacher. In this case, I was introduced to *Hailstones and Halibut Bones* and these lesson ideas while teaching an undergraduate Music for Elementary Classroom Teachers course during my doctorate at University of Illinois at Urbana-Champaign. I later adapted these ideas for my own seventh grade general music class.

PART 1

The Heart of the Fertile Ground Framework

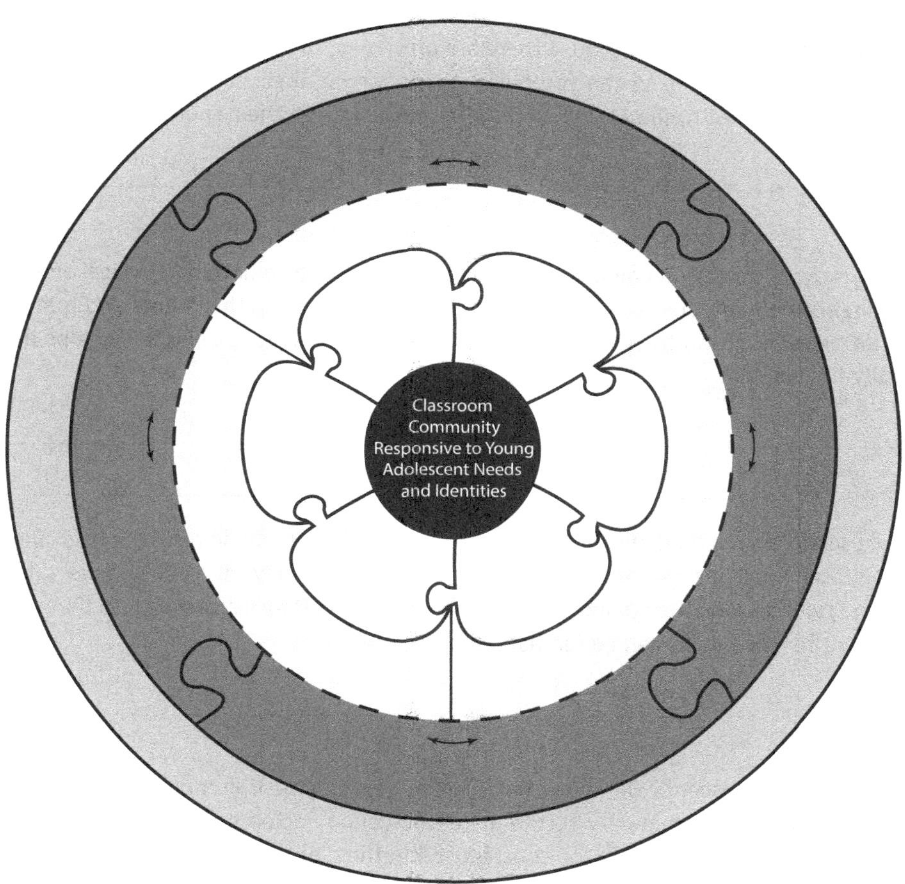

In Part 1—Chapters 2 and 3—our focus is on the core of the Fertile Ground Framework, the students and their classroom environment. Chapter 2 focuses on educating the whole young adolescent by being responsive to their developmental needs and cultural identities. Chapter 3 emphasizes cultivating a classroom community where all young adolescents feel motivated and safe to learn and grow. As an introduction to Part 1, the teachers in this book share their own perspectives on working in community with young adolescents.

> I love their enthusiasm, their willingness to learn, watching them grow. If I can just keep one kid–and I don't mean that clichè, I sincerely mean it–if I can keep one kid from putting their toes out too deep, then I've done my job.
>
> –Alexis

> Something happens in the summer of sixth grade going into seventh where they get–not lethargic, but there is like this wall [between the students and teacher]. So if there is something else you can do–because there are only going to be a handful [of kids who] will be goofy enough for you so can you put a microphone in their hand–can you give them crayons to doodle with, something so that they're busy with their energy.
>
> –Danielle

> We're always moving and doing stuff. I feel like giving them something physical and concrete helps the more abstract ideas fit better. That's why we do the chants and that kind of stuff because giving them a physical concrete [activity] is [the thing that] helps them solidify the concept.
>
> –Hannah

> Middle schoolers are kind of moody and they can be difficult, but so can little kids, and so can high schoolers, and so can adults. We all have our good days and our bad days. If you plan the right lessons they're more fun than anybody and they'll really be into things and they want to learn. They can be fantastic.
>
> –Lindsey

While all young adolescents will experience similar developmental changes (albeit at differing times), each school community serves a specific young adolescent cohort. Whether urban, suburban, or rural; public, private, or charter; multi-ethnic or homogeneous; single-sex or co-educational, each young adolescent population has its own specific needs. Even though school communities tend to serve a similar population from year to year, each group of students is unique, just as each young adolescent is an individual. Knowledge of the student population as well as the desire to develop knowledge of each unique student you teach enables the establishment and maintenance of a positive and motivating classroom community–these are the first steps to creating a middle level general music class that cultivates lifelong music learning. Thus, responding to the students' needs and identities and the motivating classroom community you cultivate for them are at the heart of the Fertile Ground Framework.

2 Educating the Whole Student

Responding to Young Adolescents' Developmental Needs and Cultural Identities

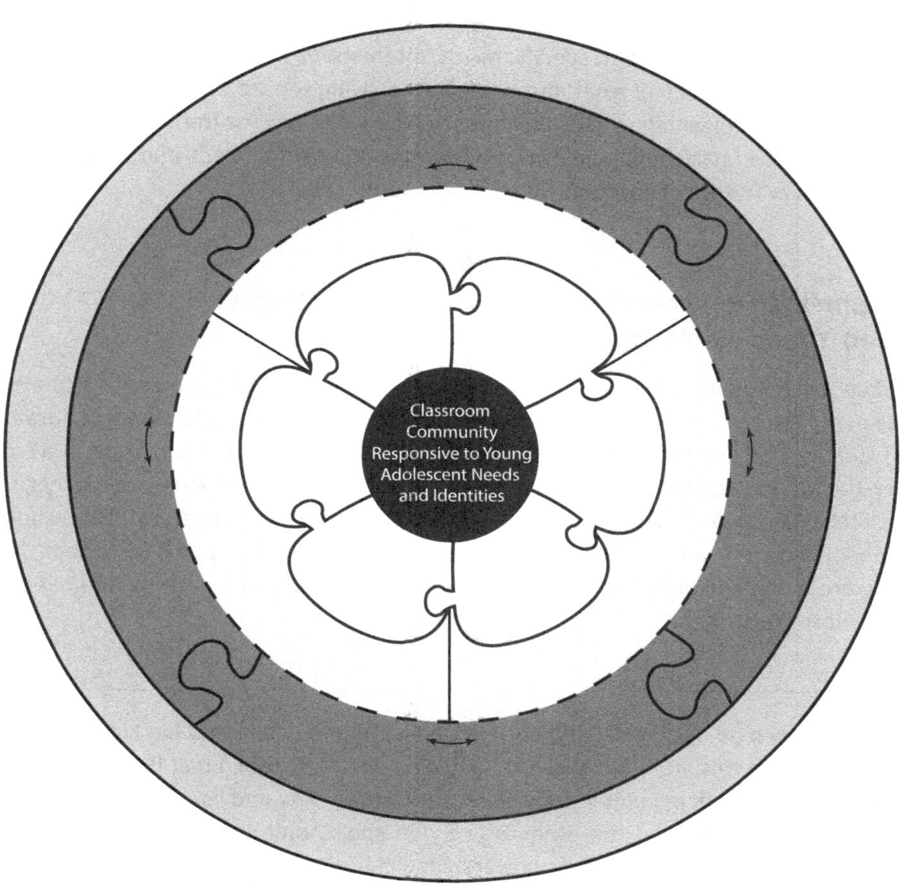

Democratic Principle #1: Educating the Whole Student

Young adolescents need teachers in all subjects who are attuned to the developmental changes they are experiencing, open to responding to students' cultural and personal identities, aware of the individual home and personal circumstances of each student, and willing to create learning environments to facilitate these evolving and vacillating developmental needs and cultural

DOI: 10.4324/9781003124245-3

identities. Put another way, middle level teachers "build relationships, design curriculum, and create learning environments that support, affirm, and celebrate young adolescents holistically" (Bishop & Harrison, 2021, p. 3). This is not a new idea. The idea of educating the *whole* student, not just enriching his/her mind, can be traced back to progressive educators such as John Dewey (1916) and William Heard Kilpatrick (1936). Yet what it means to educate the whole student has evolved with time and the needs of schooling. Modern school services such as the school nurse, counselors, and free breakfast and lunch are designed to satisfy specific student needs to enable them to perform at full potential during the school day. When students feel that their intertwined identities are not valued, they will not make themselves vulnerable in learning, an essential element for creative learning. Thus, it is our responsibility as teachers to ensure that all students feel safe and comfortable expressing their most authentic identities and changing selves in the middle level classroom.

As you read this chapter, I ask you to consider this question: How often do you think about each student as an individual with specific needs, interests, desires, and intertwined identities? This question is the essence of what music teachers striving toward the first democratic principle, educating the whole student, must ask themselves every day. For the sake of clarity, I divide this chapter into two parts, but acknowledge that developmental needs and cultural identities are intertwined in the life of each individual young adolescent.

Developmental Responsiveness: Educating the Whole Evolving Young Adolescent

For middle level students, the onset of puberty and its subsequent developmental evolution impacts every area of their lives. Adolescent researchers Kathleen Cushman and Laura Rogers (2008) suggest that the paradox of middle level learning is that young adolescents are caught between the forces of child-like reactions and their developing understanding of teacher, school, and societal expectations. Middle level students no longer need the supervision and support of elementary school nor are they ready for the rigor and responsibility of high school. The fact that they are in the middle between child-like and adult-like behaviors can be a fun and joyous time, as Lindsey describes:

> I like that they'll go back and forth between being young adults and big kids in a single day. I love to tell this story because I think it's *so* middle school; I had two eighth grade boys who were practicing guitar and I was sitting at my desk and listening in and they're like, "where is Susan" and the other is like, "oh she's home with a really high fever." "Awesome, maybe she'll get super-powers" and the other one goes, "don't be stupid, that's like a one in a million chance!"
>
> —Lindsey

Because young adolescents are caught between childhood and full adolescence, they require teachers who are consistent and firm in their expectations, but also teachers who recognize the contradictions young adolescents face as they mature and who support them in their development.

Whether we intend to or not, our actions as adult authorities impact how young adolescents are constructing their understanding of themselves in the world. Our best intentions may be missteps because of the continually evolving nature of young adolescence, or as adolescent researchers Michael Nakkula and Eric Toshalis (2006) suggest, "because development is an ongoing constructive process, ... developmentally, 'where they are' is always on the way toward somewhere else" (p. 260). Below, I briefly describe some of the major features of the physical, cognitive, emotional, and social development typically experienced by young adolescents at some point during the middle level years; however, there are certainly exceptions and outliers.

Physical

While the onset of puberty, for the majority of students, occurs during the middle level years, these physiological changes can begin as early as upper elementary school or as late as high school. Generalizations about how a specific aspect of physical development happens to "all seventh grade students" are simply incorrect. The physical changes that occur during puberty are too numerous to mention here, but include the development of secondary sex characteristics, changes in physical stature, and changes in vocal range. Growth in physical stature is, to adults, one of the most obvious physical changes. These physical changes can impact the instruments students are able to play successfully, both in general music and instrumental ensembles. Depending on the student and the time of year, hand drums, guitar, or pianos may be easy or difficult for a host of physical reasons.

Conversations about the voice change and vocal health are important for all middle level students across the gender spectrum in order to prevent physical injury and hopefully avoid social and emotional harm that might come in the form of bullying by those unaware that the vocal change is a natural process for all young adolescents.[1] Consider Abby's approach to addressing the topic intentionally with her students:

> I figured out over the years it's far more comfortable if you talk about [the voice change], because then everybody knows what's going on. When we are singing a song, I'll say, "if you need to, you can sing it in this voice." And I can sing an octave lower and they can kind of hear that. And sometimes they'll pick up on it. Sometimes you'll still have the one [kid] kind of roaming around in the middle somewhere. More importantly they're trying to make sound. So I try to recognize that like: "I hear some on-pitch singing right now. I hear some off-pitch singing, but thank you for making a sound. If you're not sure if you're right or wrong let's do a little check." And we'll do different listening-to-yourself activities. But it does have to be addressed and not doing it is a big no-no.
>
> —Abby

All students should be educated about the vocal changes they (and their peers) will experience during puberty.[2] For some students, the various physical changes, not limited to the voice change, happen rapidly, for others they gradually unfold over time, and for yet others these changes are traumatizing because of misalignment with gender identity. It is important to remember that the rate of change is uneven, often varies according to race and ethnicity, and is unique to each individual.

Cognitive

Like physical changes, cognitive development occurs differently for each young adolescent. Here, I discuss young adolescent rapid brain development, the importance of pacing, the development of abstract thinking, and how risk taking leads to creativity.

Young adolescent's brains are experiencing rapid development as well as the pruning or removal of the neural connections deemed unnecessary due to infrequent use. Developmental psychologist Deanna Kuhn describes this critical period in brain development in this way:

> Early adolescence is increasingly being recognized as a second critical period, akin to what has been widely regarded as the critical period of early childhood, when patterns are established that will be resistant to change later on.... During this second critical period, it is arguably disposition—to do or not to do x or y—as much or more than competence, that ought to be the focus of those concerned with supporting adolescents' intellectual development.
>
> (2009, pp. 181–182)

Thus, the experience of participating in many different kinds of learning experiences or activities enables young adolescents to maintain or develop a disposition or interest in a particular topic. When a young adolescent specializes in a particular area or discipline, the cognitive pruning that occurs makes engagement in certain subject areas more or less difficult in the future (Kuhn, 2009). This is the reason why it is so important to engage students in music learning in order to cultivate a lifelong musical disposition.

Two aspects of young adolescent cognitive development that are important to consider in middle level general music include their longer (albeit still relatively short) attention spans and their emerging ability to think abstractly (Mee & Haverback, 2016; Roney, 2005; Stevenson, 2002). When interested and engaged, young adolescents can spend hours fixated on a topic. However, due to their physical and social-emotional needs, young adolescents often need transitions and a teacher who knows how to pace a lesson filled with variety. Robert shares his own perspective on this:

> Pacing, pacing, pacing, pacing, pacing.... That's the number one thing I think of with [middle level students], is pacing.
>
> —Robert

Lessons that have multiple sections or activities, particularly activities where students can move around or talk to their friends, facilitate both the need for variety, but also the cognitive move from concrete to abstract. Young adolescents are *developing* abstract thought; they cannot always employ it fully. Concrete examples and activities are still necessary in order to help students understand important curricular concepts as they develop (over time) their facility with abstract thinking. Robert continues his advice:

> Those sixth graders ... they don't have abstract thought, you know, until March and then all of a sudden, they have that, which is this wonderful thing. And, even in seventh and eighth grade when they're capable of [abstract thought], they don't have a lot of practice with it yet. So, I always encourage student teachers to combine an abstract instructional thought with a very concrete example.... Show them what you mean. Do a lot of doing.
>
> –Robert

Robert generalizes by saying that the sixth graders develop abstract thought in March; this should not be taken as the rule. Young adolescents do not wake up one day able to comprehend the entire world abstractly, but rather this develops over time as they continue to practice this important cognitive skill.

Finally, young adolescents are often willing to take risks, primarily because the prefrontal cortex of their brain is still developing. Willingness to take risks, combined with their developing understanding of abstract thinking, can lead to fantastic creativity, "where they can risk novel ways of experiencing and presenting themselves" and their learning (Nakkula & Toshalis, 2006, p. 53). It is up to the teacher to harness this creative willingness and use it for successful student learning. If you design your middle level general music curriculum around the idea of creativity–not just composition, but all forms of creativity–you may find that young adolescents are willing to take musical risks and respond positively and in unanticipated ways. Cultivating a classroom that encourages creative risks will begin to show young adolescents the role music might play in their future lives.

Emotional

Unfortunately, stereotypes about volatile middle level emotions are an oft cited reason why many teachers avoid teaching middle level students. Eric admits that this is where he started as a teacher, but he learned that the emotional development of young adolescents is far more complex than the stereotypes:

> I think [my early perception] was just all the stereotypes about middle schoolers and the hormones and "they're crazy," and granted all that is true, but people usually forget that they can be really fun too.... I think it's that they're still engaged; they still want to try new things; they still want to please their teachers.
>
> –Eric

Middle level students cannot always control their reactions to particular circumstances, particularly when hormonal imbalances or social factors are involved (Mee & Haverback, 2016). As teachers, our job is to recognize the signs of an oncoming emotional outburst, whether related to our class or something that happened earlier in the day, and to diffuse the situation as quickly as possible, as Alexis describes:

> It's recognizing [in the] kid that someone just lit their fuse. And it's recognizing that and saying, "Jordan, why don't you go and get a drink?" You know, before he explodes, or before she melts in tears and it's maybe–you know–"go get a drink, go to the bathroom," or "I'm going to send you on an errand," but trying to get them out of the situation, defuse that situation, and just talking with them and being real.
>
> –Alexis

Yes, some middle level students might have emotional outbursts, but do not take them personally. This emotional expression is rarely about what is happening within the classroom at that exact moment. Being able to step back from the emotional outburst and recognize that there is something else going on is an important skill to develop when educating the whole student.

The flip side of the emotional volatility that characterizes young adolescence is a deep capacity to feel and care. Middle level students can become intensely passionate about topics, people, causes, etc. Students can become deeply emotional when discussing the lyrics of a song or when focused on their practicing. Sometimes, students become so invested in a project or activity, that when it is time to move on they become emotional and reticent to finish or put materials away. When teachers channel this passion, middle level students can commit to cleaning up parks, saving the rainforests, working at a food pantry, rallying for equal rights, or any other host of social, political, or environmental causes. Passionate support of social causes is one way that young adolescents can harness their emotional volatility for positive change in their worlds. Below, Jackie shares an unexpected story about a middle level student's ability to show that she cares.

> I was having a really bad day before my eighth grade class came in, and the [classroom] teacher kind of sensed that I was having a bad day, and she said "do you want me just to take them today?" [Jackie works at a K-8 school, so her students come to music as a homeroom]. And I said "yeah, because I'm just, I feel like a stressed out puppy right now ... I feel like I'm going to break down and cry." And so she took them [back to homeroom]. But what was interesting was one of the girls stayed back. She was one of the girls that I just was constantly having problems with and she kind of said, "why are you so sad?" I kinda went through some things, and I said, ... "do you ever have days where you just feel like you are the worst person in the world?" She said, "yeah." And I said "well, I'm having one of those days." And I said, "I'm feeling not like a teacher right now." And this is where I found out really the capacity of middle school kids to be some of the best kids in the world, she just came up to me and gave me a hug, and she said, "I know I don't show it, but I think you're a really excellent teacher, and I love being in the class with you." And I'm like [crying]–because I would never have expected this particular student to say that.
>
> –Jackie

As music teachers, it is important for us to learn to "read the room" emotionally and build off the energy and emotion coming from the students (Sweet, 2016). The seventh graders in second period may need one emotional energy from their music teacher on Tuesday and an entirely different emotional energy on Wednesday. Your ability to read and respond to this emotional energy will reap significant benefits for the success of your middle level general music classroom.

Social

As students move from childhood into young adolescence, their relationships with peers become primary. Young adolescents need time to think aloud and engage with their peers in settings that foster positive interactions (Mee & Haverback, 2016). Most young adolescents want to work with their peers; however, there are always a few who would rather work alone. This is why group work can be an important but also challenging component of middle level learning. When guided properly by adults (see Chapter 3), social learning can lead to productive work and creative musical products.

At the middle level, peer pressure also becomes a force for either good or ill. Peers can convince a reticent friend to try something new, like auditioning for the musical, or to engage in risky behavior, like smoking or drinking. Because recognition from peers is important to most young adolescents, they sometimes do things that are surprising and out of character. A teacher, like Jackie, who can acknowledge that social pressure may contribute to unusual behaviors by a particular student is more likely to react in a way that will help the student and the rest of the class refocus.

> You know, it's like sixth, seventh, and eighth grade, be prepared for hormones because man when it hits you just sit back, and you go, "REALLY?" You know, part of those discipline problems aren't necessarily the kid, but the phase they're going through. They're trying to be such-and-such because they're trying to impress so-and-so.
>
> –Jackie

As music teachers, helping young adolescents develop positive peer relationships is important. It is equally important to know that middle level students' need for peer interaction can be harnessed to make the learning environment positive for everyone.

Cultural Responsiveness: Educating Students' Developing Multifaceted Identities

Young adolescence is a time of identity exploration and identity construction (Nakkula & Toshalis, 2006). Their developmental changes propel them toward independence and a desire for autonomy over themselves and their learning experience while they simultaneously try to figure out who they are as individuals both separate from and related to their nuclear family or primary caregivers and their cultural identities. Culturally responsive teachers recognize the various aspects of each student's identity that they bring to the classroom and value and celebrate those differences within the learning environment. In addition, culturally responsive teachers draw upon school resources such as students' Individualized Education Programs (IEPs) or 504 plans (US specific learning plans) and relevant school personnel in order to serve each student's needs.

Cultural responsiveness begins with an awareness of the cultural norms that schooling, and by extension music education, place upon students, norms typically aligned with a White middle-class perspective (Vagle & Hamel, 2019). As Harrison, Hurd, and Brinegar remind us, "to be developmentally responsive to young adolescents from marginalized backgrounds, one must be culturally responsive as well" (2019, p. 8). Developmentally responsive and culturally responsive approaches go hand-in-hand to creating a classroom environment designed to educate the whole young adolescent. The sections below highlight some—but certainly not all—of the multifaceted identities that contribute to each unique middle level student.

Race and Ethnicity

According to multicultural education scholar Geneva Gay, "in addition to dealing with the general developmental changes characteristic of the age group, African-American, Hispanic, Asian-American, and Native-American young adolescents have to fashion for themselves a clarified ethnic identity" (1994, p. 151). In the growth of individual identity development, students often struggle with integrating their racial and ethnic identities, often seen as "home" identities with the expectations and norms of school, particularly if schools are not sensitive to these developing identities or expect all students to dress or behave according to specified norms that do not align with cultural norms. Gloria Ladson-Billings' (1995) theory of culturally relevant pedagogy focuses on the importance of helping all students, but particularly students of color, achieve academic success, develop or maintain cultural competence, and build a critical consciousness that equips them with the ability to examine existing social norms critically. Cultural competence and critical consciousness are important because, too often, the multiplicities of students' identities may clash with what they perceive (or are told outright) are the norms of school.

In music education, norms of Whiteness found in schools are extended and perpetuated through the Western music paradigm. According to music education scholar Deborah Bradley, many music teachers:

> teach from a perspective of Whiteness as ignorance, ignoring the realities of lived experience for children of color or those who are minoritized for other reasons, and/or ignoring other forms of music that may be more relevant to the student in their charge. Having never experienced music outside the Western canon, or only superficially so, teachers may react defensively at the very suggestion of including music from another culture or musical tradition.
>
> (2015, p. 195)

While the use of the Western music canon is just one example of how Whiteness is perpetuated in the music classroom, one of Bradley's most important points for middle level general music is the importance of the lived experience(s) of the students in the classroom and the influence of those lived experience(s) on the selected curriculum.

Consider Tyler's explanation of how his hip-hop unit emerged while working with his students, the majority of whom are African American or Afro-Caribbean:

> [My] whole hip-hop unit kind of came out of trying to really immerse myself in what [my students were] listening to and coming up with something where I could ... take them where they are and move them a little bit forward in their musicianship through something that they already know. So, like if I had a bunch of middle schoolers right now who were in a room and didn't want to be there—or maybe they did want to be there but don't have [many] skills—I would try and figure out what they're into and then what they know.... Maybe even involve them democratically—I do that an awful lot in my classes—I will make time for some kind of whole group discussion or do a partial group discussion and find out what [the students are] interested in doing.
>
> —Tyler

Although Tyler was unfamiliar with most of hip-hop music and culture, he has found a way to honor his students' racial and ethnic backgrounds, and their experiences in a multicultural urban community by learning about the music important to them. Tyler also works to give his students voice in the classroom and thus create a culturally responsive classroom that responds directly to the identities of students in a given class.

Language Background

While the predominant language of school in the United States is English, English is not the singular language identity for many students enrolled in schools. Both English Language Learners (ELLs) and multilingual students bring unique identities to their experience with school. Yet we must not assume that all students of a particular racial or ethnic background are ELLs or even speak the language of their ethnic heritage. Young adolescents learning English "are in a unique situation in that they are acquiring English as a new language while they are in the stage of identity formation and development in a new context" (Yoon & Uliassi, 2019, p. 240). For a middle level learner, already experiencing heightened social and emotional pressure due to age appropriate developmental changes, being unable to fully understand the world of school or to make friends often leaves ELLs isolated and behaving in ways that may appear uncooperative as Katie describes:

> [Last year] I had five ELL students who had just moved here.... three of them were Asian and two were Brazilian. The two Brazilian kids, one was just kind of doing nothing and would sit there and chat with [the other one], but then would kind of run around and grab a drumstick and start hitting everything he touched. So, the first time that happened I sent him to the office, the second time that happened I sent him to the office, third time that happened, I sent him to the office. [I went to the ELL teachers] and said "I need some ideas of what to do here," I had a long conversation with them and that was actually really helpful because the ELL teachers [told me] that [this] kid had been living on the street

in São Paulo. When I heard that, I was like, "that explains a lot of things and also [why] sending this kid to the office is probably not super helpful because he has no idea what's going on, so he's not feeling punished so much as constantly confused." [Later the ELL teachers] translated the critical listening sheet [a daily warm-up] into Portuguese. [The better-behaved student] actually did play with his band [in the final assignment]; he was playing good guitar already. [The other student] stopped hitting things, [but] he didn't really ever participate with anyone in any meaningful way. So, you know, it's not the success story of all time.

–Katie

In middle level general music, language barriers can sometimes be a major struggle for teachers, particularly in courses that last only a few weeks. My best recommendation is to be aware of whether and what kind of language supports students need in your classroom. If your school annually has a large population of students who are native speakers of an additional language, preparing handouts and other materials in both English and the other language can prove very useful as they can be reused from year to year. However, it is also important to be prepared for ELL students to appear in your class without notice due to a schedule change, as Jessica experienced:

I had five [ELL] kids put in my [year-long guitar-focused] class within one week. It was the third quarter and it was really rough for a little bit because of the language barrier. Then, once they realized that I wasn't trying to talk down to them or anything like that, that I was trying to kind of catch them up and bring them along to where we were ... then they really took to [guitar] and they were more willing to try. I had one student, he just really took to me once he gave it a try and he started learning some on his own. Then he would try to hide when he was doing his own thing, and I was like, "it's okay for you to play what you want to. You just have to make sure that you prepare for the test material too," and he's like, "okay Miss, okay."

–Jessica

While they both admit to being imperfect examples of involving ELL students in middle level general music, both Katie and Jessica tried their best to recognize and honor the language identities of their students and to meet their needs as learners within the confines of their existing curriculum.

Religion and Spirituality

Another facet of young adolescents' cultural identity is religion or spirituality, emerging from family traditions, discovered through peers, or evolving independently. Young adolescents may begin to question the religious or spiritual beliefs of their upbringing or become more emotionally invested in these identities. As music educators, being culturally responsive to students' religious and spiritual identities is complicated and goes far beyond ensuring that there is a

Hanukkah, Kwanzaa, or Diwali song on the fall concert. The separation of church and state is expected in most US public schools and yet the nature of our discipline, particularly the Western classical tradition, is steeped in the Christian church. In fact, music from around the world is often connected to the religious or spiritual practices of the music creators, and thus discussions of the intersection between music and religion are hard to avoid and must be handled sensitively by an educator attuned to the identities of the students in the room. One (of many) challenges faced by music teachers is that students' religious or spiritual identities may prohibit them from participation in certain music-related activities. A culturally responsive music teacher knows each student individually in order to ensure that the musical choices made will enable all students to participate.

Gender and Sexuality

Culturally responsive teachers are aware that the exploration of sexual and gender identities is an important, age appropriate, aspect of young adolescent development often catalyzed or accelerated by puberty. While gender and sexual identities are discussed here together, I want to be clear that a person's sexual identity and gender identity are not the same, nor can a specific sexual identity be linked to a particular gender identity. Young adolescents often need to explore these identities and failure to understand themselves in terms of gender and/or sexuality can have lasting psychological impacts into adulthood.

Creating a welcoming space for all students to express themselves freely is one of the things that arts teachers do best. In fact, several research studies have shown that music classrooms are seen as safe spaces for high school LGBTQ+ students (Bergonzi, 2015). The best thing a music teacher can do for a student exploring gender or sexual identities is to welcome the student into the classroom, be open to day-to-day changes in appearance or behavior, and prohibit offensive language such as "that's so gay" in the classroom. Teachers can begin by adding a simple statement as part of their introduction on the first day of class:

> My name is Ms./Mr./Mx. ________ and I prefer you to use these pronouns ______ when talking about me. I am going to call the last names that are listed on my roll. When I get to you, please tell me your preferred first name and what pronouns you would like me to use.

Music education researcher, Louis Bergonzi (2015) also suggests that "music education for gender-sexual diverse Others would also anticipate choral opportunities for student singers who are transgender, develop travel and housing policies that are gender-sexual diverse, and consider gender expression in selecting ensemble concert 'dress'" (p. 226). The only reason why concert attire consists of tuxes and dresses is tradition. Tradition can, and in this case should, be broken. Music teachers can also move the music education profession forward by thoughtfully considering whether other traditions in the field of music education assume heterosexuality or a gender binary. For example, is it critical to students' understanding of a folk dance that all partners must be of the opposite gender? When studying West African drumming, can you explain the cultural gender binary between drumming and dancing as a cultural norm and practice, but not reinforce this norm within your classroom? These and other small changes can go a long way toward helping a student exploring gender or sexual identity to feel welcome in our classroom.

When you are faced with a situation involving a student exploring gender or sexual identities and are not sure how to proceed, find a private moment with the student and ask what would make the student feel most comfortable. Jackie describes her own experience with a student in transition where she was not sure how best to proceed,

> This past year I had an eighth grade student who [was transitioning] from a girl to a boy. Well, nobody ever taught me [how to handle] that. But I had to be very sensitive about it.... Number one, I would refer to him as Jonathan, but her [birth] name was Alexis. I talked to [him] and said, "you know, I'm going to start putting up certificates for eighth grade." I said, "you know I want to write Jonathan [on this certificate], but I also know that your Grandpa is gonna want to see [your name listed] as Alexis. Are you okay with that?" And [he] said "yeah, I'm fine." [He] said, "because if [Grandpa] sees that he'll hit the roof." I said, "you know I understand."
>
> –Jackie

Jackie's story is just one example of how a music teacher attempting to be culturally responsive to his/their/her students' individual needs might address an issue directly with an individual student exploring gender or sexuality identities. In this instance, Jackie was both sensitive to the student's needs and to what she knew about the student's family life. Sometimes students have not shared their gender or sexual identities with family members even when everyone at school is aware.

Socio-Economic Status

Young adolescents' socio-economic status and subsequent living situations–from homeless shelters to foster care, crowded apartments to two separate houses–impact their development and identities, their access to supplies, whether they can return to school for evening events, and their ability to learn. While they did not expressly state this, socio-economic status and home life might be one reason why some teachers featured in this book choose not to assign homework and choose to keep students' materials in the music classroom.

The US government designation, "Title 1," is given to public schools that receive government funds based on a specific percentage of low-income students served by the school. Alexis shared,

> I'm not exactly sure of the free and reduced lunch rate, but I know [at our school] it's probably at least eighty percent if not higher than that. It's a small farming community. A lot of parents are factory workers or that sort of thing, so, more on the lower socio-economic class. [But the school community is] not poor in family support [of schooling] which is nice.
>
> –Alexis

In addition, Katie described the three elementary schools that feed her middle level school as dramatically different from one another, thus resulting in a mixed socio-economic profile for her middle level school:

> There are three schools that feed into mine, one of them is super wealthy, one of them is more of a range [of socio-economic statuses], and then one of them is probably the only school in [the district] that has a homeless shelter that feeds into it.
>
> –Katie

While Katie did not tell me anything more about the students living in the homeless shelter who attended her school, these students' economic circumstances certainly contributed to her school's Title 1 designation.

Culturally responsive music teachers understand that students with certain socio-economic identities will be unable to complete internet research at home, provide a telephone number on a form, watch certain videos or TV shows, rent instruments, or purchase materials. As a culturally responsive educator, it is important to be aware of the socio-economic factors that present barriers to students succeeding in school and make the music program as accessible as possible to students with limited access to monetary resources.

Exceptionality

Students with exceptional identities, those with diverse neural, physical, and emotional needs, or what schools often label as "students with special needs," are often integrated (both with and without paraprofessional aides) into the middle level general music classroom. The focus here is on student strengths, rather than weaknesses, despite the language that might be used at your school. Neurodiversity, according to Thomas Armstrong (2010), emphasizes that everyone (regardless of diagnosis) has different brain-based strengths (and consequently weaknesses or challenges). I extend this concept to emotional and physical diversity to again emphasize the strengths of the individual rather than his/her emotional or physical limitations. In addition, I also include gifted and talented students (such as those regularly taught by Robert) as those with exceptional neural identities.

In welcoming all students into middle level general music, culturally responsive teachers plan for differentiation, in part because differentiation has a "unique fit with a middle grades philosophy that centers on students first and foremost" (Tomlinson, 2013, pp. 217–218). I believe culturally responsive teachers assume that the learners in their classroom each possess diverse strengths and weaknesses and thus plan for this differentiation for all students at the outset, rather than as an afterthought or add-on in order to meet a specific IEP or 504 plan.

While US law specifies that all students need access to a free and equal educational experience (IDEA, 2004), access to music education is handled differently in each school community and administrative decisions are often not shared with the teachers who must respond to accommodate the students' needs regardless of circumstance. Yet, as Abby points out, the IEP or 504 "can [sometimes] be really informative and sometimes not at all," making things challenging for busy music teachers. The general music teachers in this book most commonly experienced students with exceptional identities integrated into the general music classroom either with or without a paraprofessional aide. In addition, some school administrations chose other options. Both Abby and Nicole taught self-contained general music classes for students who spent most of their day in a self-contained classroom. In addition, Hannah's middle school developed a peer tutoring leadership program whereby students selected for the program were trained and then attended general music to support the student with an exceptional identity. My hope is that whatever administratively imposed scheduling situation you face regarding students with neural, physical, and emotional diversity, you will focus on the unique gifts and strengths each student brings to the classroom.

In Chapters 4–6, I present a limited selection of differentiation suggestions aligned with the featured lesson plan presented in each chapter. When you choose a culturally responsive approach that views students as possessing diverse strengths, I hope you will find yourself full of stories like Hannah's and Eric's:

> Well I think sometimes [students with learning disabilities] can do a lot more than we think that they can do. I've had a lot of kids where [administrators are] like, just have them in there, they don't really need to do anything, they just want to be a part of the music. But I've had students that have been able to figure out notes on the staff and figure out intervals. They really can do more than I think a lot of people give them credit for, so let them try things and don't expect that they're going to sit there, expect them to get up and move with everyone and sing with everyone because they really can do more than what we think they can.
>
> –Hannah

> I've had some students from the partnership program [special education] that are amazing with the Scratch and Makey-Makey projects. They're just so good with computers and so good with the engineering principles. I've had other students that just love music so much. I had a girl a few years ago who is very shy and for her cover song she played and sang "House of Gold" by twenty øne piløts entirely by memory, in front of the whole class. The aides and [I] were holding back tears; it was amazing! Some of those kids are just the warmest, sweetest kids.
>
> –Eric

Wrap-Up: The Whole Student

This chapter addressed the multifaceted developmental needs and cultural identities young adolescents in our classrooms embody. While whole student needs do not supersede the musical knowledge and skills the music teacher is trying to convey in the lesson, middle level students need teachers aware of students' individual developmental growth and evolving cultural identities in order to employ curricula and pedagogical approaches that navigate potential barriers to successful learning. Consideration of students as whole persons with multifaceted needs and identities, the first democratic principle outlined in Chapter 1, is an essential foundation upon which successful middle level education rests. Without knowledge of students as individuals, music teachers cannot create a classroom community based on young adolescent needs. As you think about your students, where are you succeeding and/or falling short in addressing them as whole persons? What is one thing you might ask all students in your class in order to get to know them better? Which personnel in your school might be resources to help guide your work as a culturally responsive educator?

Notes

1 Vocal development must be discussed with both male and female students. While the male vocal change often receives the most attention, female students who are unaware that their voices also change during puberty may feel frustrated when their range shifts or they are moved to a different voice part.

2 For more information about the vocal change, I highly recommend Bridget Sweet's book *Thinking Outside the Voice Box: Adolescent Voice Change in Music Education* (2020).

3 Creating a Motivating Learning Community on Day One and Every Day

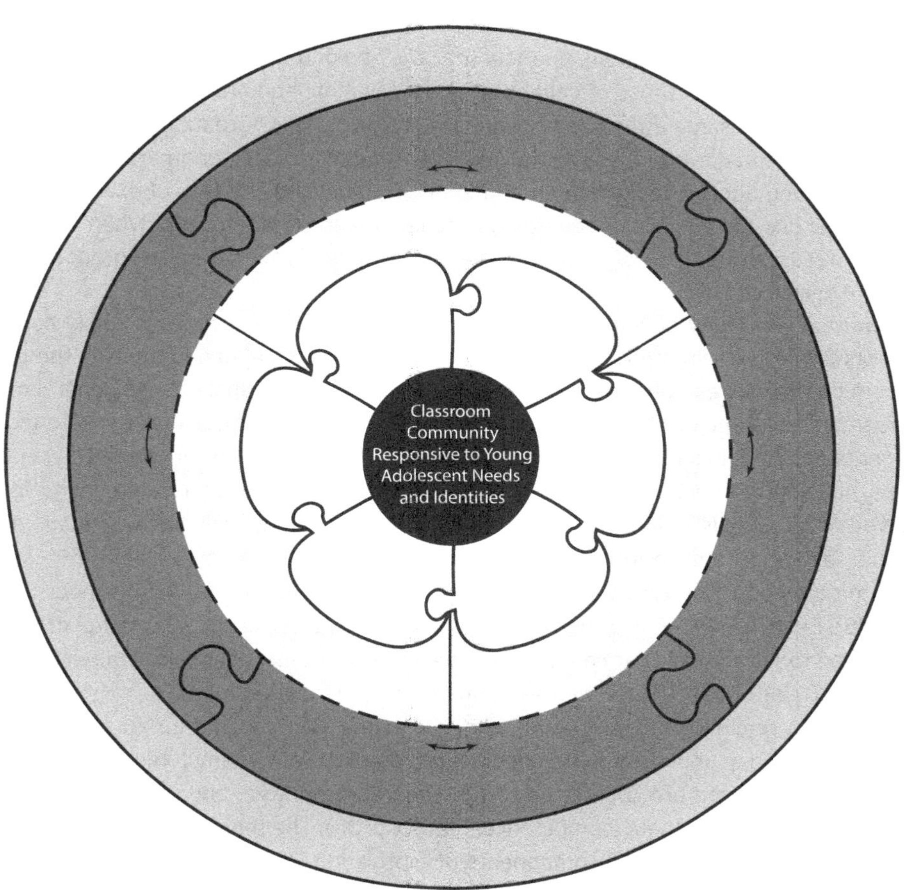

Democratic Principle #6: Teaching all Students

Consider for a moment what the word community means to you. While community can be defined in many ways, at its heart, community is a familiar place where individuals feel a sense of belonging to something beyond themselves. As an adult, where do you find community in your life? Perhaps you find community with your nuclear or extended family, in your local

DOI: 10.4324/9781003124245-4

neighborhood, in your religious life, or through a social activity or form of community service. What defines or shapes this community? In your neighborhood, this might include the smell of the local coffee shop, the neighbor who walks his dog at the same time each day, or the shop clerk who knows you by name. At your faith community, this might be the sense of tradition, the order of worship, or the person who greets you upon arrival. For each community, the list would be different, but the effect is the same. The people, places, things, and events that you expect within your community contribute to the sense of belonging that you feel within each of your chosen communities. This feeling of belonging in turn helps you to feel safe, enables you to feel recognized as an individual, and motivates you to make your own contributions to the life of the community.

As musicians and music teachers, we know the importance of establishing a community of musicians who work together toward a common musical goal. Most music making is collaborative and thus requires a community of individuals who respect each other, recognize what each individual contributes to the whole, and feel that they belong to the group. Most music teachers strive to cultivate this sense of collaboration, motivation, and group identity in ensembles. But do you make the same efforts in your general music classes? Creating a community in the classroom is key to addressing young adolescents as whole people, and particularly for satisfying many young adolescent social-emotional needs, including the fear of exposing personal vulnerabilities due to insecurities regarding knowledge and skills in music. When these social-emotional needs are met, music teachers are better able to motivate young adolescents to participate in learning.

Classroom community begins on the first day of class, but must be continually cultivated. If students do not remain motivated to participate in middle level general music, the positive classroom community established on the first day of class can fall apart. When general music is a requirement for some or all students in a grade, music teachers must find a way to motivate *all* students enrolled, including those who appear uninterested, those for whom the content is too easy, or those with behavioral, cognitive, physical, or other identity-related needs. In many cases, you must establish this motivating classroom community quickly because many general music classes are scheduled for a limited timeframe, such as Jackie's 15 class periods scheduled during a meagre three weeks of the school year. Drawing on motivation theory (Deci & Ryan, 1985), Erika Daniels (2010) suggests that motiving *all* students in any subject or schedule configuration requires a teacher committed to developing a classroom community centered on three facets: (1) autonomy, (2) relatedness, and (3) competence.

According to Daniels, students are "looking for clear and specific instruction from their teachers so that they know what they need to accomplish (autonomy), knowledge that their teachers care about and are committed to the class (relatedness), and a belief that they *can* do what is being asked of them (competence)" (2010, p. 25). The teachers featured in this book instinctively address these three components of motivation to create classroom communities centered on the specific young adolescents they teach. This chapter highlights their work in honoring young adolescents' need for autonomy, relatedness, and competence.

Autonomy

While teachers interviewed for this book use a variety of terms to describe their classroom community, many of these terms can be distilled into a singular idea: the music classroom must be a safe space. Creating a safe space in middle level general music requires the cultivation of a classroom community where students feel recognized as individuals, comfortable being themselves, and open to taking musical risks. Teachers who do this well not only support students' cognitive and musical development, but also their development as whole persons.

Regardless of whether middle level students move to a new school building or remain in their elementary school building, nearly all young adolescents at fifth, sixth, seventh, and eighth grade experience increases in the number of teachers they interact with, the number of classrooms they visit on a given day, and the level of academic expectations placed upon them. Most middle level students no longer have a teacher or a classroom that they consider their in-school "home," as is often the case in elementary school. As a result of these changes to the school structure at the middle level, many young adolescents no longer feel recognized and honored as individuals. This absence in their lives as learners directly conflicts with their developmental need for autonomy, to become (with support) more independent as people and learners.

In *Growing Musicians: Teaching Music in Middle School and Beyond,* Bridget Sweet describes safe music classrooms as "nonthreatening places where adolescent music students can escape the scrutiny (real or imagined) of others" (2016, p. 77). She discusses how the characteristics of the instructor, classroom peers, and the individual learner are joined with the physical space in which the music learning occurs to cultivate a safe space for music learning. Sweet goes on to describe the outcome of this safe musical space as:

> a music classroom environment where adolescent students are not belittled, where they feel free to push the boundaries of musical thinking and performing, and where they feel empowered to be themselves—their varied, unique selves.... Within safe musical spaces, musicianship [flourishes] as adolescents take more artistic risks and [support] is received and mistakes are honored.
>
> (2016, p. 80)

Thus, the safe music classroom Sweet envisions allows all young adolescents to have an autonomous voice and to feel socially and emotionally supported, recognized as individuals, comfortable being themselves, and open to taking risks.

A safe place for belonging is not guaranteed, particularly if students do not feel that their unique identities are recognized in the classroom. Sweet (2016) wants all students to be able to be their unique, varied selves in the music classroom, but this is only possible if each student's multiple identities are honored. Thus, a truly safe space that honors students' autonomy as learners must ensure that the identities of *all* students are recognized, as Geneva Gay (1994) describes when discussing the learning needs of students of color:

> Teachers will be better able to create authentic, developmentally appropriate, and effective educational experiences for youths of color if their curriculum content, instructional strategies, performance appraisals, and classroom climate reflect cultural diversity, and are responsive to the various stages of ethnic identity. (p. 154)

Each young adolescent who enters the middle level general music classroom brings with him/her/them multiple identities that influence their responses to music, their willingness to participate in performance, and their openness to being personally creative. The cultivation of a safe space to belong requires a music teacher attuned to all of the diverse identity characteristics each young adolescent embodies.

In the following sections, I discuss various ways to encourage student autonomy through the establishment of classroom procedures that require students to take responsibility for their own learning. The time devoted to establishing procedures can maximize instructional time, encourage mutual independence, and potentially avoid behavioral disruptions.

Supplies and Materials

When establishing expectations regarding supplies and materials in the music classroom, be sure young adolescents understand that you expect them to take responsibility for the music classroom. Remind students that use of classroom materials, particularly musical instruments, is a privilege that can be taken away if they do not behave responsibly. By doing so, you give young adolescents autonomy to act with maturity over their own preparation for learning. The more responsibility you give to the students for set-up and clean-up, the more time you have to manage other issues and to focus on teaching.

One aspect of set-up and clean-up that young adolescents can do themselves is to collect and return musical instruments to their storage spaces in the music classroom. While young adolescents are capable of taking on this responsibility, they need to be taught how to correctly care for the instruments in order to avoid damage. In particular, you need to ensure that young adolescents who are often unaware of their own strength or clumsiness can safely move around the classroom. For any class set of instruments, such as guitars or ukuleles, name or number each instrument and assign each student to always use the same instrument. Should something untoward happen or an instrument go missing, you will know which student to talk to from each class period. When instruments are kept in cases, insist that students place the case on the floor, sit in their chair, and then remove the instrument while seated. This will avoid instruments being dropped from a standing height, cases slipping off chairs, or students accidentally falling while walking with an instrument. If instruments are hung from the wall or kept in cubbies or drawers, ensure that aisles are kept clear and develop a procedure for carefully moving around the room to avoid students accidentally running into one another or dropping their instrument while returning to their seat.

Another aspect of set-up and clean-up involves folders or binders containing handouts and other supplies. While many middle level schools strive to instill young adolescent responsibility by requiring students to retrieve the correct materials from their lockers each class period, several of the music teachers featured in this book have chosen to establish a place in the music classroom where students keep their music folder or binder. When asked why he chose to store students' folders in the music room, Eric said:

> I don't remember, but it might have just been kind of trial-and-error. [Maybe] right away I decided, let me hold onto [the folders] because they're going to lose them. I have one section that's right before [the students] go to lunch and recess [so it is easier if I keep the folders in the room].
>
> —Eric

Similarly, Alexis said she learned as a beginning teacher that storing student materials in the classroom was advantageous to successful classroom functioning.

> I learned very quickly in my first few years of teaching, that if I give them something, since [general music is] not an "important" class, it never returns. So, [the students] each get a folder at the beginning of the semester. [They] put their name on it [and] they can decorate it however they want to. [That is] one of those first few day's activities that I give them time to do, [we] listen to music [and] just kind of hang out a little bit. They have a slot [in the classroom] that they put [their folder] in. I have them put in ten pieces of lined notebook paper. I [also] give them twelve listening logs [to add to their folder].
>
> –Alexis

In addition to handouts, blank paper, and course related work, Hannah also gives each student a dry erase sheet and dry erase marker to keep in the binders they store in the classroom. Hannah uses these dry erase sheets for quick response activities throughout her instruction. Thus, when students enter or exit the room, they collect or return their folder or binder to a designated bin, cubby, shelf, or drawer in the classroom labeled with their class period and students avoid requesting to return to their lockers or accidentally bringing the wrong materials to music class. By developing a start of class and end of class procedure for collecting and storing folders and other materials, young adolescents can independently prepare for learning to begin and take responsibility for organizing the music classroom.

Do-Nows

One effective technique for maximizing curricular time is to establish a regular practice of using a "Do-Now" to start the class. Do-Nows, sometimes called "bell-ringers," are daily warm-ups that students take responsibility for completing, without teacher instruction, in the first 5-10 minutes after they enter the classroom. Do-Nows provide you time to complete start-of-class tasks such as taking attendance or passing out materials without wasting valuable instructional time. When students enter the classroom, the instructions for the Do-Now are displayed on the board. Due to practice of this procedure, the students know that when the tardy bell rings (if your school has one) they should be working on the Do-Now.

Do-Nows can be used to review content, quickly assess student knowledge of a new topic, or ask students to apply knowledge in a new way. For example, Alexis often uses a quick online quiz to check students' understanding of content learned previously. Alexis also uses Do-Nows to quickly review a new vocabulary word learned in the previous class:

> A lot of times we'll have a really good discussion, and then the next day as kind of a bell-ringer, I'll say what was the definition of this [word]. Sometimes [the students] panic because they don't remember. I say, "sure you do. Maybe you don't remember the word, [but] what were the things that we talked about?" They can usually always tell me, they may not remember the actual term, but the [main ideas], yes.
>
> –Alexis

In contrast, Tyler, Danielle, and Hannah prefer to use vocal or other musical warm-ups to get their class started. Danielle also sometimes uses quick rhythmic dances that the students in her K-8 school learned when they were in elementary grades. This immediate physical musical engagement is a great way to get class started if you are in the middle of a unit focused on musical performance. For example, you might display a set of "warm-up" ukulele chords, drum patterns, or a solfege melody that students can practice on their own for the first few minutes of class. If students cannot accomplish the Do-Now independently, then perhaps the activity you have chosen is not an ideal Do-Now in your circumstance.

Student Leadership Responsibilities

Another way to motivate student learning through autonomy while also managing the classroom is to establish student leadership positions or responsibilities that students earn through positive behavior or academic success. When students take on particular leadership roles within the classroom, you are free to attend to other administrative responsibilities or provide individualized support to students in need.

There are many possibilities for student leadership responsibilities in the middle level general music classroom. In many cases, these responsibilities may emerge as you develop your curriculum and pedagogical approach. Eric describes how student leadership over ukulele tuning often emerges in his classroom:

> I do all the tuning unless there are some students that are really showing aptitude or interest. [If so,] I will give them a tuning quiz; I'll detune the ukulele, give them the tuner and tell them to fix it, and I'll show them how and then see how they do. If they are capable, I will allow them to start tuning other students' ukuleles.
>
> –Eric

This leadership responsibility for tuning ukuleles emerges each year based on student interest, rather than as a leadership responsibility Eric establishes outright. Other leadership responsibilities might include taking attendance, monitoring the instrument storage closet, passing out work or handouts, etc. In my own seventh grade general music teaching, student desire to "lead" the opening drum circle (see Do-Now 6.1) motivated students who were often tardy to begin to arrive to class early. Added responsibility can motivate some young adolescents to participate in class, change their chronic behaviors, or strive for higher levels of achievement. As with all other aspects of the classroom, student leadership responsibilities should cultivate a positive environment and motivate students to behave in positive ways. If student leadership responsibilities are creating divisiveness or dissent among the students, then these leadership responsibilities should be suspended or re-envisioned.

Relatedness

Teacher and student relationships emerged from the interviews conducted for this book as one of the most important facets of successful middle level general music. For the teachers in this book, relationships with students are key to building a positive classroom community. As Katie mentioned in Chapter 1, being able to connect with young adolescents may be more important than the subject in creating a positive and motivating middle level classroom environment. Lindsey agrees:

> We'll often have a kid who I'll think is like amazing and [other teachers will say], oh he didn't turn in his homework for sixteen days, and I had no idea because he's such a hard worker [in music]. So, I think kids like to have success in some things, and I think that if you have that relationship and you're having success and you're on the same team, they'll go above and beyond.
>
> —Lindsey

When young adolescents have a feeling of relatedness, to the subject, the teacher, and their peers, their motivation increases and they will, as Lindsey notes, "go above and beyond" to demonstrate their musical knowledge and skills. Young adolescents want to be seen by adults as unique individuals who deserve respect and autonomy. They also want teachers who appear knowledgeable, excited, and positive about the content they are teaching. Young adolescents want to feel that their teacher knows them as individual persons, not just a member of a particular class. The following sections discuss some ways that relatedness can be cultivated within the middle level general music classroom.

Getting to Know Individual Students

While developing individual relationships with students requires continual respect and rapport building, there are a variety of techniques that you can use to get to know students individually. Young adolescents who like and respect their teacher and who feel valued and respected in turn are more likely to participate in class and demonstrate positive behavior in the classroom, regardless of their interest in the curricular content. Getting to know individual students and demonstrating your support for them as individuals often requires little to no instructional time.

Perhaps the foremost technique for getting to know individual students is learning students' names as quickly as possible. As a teacher, I began my middle level general music classes by asking each student to fill out a note card answering a few easy questions about themselves, their likes and dislikes, and often a question or two about their previous musical experiences and musical preferences. These cards helped me get to know each student personally, modify the curriculum to include students' preferences, and learn names. Hannah also strives to learn students' names as quickly as possible and makes it a game with her students:

> I make an effort to learn every single student's name within the first two weeks of school and if I forget their name after the first two weeks, they earn candy. So, they really like that!
>
> —Hannah

When you do forget a student's name, admitting your fallibility through a "reward" or some other means is important so that young adolescents understand that you are making every effort to learn who they are as individuals and that everyone can make mistakes in your class.

Also, it is important to involve every student in the classroom by letting each student feel heard and seen by the teacher. This moment of connection with an individual student can be so brief that it seems insignificant to the teacher but it is essential and meaningful to the young adolescent. For example, I once observed a teacher on the day after the Super Bowl (American football championship) as she circulated around the room to tune guitars. Amidst students' practicing of the warm-up exercise, she tuned each guitar and asked each student whether they had watched the Super Bowl and if so, what they liked best about it. During the thirty seconds or so she tuned each guitar, the student was able to share his or her experience (or not) with the Super Bowl and feel heard by a teacher, perhaps for the first time that day. Yes, the music teacher asked the same question over and over all day long, but for each student, the question was new and personalized.

Another approach involves interacting with students outside of the music classroom. By attending events such as athletics, theatre, debate, dances, and other activities in which the students are involved, the students see that you support them in their endeavors and interests, as Hannah describes:

> I try to go to school events and get better involved in their sports and stuff. I always try to go to at least a few [sports] games so that they can see me there.
>
> —Hannah

Regardless of the nature of the event, when young adolescents see you and are able to engage with you outside of the music classroom, they know that you support them in their interests. Depending on how your school operates, this could be as simple as greeting students in the hallway between classes or spending time in the cafeteria before school or during lunch. Attending a student work presentation when invited by a student or colleague is another opportunity to support students in their learning outside of music and to learn more about what students are achieving in other subjects.

Finally, it is paramount that music teachers develop relationships with those students who struggle academically, socially, or behaviorally, relationships that should go beyond simply understanding what is written on a student's IEP. The relationship you develop with students who face learning challenges can be the difference between a classroom environment filled with regular and uncontrollable behavioral interruptions and a positive and respectful classroom environment. Both Lindsey and Eric have noticed that building relationships with students who face these challenges can often eliminate classroom management issues before they begin.

> I have an autistic student who [has] difficulties with the group work or with something abstract. I've had to exempt [this student] from writing their own composition, because even though it's [a] small [task], there is freedom and there is no one right answer. It's so overwhelming to them that they just can't [complete the composition assignment]. [This student] might give me behavior issues until I figure out what was going on [and can adjust my expectations].
>
> —Lindsey

> I had a student in eighth grade a few years ago who had behavioral issues where he couldn't control his temper. The very first day of class he got upset about something and started yelling profanities. The aide took him out of the class, and when he calmed down, he came back in. When there was [a break] he came up and apologized to me. I told him, "look, I'm not going to go and tell the Principal, but you have to work with me; you've got to meet me halfway." We got along great for the rest of the year. I never had to send him down to the Principal. There was maybe one other outburst, but he knew when he was wrong and he knew he couldn't control it, but when he calmed down, he always knew that he'd screwed up.
>
> –Eric

Once Lindsey and Eric established relationships with the individual students they describe, they were able to make lesson modifications that were more individualized and appropriate to the specific students' needs. Although IEPs or 504s (in the United States) often provide lists of recommendations, middle level students who feel comfortable with a teacher are capable of articulating their needs in particular contexts and should be given the opportunity to work in relationship with the music teacher to create a modification that will best suit the particular situation or assignment.

Collaboratively Setting the Tone

Another way that teachers featured in this book focused on motivation through relatedness was by working with students to collaboratively set the tone of safety and belonging in the first few days of class. Katie explains that she considers her students her colleagues because "we're all in this together, there's nobody else in the room, so, we have to be invested in each other." Thus, striking the right tone on the first few days of class and working with, rather than against, the students to create an inclusive classroom community is important to the success of a middle level general music class.

Whether your middle level general music class meets for only a few short weeks or for the full school year, the first few days of class should be focused on involving all students in the classroom and collaboratively setting a positive tone for your remaining time together. Both Lindsey and Alexis describe how they specifically use the first three class periods of middle level general music to set and reinforce the tone. Because they choose to set the tone over three class periods, they are able to intersperse the important classroom rules and procedures with getting-to-know-you activities that integrate musical content.

> The sixth graders all come into the room and I always try to start very quickly with an activity. I think having an intensity in your purpose of what you're doing helps set behavior expectations. [For example] I have a set of drums and we do some simple drum patterns. I'll teach them right away, okay if I hold the drumsticks together, this is ready [position]. And we'll practice that [on the first day]. Also, I'll give them an overview of the room, what they should be touching, what they shouldn't. [This gives them] a preview of the units [by] showing [them] where the different things are in the room. [On the second day], we'll talk about tardies and I'll do an example of what it means to be on time. [Then

on] the third day, I'll do a music room scavenger hunt where I'll have [questions] like "how many chairs are in the room," "what do you have to do to be prepared," [and so on]. I think that first week I probably spend a third to a half of every day on discipline and expectations and then we don't have to do it again.

–Lindsey

I bought one of those vinyl stickers [shaped like] a tree, and I have it on my wall. I have these little dye-cut [music notes] and I write down their names on the [music notes] and then set those in their seats, so they know exactly where to sit on the first day of class. Then, [as I call roll, each student] puts a piece of tape on their note and they go and tape it on my tree. So then, my tree has all of my students' [names] on it. [After I introduce myself and we go over the rules and procedures], I hand out a Bingo sheet. [It has things] like "find a musician who can name this note," or "knows a composer whose name starts with B." They have to go around the room and ask their classmates and then their classmates will sign the appropriate box on the Bingo sheet. On the second day, we make the folders [we'll use throughout the class] and then I pass out post-it-notes [and ask] them to write a song that they would like to listen to on a Monday [for our regular listening day]. Then the third day, we'll practice getting out our folders and we talk about the three ways of listening: casual, mood, and concentrated listening. We talk about how we will be doing concentrated listening mostly in this class and we start listening very quickly.

–Alexis

Another approach to setting the tone focuses on helping young adolescents understand rules and grading. Following active getting-to-know you activities similar to Alexis' Bingo cards above, Abby and Nicole both implement techniques to help young adolescents understand these mundane aspects of a learning community.

In elementary school [students are told] here is what we do in this classroom and what we don't. But I feel for teenagers, because they start to question every authoritative thing you say, [they need to know why]. I have them tell me why they think something is a rule because I find if they know the rationale behind things, they'll go with it. If you're just telling them a rule, [young adolescents] don't seem to care as much.

–Abby

I say, "grading in [middle level general music] is very similar to all of your other related arts classes: Are you doing your best? Are you being kind to yourself and each other while you are doing your best? If you failed at something, did you try again or did you just give up?" I try to impress upon them, we're always working as a class, once that [learning] opportunity is gone, it's gone, so use it now [in the moment of class as we work together].

–Nicole

Both Abby and Nicole honor the young adolescent developmental need for autonomy by helping students see the rationale or logic behind the rules and grading procedures. Rather than presenting these important aspects of the classroom in an authoritarian fashion, these teachers wisely collaborate with the students in an attempt to secure student buy-in and positive understanding of the classroom expectations. This effort honors the transition to middle level learning and also sets a tone that hopefully persists, one of collaboration and relatedness among students as well as between the teacher and the students.

Learning Together through Group Work

Cultivating relatedness in a positive classroom community also involves helping students to learn from one another and work together in positive ways. While some music making can be done individually, much music learning is a collective effort, and thus part of a classroom community is helping young adolescents learn to work together, teaching students how to provide useful peer feedback, and guiding students to help one another without disrupting the class. Music teachers can make this a natural part of the general music classroom "by adding explicit steps to lessons where students consult peers for feedback on their work" (Milner et al., 2019, p. 86). When students begin to feel comfortable asking for and receiving feedback from peers, student relatedness increases and young adolescents are primed for positive learning through group work. Given access issues and home lives, it is imperative that middle level students are given ample in-class time to complete group work.

When appropriate to the project, I encourage you to allow students to form their own groups for projects. Young adolescents are often motivated when allowed to work with their friends, particularly when their shared interests are integrated into the project. Allowing students to form their own groups also demonstrates to students that you trust their judgment and their ability to work toward the learning goal and not just hang out with their friends. Some projects require that each group has students with specific skills and thus you may need to assign groups in order to ensure each group is successful in meeting the learning goal. However, whenever possible, allowing students to choose their groups gives young adolescents a level of autonomy over their learning, increases relatedness within each group, and likely improves student motivation to meet the learning goal.

Whether students choose or are assigned groups, I strongly recommend establishing leadership roles and responsibilities for each student in the group. Assuming that each group for a particular assignment contains the same number of students, you can determine the leadership roles in advance and then allow each group to collaboratively decide which student will take on a particular responsibility. For example, for a cover song project in my eighth grade general music class, I established roles that mimicked careers in music: Conductor, Manager, Producer, and Publicist. Leadership roles like the Conductor, emphasize the musical aspects of the project, while leadership roles like the Producer, emphasize the collaboration or organizational aspects of the project and thus allow students to choose the role most suited to their abilities and to take serious responsibility for helping to manage the group's success. When each person in the group has a leadership role, contributions to the group by each student are often more balanced. Students who are often afraid to speak up are often willing to do so when their role is defined, and the collective group can more easily overcome a dominant member of the group when he/she oversteps their assigned leadership role.

Third, allowing some students to work independently on a group project can lead to unforeseen collaborative learning and the emergence of leaders in the classroom. Lindsey noted that she rarely has students who choose to work independently during a group project, but that when she does, these individuals often end-up taking on additional leadership by helping other groups:

> If they're a really strong student [working on their own] sometimes they'll end up doing two projects. They'll do theirs and then some other group will try to recruit them to help them do theirs too. So [then] they'll work in more of a leadership role, and they end up doing twice the work.
>
> –Lindsey

In Lindsey's case, some strong students who did not want their grade dependent upon other students, end up helping other groups in addition to completing their own work. While this leadership role emerges naturally within the classroom, it can encourage those students who choose not to work with others to engage with peers in a positive way that does not directly impact their own individual grade or project success.

The success of group work is largely dependent on the classroom community already established. Student relatedness within the classroom is not a given, but it must be cultivated by the teacher who encourages peer to peer interactions, feedback, and critique. If your middle level classroom is a safe space of belonging for students who are encouraged to work in relationship with one another, their motivation to succeed in the class will transfer to individual work and collaborative learning situations.

Competence

A feeling of competence is the third facet of a positive and safe learning community designed to motivate young adolescents. A feeling of musical competence, like competence in any academic subject, is individualized, developed over time, based on previous experiences in the subject, and dependent on the actions of the teachers a student encounters. Young adolescence is an important time for the development of musical competence, particularly the belief that, as individuals, they can develop and share knowledge and skills in music in their future lives.

Unfortunately, many young adolescents enter the general music classroom with the preconception that they lack individual competence in music. Young adolescents who chose not to participate in available school ensembles may not view themselves as musical or may (unfortunately) have been told by an adult that they were not musical. According to Jo Saunders (2010), researcher at the University of London, "It is in relation to the dominant school-based genre that pupils form judgements of musical worth, have musical encounters and ultimately decide if the understanding of 'musician' presented in the school context relates to their own understanding of themselves" (p. 74). In the United States and elsewhere, the dominant school-based music genres are primarily the ensembles aligned with the Western paradigm: choir, band, and orchestra. Students who do not or choose not to "fit" in these ensembles may feel that they have no musical competence recognized by what schools call "music."

Most young adolescents possess some form of musical competence, but this may not be evident unless music teachers make an effort to understand how their students engage with music outside of school. Modern middle level students have constant access to music through their devices and access to a greater variety of music from around the globe than students of any previous generation. Since music is a daily component of middle level students' out of school lives (Campbell, 2009), each student already possesses some level of knowledge about particular forms of music and thus possesses musical competence. Music teachers can leverage this musical competence to engage students in the general music classroom by allowing students to share their musical interests and knowledge at appropriate points in the curriculum.

One way that young adolescents may perceive themselves as developing musical competence is based on whether the work they complete in middle level general music is ever seen or heard by anyone outside of the immediate classroom. Students who participate in ensembles know that they will eventually perform music in a concert. However, for a great many middle level general music classrooms, there is no public knowledge-display requirement. In referring to the public performance, I am separating performances in front of an audience (i.e., concerts) from in-class performances either as a whole class, small groups, or individuals. In-class performances should occur often in middle level general music as students practice, refine, and finalize their work. While the absence of a required public concert provides great freedom in the curriculum, and perhaps relieves pressure for general music classes that only meet for a short wheel-type schedule, students still need opportunities to share their developing musical competence with others. Without doing so, your colleagues and administrators may not understand the importance of general music learning to the development of well-rounded young adolescents and thus may devalue your work and students' developing competence.

Informances and Displays of Student Work

One option for sharing musical learning with others is to use an informance to share and/or display student work. The term *informance* is a combination of the word performance and the word inform. The point of an informance is to help parents, teachers, and administrators know how music learning occurs within the music classroom and to help them understand the process, not just experience the product (Zaffini, 2015). Music educator Mary Pautz (2010) explains that an informance is "an opportunity to show parents what the music curriculum really is and how the concepts are being developed" (p. 20). This is, in Pautz's (2010) language, likened to a musical "show and tell," a chance to help parents and other school community members understand what students have learned in order to be able to share their work with the audience.

Informances can improve motivation because young adolescents can participate in the preparation of these events to further develop feelings of musical competence. First, you can ask your students what they think they should perform or present in order to best demonstrate what they have learned thus far in the course. If you create a list of all things that were learned on the board, students will have several ideas for what to share at the informance. Second, once the demonstrations or displays are selected, students can help the teacher decide how best to practice or prepare for the presentation. Depending on the focus of the class, students may select to rehearse a piece as a whole group, practice compositions in small groups, prepare posters, bulletin boards, and video or audio recordings for display, or any other host of possibilities. Third, students can write program notes or explanatory remarks in order to help the audience understand what they are seeing and hearing. Fourth, the teacher can look to the students to direct the teacher's participation in the informance. If the students feel they need a conductor, the teacher can serve that role, assuming no student desires this responsibility; alternatively, the teacher might perform alongside the students or simply welcome the audience and step off stage. In essence, when you ask students to plan informances, you motivate them to articulate and demonstrate what they learned, thus deepening their understanding of themselves as competent musical individuals.

As a middle level general music teacher, I was required to present a concert every semester and in my research, I have encountered numerous teachers who also face a similar administrative requirement. If you are faced with a required concert for your general music classroom, I urge you to shift your thinking and work with your administration to alter expectations. Personally, I had great success moving my required semester concert from a performance to an informance. One semester, students decided they wanted to demonstrate their learning with an improvised drum circle (see Do-Now 6.1). They elected a student-leader to set the tempo, determined how other students would enter or exit the improvisation, and planned the prepared comments for the audience. The students decided that I should read their prepared comments, the "script" they wrote to introduce the project, because they wanted to focus on being ready to play. Another semester, after building ukuleles, the students only felt prepared to share one short piece of repertoire, but they also wanted to share poster boards of in-progress *Peter and the Wolf*-inspired fairytale leitmotif composition projects they were working on. These projects were unfinished, but each student was able to put their compositional planning on display on a poster board. And, because each student had built a ukulele, their ukuleles were also on display for the audience to examine. During my time at this school, the attitude regarding the semester performance shifted away from a music-only concert to an arts-showcase evening where music, visual art, drama, and applied arts all prepared displays and presentations for parents. This informance approach deepened the connections between all of the art forms, shifted expectations of parents and administrators, enabled students to publicly demonstrate their competences in a variety of art forms, and made for a joyful evening where artistic products at all stages of the artistic process were celebrated.

School-Day Sharing Events

Another way for students to develop feelings of competence is for them to share their musical learning in a school-day cabaret-style performance. School-day sharing events have several advantages. First, these performances only involve one class period of students at a time making them easier to manage. Second, students are already present in school and do not need to return to school at night, which can sometimes be challenging for families. Third, administrators, staff, and faculty are already on campus and are potentially more likely to attend. Finally, because they happen within the school day, these events are more easily integrated naturally into the curriculum of a middle level general music class.

In Jessica's year-long general music classroom, which is guitar focused, she does two school-day sharing events that she calls "Coffee Houses" where all students are required to select and prepare a short guitar performance of their choice. Typically, Jessica is able to hold this event in the media center and she advertises it on the school's morning news bulletin. Although not required by her administration, Jessica has gone out of her way to make this Coffee House a big deal for students, thus allowing her young adolescents to develop pride in themselves and share their emerging performance knowledge with a supportive audience.

> The [first Coffee House] recital is held in February usually, so I give [the students] a choice. They're allowed to choose whatever melody they want. [Their melody] has to be at least fifteen seconds, so they play like two lines [of the song]. Some kids really get into it and they do medleys that they've arranged themselves, like from *Pirates of the Caribbean*, and that's been really cool to see.
>
> I make it a big deal and [the students] have [formal] invitations [to distribute]. That really gives them some ownership because they know they're performing for their families. Let's say I teach period-2 for guitar so the period-2 students know that on Wednesday, whatever the date is, during period-2 I have a performance I can invite anyone in my family, I can invite any teacher, and I'm allowed to invite one friend to miss class, if their teacher allows it. [The invited friend has] a little pass that I make. I do have a lot of staff members who like to come, which is really cool. My administration has never come, but you know that's the game, right. Actually, a lot of the parents do come; some of them will email or tell the kid to tell me that they're running late and I try to do the schedule [of performances] to best accommodate everybody as I can. [Sometimes I] have [the student] play again when the parent shows up, which [the students] hate, but the parent loves.
>
> –Jessica

Jessica's approach to this school-day sharing event puts emphasis on the students' successes and developing musical skills. Students are able to choose what they play, thus integrating their perspectives and helping them feel comfortable demonstrating their emerging knowledge and skills. By allowing the students to invite a friend and their teachers to the Coffee House, Jessica implicitly instills in her students the message that they are musically competent and have musical skills to share with those people they trust. In Chapter 7, Jessica describes in more detail how these performances are an integral part of her assessment plan.

Service-Learning Performances

Finally, middle level general music students can develop feelings of musical competence through sharing their music learning in a service-learning setting. At the middle level, service learning is an important component of the curriculum, because young adolescents, while capable of many things, do not have a fixed role within the larger society. Many middle level schools have a community service requirement in order to help young adolescents develop a sense of responsibility and the importance of giving back to their community. However, service learning takes community service one step farther by connecting "an identified community need with academics" through "real life, community-based problem-solving" (Thompson, 2013, p. 248). Although a musical performance or informance might not directly solve a community problem, it might bring joy to a senior citizen or provide important musical instruction to an underserved elementary school.

Service-learning provides young adolescents with an opportunity to use their developing musical competence to contribute productively to their community and develop a sense of the importance of giving back (Jagla, 2016; Thompson, 2013). Rachel, a music teacher who served as a participant in my dissertation study, used service-learning performances in her general music classroom (Cronenberg, 2016). Rachel noted that, due to the low socio-economic status of many of her students, these performances were one of the only ways that many of her students felt like they could contribute to the community. For young adolescents, developing a sense of pride in the ability to give back to the community is an important life lesson that impacts their future desires to be involved in their local community. When students can bring joy to someone else through the musical knowledge or skills they have gained in general music, their feelings of musical competence will increase.

Wrap-Up: Creating Community

Key to creating a positive classroom community is motivating *all* young adolescents to engage, learn, and grow as members of the classroom community. Music teachers who develop a classroom community centered on autonomy, relatedness, and competence are most likely to motivate students to learn. This motivation, in turn, cultivates a positive classroom that is safe for young adolescents to try, fail, and try again. While it may be impossible to create such a space for every individual student every day of the school year, this goal of a safe space for belonging is achievable through daily, consistent efforts. Placing students at the center of the middle level general music classroom is not a one-time event. It requires a daily commitment to the individual students in the classroom and the creation and maintenance of the collective classroom community. When you place your students' identities and the establishment of a positive and motivating classroom community at the center of your work in middle level general music, you may find yourself making curricular choices that emphasize more diverse musical cultures and experiences (democratic principle #5). Please feel encouraged to expand your music teaching knowledge by embracing new musical cultures, new ways of understanding and interacting with music, and new strategies for engaging students. In what ways are you making your classroom community a safe space for each individual student and his/her multiple identities? Are students in your middle level general music class motivated to learn? Is performance preparation or project completion putting undue pressure on students and impacting their motivation? Is your class unbalanced in terms of autonomy, relatedness, and competence? What steps can you take to make your classroom community a more motivating environment for students?

PART 2

Reconsidering Curriculum and Pedagogy through the Fertile Ground Framework

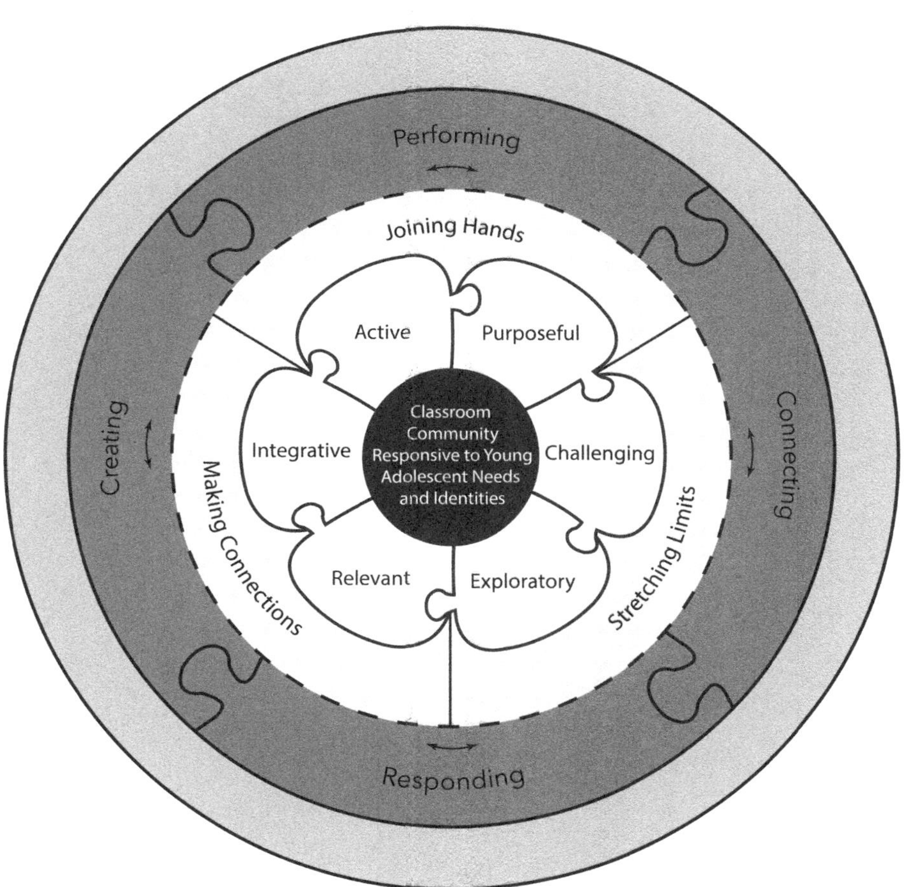

In Part 2–Chapters 4-6–our focus is on the six middle level pedagogical essentials and the four artistic processes featured in the modified Fertile Ground Framework figure above. Each chapter focuses on an overarching theme–joining hands, making connections, and stretching limits–that connects the paired pedagogical petals of the Framework. Possible applications of each theme are highlighted through an activity idea, a lesson plan sequence, and a Do-Now. As in Chapter 1, a brief section introducing the featured artistic process precedes the lesson plan sequence. Each chapter begins with a modified version of the flower-shaped portion of the Framework diagram highlighting the artistic process and pedagogical essentials featured in the chapter. Following a brief introduction, each chapter opens with two *imagined* classroom vignettes developed from what the teachers told me about their classrooms, their students, their preferred teaching style, and the lesson described. I have *imagined* these opening scenes from interview data; they are not factual step-by-step narratives of an observed in-class occurrence. These vignettes are presented for illustrative purposes to engage the reader and to highlight aspects of the Framework discussed later in the chapter.

4 Joining Hands

Active and Purposeful General Music Learning

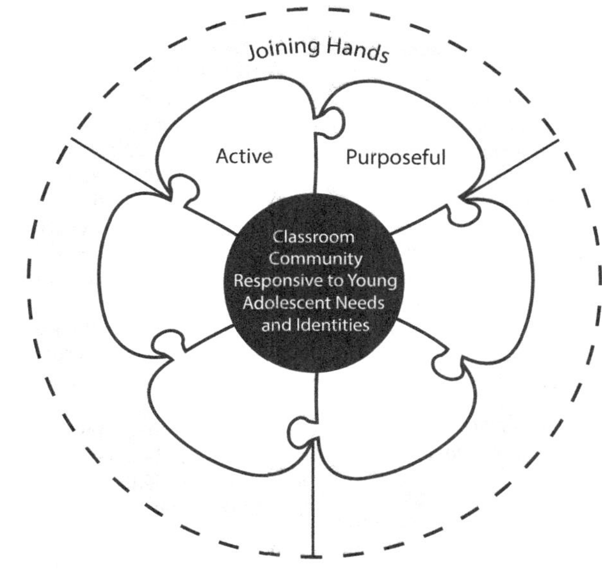

Democratic Principle #2: Integrating Students' Perspectives

Once a classroom community designed for our specific young adolescents is established, it is important to remember that this classroom community must be regularly maintained, not only by our relationships with students, but also by how we think about teaching and learning within the community. If, as I believe, the goal of middle level general music is to inspire students to continue their musical journeys once they leave our classrooms, students cannot achieve this learner independence without help, guidance, and support from teachers. Thus, a middle level general music teacher must foster a learning environment where students' perspectives are valued (democratic principle #2), students are actively and mindfully involved in learning, students understand and contribute to designing the purposes of learning activities, and students accept increasing responsibility for their own learning. This is joining hands with students.

DOI: 10.4324/9781003124245-5

Hannah

As we enter Hannah's classroom, the seventh grade students are moving around the classroom in time to the music played by Hannah on the piano. Suddenly, the tempo of the music changes and the students, trying to avoid bumping into each other, are moving faster. Some students laugh as they take giant, almost running steps around the room while others are quietly using only a small space in the classroom. The music stops and Hannah invites all of the students, some of whom are slightly out of breath, back to their chairs.

After everyone is seated, Hannah passes out a piece of paper, face down, to each student and tells them not to turn it over until she says go. The room has fallen silent as the students anticipate what is to come. Hannah says, "remember how we began talking about 20th century music last class?" Some students nod or say yes while others give no outward indication that they remember. "Today, we are going to use our bodies to create a composition using this sheet of paper as the instructions. After we complete that, we'll talk about it and learn some more about 20th century composition. Tomorrow we'll do a different kind of 20th century composition using instruments. Now, please turn over the paper and begin reading it silently. As you read, please do or say aloud whatever the paper tells you to do." The students turn over their sheet of paper and read:

> "Humming and Whooping a piece for singers by Carol Erion modeled after *Doodling*, by Tom Johnson"

"This piece is for many singers who can listen to each other while reading these directions. Often singers begin by clearing their throats. Clear your throat now" (Erion, n.d., para 1).

As the fastest readers in the class reach the first direction to clear their throat, they do so tentatively. Other students look around and, as their eyes return to their paper, they smile as they reach the same instruction. The throat clearing becomes louder as students gain confidence and read the next line, "since we are reading at different speeds the throat clearing sounds will occur at different times." Throat clearing and sniffing continues around the room as the instructions continue. Then someone makes a "t" sound that evolves into a "p" sound and suddenly the room is filled with snake-like "S's." Then, suddenly everyone is humming as the composition continues.

When Hannah is certain every student in the room has reached the end of the instructions, she cuts off the class and asks, "who wants to tell me what they observed during that activity?" and suddenly smiles appear on dozens of faces and nearly every hand in the room is in the air as class continues.

Alexis

At Alexis' K-12 school, the sound of chatter, movement, and energy reaches us while we are still in the hallway. When we open the door and enter, we see seventh and eighth grade students sitting, standing, and moving around the room. Some students are talking to classmates while others hold items in their hands or are making sounds by hitting strange objects. On the walls are images of musical instruments from around the globe. The instrument images are categorized and labeled as aerophones, chordophones, ideophones, membranophones, and electrophones. At first glance, this classroom appears like "mass chaos," yet, as we look closer, we notice a purpose to each student's movements. Even though no student is doing the same thing, it is not really mass chaos, but rather organized, creative chaos.

Alexis's students are in the middle of a project and each student appears to know what he/she needs to be doing. In one corner of the room three students are bent over an object that looks like an old coffee can as one of them uses a hot glue gun and another holds some kind of stick. In another corner of the room several students are drawing as they discuss a design. On the far side of the room, four students are holding various lengths of PVC pipes and having a detailed discussion.

A student near the door stands up and says, "I'll go ask," as she walks across the room to someone seated at a table with three male students, but with their back to the door. It is only when the person seated at the table stands up that we realize that it is Alexis, the teacher, who was working alongside these three students on a giant length of PVC pipe. The student who walked across the room asks, "can we see that Kahoot from the other day again?" and Alexis helps the student access the exercise from the beginning of the unit using the classroom computer.

We approach a group of three boys working nearby who are bent over a large cereal box with some plastic straws glued on the front of it, out of which a length of PVC pipe emerges. Three large rubber-bands run the length of the pipe to the box. "Can you tell us what you are doing?" we ask. All three boys look up and excitedly begin talking at once:

"We are making an instrument," says one boy.

"See this part's a chordophone," says another, plucking the rubber bands.

"And this is our idiophone," chimes in the third, scraping the row of plastic straws with the back of a plastic spoon.

"Now we are trying to decide how to include a membranophone," continues the first. "We are supposed to figure out how to have the four main types of phones on our instrument. Next week we will share them with the class."

Joining Hands

I adopt the joining hands metaphor from a brief mention of "hands-joined" learning in the section of the 2010 *This We Believe* that addresses active, purposeful learning:

> Developmentally responsive middle grades educators take the concept of hands-on activities further by promoting what might be termed "hands-joined" activities, ones that teachers and students work together in developing. Such activities foster student ownership and lead to levels of understanding unlikely to be achieved when students are simply completing teacher-made assignments.
>
> (NMSA, 2010, p. 16)

Young adolescents' desire for autonomy and independence can lead to a need to make their own choices and chart their own course within the learning environment. Classroom environments that are strictly controlled—where all decisions are made by the teacher—do not provide young adolescents with their desired autonomy and often lead to disengaged students. As a consequence, most middle level students seek out teachers who genuinely listen to their ideas and views on almost any topic, including the curriculum. Offering students autonomy over their learning decisions is part of helping them develop a sense of themselves as individuals and as independent learners (Mee & Haverback, 2016; Nakkula & Toshalis, 2006). When students are given a voice in the classroom and their perspectives are honored and integrated, young adolescent developmental needs and cultural identities are acknowledged, and hands-joined learning begins.

Joining hands in learning, as I describe it here, is rooted in constructivist theories of education which put students' experiences and perspectives at the center of the learning environment. Constructivist approaches to learning emphasize the importance of students constructing their own understanding of the world or the subject under study by integrating new knowledge into their preexisting understandings (Scott, 2011; Wiggins, 2015, 2016). Students cannot construct their own understandings if they are disengaged or unable to see how classroom learning connects to them personally. Learning begins with students' knowledge of and interest in a particular topic. We begin with our particular students and their relationship to the topic. What do the students already know? What do they want to learn? How can we help them achieve their goal? How can we involve them in the learning environment?

Active Learning as Hands-On and Minds-On

Active learning often is equated with hands-on learning or learning that engages students physically in music making, as described by Lindsey, Nicole, and Katie:

> I think for general music [it is] active because I definitely believe in a hands-on approach. That's so important for music making.
>
> —Lindsey

> [My class is] definitely active or always hands-on. Every day with an instrument, learning a concept—hands-on.
>
> —Nicole

> I think being active and hands-on at the middle school level is the best way for [young adolescents] to learn, they are so wiggly and so the more they can be active and doing stuff, the more fun they have and the more focused they are, there's no question about that.
>
> —Katie

The young adolescent need to physically move as part of the learning experience and to embody their learning should not be overlooked. Middle level general music classes where students sit quiet and still all period will likely not be successful. In the classroom vignettes at the opening of this chapter, both Hannah's and Alexis' students are engaged in active learning, albeit in very different forms. Hannah's students embody their emerging understanding of twentieth century compositional styles as they perform Carol Erion's *Humming and Whooping* prior to Hannah introducing John Cage and experimentalism. For Hannah and her students, it is this concrete embodiment of the musical style that helps convey understanding of the abstract concept, an approach Hannah employs throughout her Western classical music history unit.[1] In the second vignette, Alexis' students are engaged in an active hands-on learning environment where each student is working independently or with a small group of peers to build an instrument.[2] These students are not doing the same thing at the same time, but are still involved in a hands-on learning community. In physically active learning environments, a student's lack of participation in the hands-on activities, whether independent or teacher-guided, will likely result in the student's failure to connect the lesson to prior knowledge.

According to music education researcher Jackie Wiggins (2016), constructivist learning is not only hands-on but also "minds-on." While students who are actively playing instruments or are otherwise physically engaged may appear involved in the classroom, hands-on activity alone does not guarantee that they are actually learning through the independent construction of knowledge. They could simply be imitating what the teacher has demonstrated and playing their instruments rather mindlessly while daydreaming about lunch, a new crush, or some after school activity. In Alexis' classroom above, students are physically involved as they build their invented musical instruments, yet their group discussions also indicate mindful engagement with the classroom topic. Likewise, in Hannah's classroom setting, the students' eagerness to discuss after the activity suggests minds-on engagement.

As another example, although students are often wearing headphones and working alone on a computer in her class, Jackie considers her classes active:

> Are they active while they're working on something? Oh, yeah. They're basically on a computer, they're actively engaged, their brain is engaged trying to figure out the best way for this [composition] to happen.
>
> —Jackie

In contrast to the student who is daydreaming while playing the guitar, Jackie's students are actively trying to use the computer to produce the musical sound they hear in their heads. In solving musical problems (Wiggins, 2015)—whether building instruments, composing on the computer, or some other topic altogether—students practice applying their existing knowledge to some new context or musical task while engaging actively, both hands-on and minds-on, in music.

Purposeful Learning through Teacher and Student Collaboration

In order for students to be actively engaged in the learning process, they must understand *why* they are being asked to complete certain tasks. A teacher might do this by revealing to the students more of the "teacher thinking" behind a particular lesson or unit. When students understand the purpose of the learning activity, they are more able to connect their prior knowledge to the content being taught.

Many schools or districts mandate that teachers clearly articulate the objective or central purpose of a lesson, perhaps even requiring that this statement be posted on the classroom wall. However, posting the objective statement in the classroom does not necessarily ensure that the students understand the purpose of the lesson. Many teachers, like Abby, believe that they have a music classroom that is purposeful:

> I feel like every task that I ask them to do is done with intention.... I never ask them to do things just because. I feel like it's always got to be leading somewhere, and I don't mind telling them, we're doing this because this is where it's headed.
>
> —Abby

Knowledge of an activity's purpose gives young adolescents autonomy over their own learning and thus leads to greater motivation. The inverse is also true: young adolescents who are unaware of the learning purpose(s) are more likely to reach the conclusion that middle level general music is irrelevant and, at a minimum, disengage from the learning.

Joining Hands: Collaboratively Constructed Learning Experiences

Students and teachers begin working side-by-side when students help to develop the purposes of a particular learning exercise, collaborate with their teacher in developing assignments, and "routinely assume the role of teacher" within the classroom (NMSA, 2010, p. 16). While stating or posting the objective or purpose is an important step in helping students understand why they are completing a particular activity, I hope that middle level general music teachers move beyond this teacher-directed way of thinking about learning. When young adolescents are given the opportunity to collaborate with their teacher in developing the objective or purpose or to direct, co-construct, or choose the learning activity, engagement increases and students move toward autonomous music learning.

In a hands-joined learning environment, the shared awareness of the purpose of the learning activity enables any member of the classroom community to take on the role of teacher at various times. Of course, while teachers are still responsible for maintaining classroom order and ensuring that learning is proceeding, students can still support one another, monitor themselves, and even teach their teacher. In the classroom descriptions above, it was clear that Hannah was leading her students, whereas at the beginning of Alexis' description we were unaware of the teacher's presence in the room. Alexis, while still maintaining a productive learning environment, was working *alongside* her students to help them meet the learning goal. When and how teachers lead or work alongside will, of necessity, vary based on the particular learning goal.

Hands-Joined Learning and the US National Core Arts Standards

This shift in the power relationship between teachers and students may at first appear misaligned with the learning that occurs in your school community, but this approach is already embedded in the US National Core Arts Standards. Consider these two seventh grade general music standards:

- MU:PR4.1.7a: "Apply collaboratively-developed criteria for selecting music of contrasting styles for a program with a specific purpose and/or context and, after discussion, identity expressive qualities, technical challenges, and reasons for choices" (SEADAE, 2014c, p. 4).
- MU:CR3.1.7b: "Describe the rationale for making revisions to the music based on evaluation criteria and feedback from others (teacher and peers)" (SEADAE, 2014c, p. 2).

In the performing standard (MU:PR4.1.7a) above, students and the teacher *collaboratively* develop criteria for selecting music based on their understanding of the purpose of the learning activity. Likewise, in the creating standard (MU:CR3.1.7b), the teacher is not the sole source of feedback on a student's composition. The student can independently apply the evaluation criteria to his/her own composition and can provide feedback to a classmate based on this criterion. When students and teachers are aware of the purpose of a musical activity, they can work *together* to develop criteria for selecting music for performance or evaluating the compositions of any member of the class.

Many of the middle level general music Standards indicate an increasing emphasis on a different kind of relationship between teacher and students. If you read a particular standard across from fifth through eighth grade, you will see an emphasis on gradually moving students away from reliance on their teachers to increasing student autonomy in musical decision-making. So, while fifth graders may not be ready for accepting all of the responsibilities of a hands-joined learning environment, this responsibility and ownership over learning can and should increase each year of middle level learning. This is how music teachers can help guide students to increasing levels of musical independence and strive for the ultimate goal of students pursuing their own musical endeavors after they leave the general music classroom.

While the US National Core Arts Standards set grade level targets, teachers who are well-attuned to the specific students in their classroom community know whether these targets are too easy or too difficult for their specific students and adjust accordingly. This is particularly important when general music learning is not available or required across all four grade levels. The progression suggested by the Standards will, of necessity, be interrupted.

An Example: Purposeful Learning on the Way to Hands-Joined

In fully hands-joined learning communities, the teacher to student hierarchy dissolves because "teachers and students work together in developing" the learning purposes and activities

(NMSA, 2010, p. 16). Robert provides us with one description of how his role as teacher has altered as he gives students more autonomy within his classroom community:

> I guess I can describe my style as, it's not so much that I teach, it's that I coach. And, I sometimes challenge [the students] pretty hard to the point where it's a little bit too hard for them, and they're starting to feel that frustration. [In general music] the work the kids do is fairly project-based, they do have a lot of their own time too, where they're working on something and I can, I just sort of come around and offer advice or expertise.
>
> –Robert

While Robert sets the learning goal or project, rather than working with his students to set the goal, his coaching style presents a less hierarchical relationship and meets many of the criteria for a hands-joined learning community. Robert did not specifically articulate that he is learning alongside his students, but we might assume that he sometimes learns something new as he guides a student in his/her musical work. In addition, we might assume that, given his coaching style, he might easily choose to establish the learning purpose *with* his students rather than *for* his students. Creative teachers will think of many possibilities for shifting power to the students and joining hands to cultivate an active, purposeful learning environment guided by students' perspectives.

A Hands-Joined Approach to Project-Based Learning

In project-based learning, students are learning musical content, potentially across multiple standards, while completing a clearly defined project that will demonstrate their knowledge. Project-based learning is experiential, hands- and minds-on, and student-focused. In project-based learning, teachers like Robert act as a knowledgeable guide or coach rather than as a director or conductor. Often project-based assignments also address a problem or other real-world scenario, thus making these assignments more relevant to students. In project-based learning, students should understand the purpose of the assignment from the outset and should be able to articulate the purpose, like Alexis' students in the opening vignette, when asked at any point during the completion of the project. Jessica DeMink-Carthew, middle grades education scholar at the University of Vermont, and her colleagues have applied the concept of hands-joined learning to project-based learning (DeMink-Carthew & DeMink, 2016; DeMink-Carthew & Olofson, 2020). DeMink-Carthew and her colleagues admit that project-based learning can easily become overwhelming for teachers, particularly those who would like to join hands with their students in this form of learning. Thus, they have recommended five steps teachers can implement to help make a project-based learning assignment more hands-joined, each elaborated briefly below.

Step 1: Identify a Theme of Student Interest

Teachers review the curriculum and standards to find encompassing themes they believe students will find interesting and engaging. Hands-joined teachers then engage students, perhaps through a vote, in the final selection of the theme from among a few possible topics. Willingness to move forward with the students' choice is key. If you teach multiple class periods of general music, you will need to decide–in advance–if votes will be tallied across class periods or if it is feasible for each class period to choose a different topic.

Step 2: Co-Develop Inquiry Questions

DeMink-Carthew and DeMink (2016) suggest that the second step is to work collaboratively with students to develop a set of questions, derived from teacher-selected standards, objectives, and essential questions, to guide the project. In discussing the essential question(s), students brainstorm possible guiding questions for the inquiry using prompts like "'I wonder why ...' or 'I wonder how ...'" (DeMink-Carthew & DeMink, 2016, p. 36). The size of your general music class may impact how you choose to co-develop inquiry questions. One technique that might be useful here is to have each student work independently to generate six "I wonder" statements. Then, ask each student to join with a partner to "pair and share" their list of statements. As a pair, the students then discuss and perhaps vote to create a combined list of their top four "I wonder" statements. Each pair joins another pair and, following discussion, decides on their top two "I wonder" statements that are then written on the board. In this way, a large class of 30 students can quickly generate 180 "I wonder" statements and in the course of about 20 minutes (or less) narrow that list to approximately 14 "I wonder" statements–a far more manageable number for whole class discussion.

Step 3: Co-Planning

In the co-planning phase of the process, the teacher prepares a series of exercises, worksheets, instructional centers, graphic organizers, or other forms of scaffolding that help the students move through the process of: (1) choosing an inquiry question individually or through a class vote; (2) selecting a project, perhaps from a class menu–such as building instruments, producing a music video, researching the history of a musician for a report, or creating a podcast or video for younger kids about the topic–to demonstrate their new knowledge or skills; and (3) co-planning the steps necessary to accomplish the proposed project. While the students already have access to the standard, objective, and essential question(s) that guide the project, the students now need an evaluation tool (e.g., a rubric). The evaluation tool will help the students make choices about their individual or group project. To enhance the hands-joined efforts of this project, students might co-plan the rubric with their teacher (see Chapter 7).

Step 4: Facilitating Inquiry

In the fourth stage of a hands-joined project-based learning experience, teachers need to provide the time and space for students to complete their project. According to DeMink-Carthew and DeMink, "this phase is where many 'student-centered' projects fall apart since it can be difficult to find the appropriate balance between providing developmentally appropriate support and active, purposeful learning" (2016, pp. 37-38). Young adolescents desire autonomy and an opportunity to demonstrate competence, but this desire does not always equate with their cognitive abilities for abstract thought and planning. Thus, they need support and direction from their teachers, particularly in the setting of short-term goals and using their time wisely in class. Now is the time for the teacher to work as a facilitator or coach. Posting a schedule in the classroom will help students judge their own progress against the overall deadlines and goals of the project.

The balance of space to work and guidance through specified deadlines will be determined, in part, by the amount of class time available to this project. If your middle level general music class meets only once or twice a week, this project may require all or nearly all of your class time for several weeks. However, if your class meets every day, you might choose to create a schedule where students are working on their projects on specified days of the week but are engaged in some other musical learning on the other days of the week. Young adolescents will value a predictable schedule where they can anticipate the day's work. Once students are invested in their projects, you may find students entering the room with the question: "Are we going to work on our projects today?"

Step 5: Authentic Sharing

Authentic sharing is the final phase of a hands-joined project-based assignment. While sharing projects within class helps students build their public speaking abilities and facilitates grading, authentic sharing focuses on opportunities to present work beyond the walls of the classroom. According to DeMink-Carthew and DeMink (2016), authentic sharing is motivating to students because the audience listens to them as knowledgeable experts. When students share in authentic settings, such as an informance, concert, or visit to an elementary school, they are the experts and have an opportunity to see that their knowledge and skills are valued beyond the walls of the music classroom. To further motivate students, those who complete their projects first can work together to begin planning the event. Of course, it would be impossible to complete the authentic sharing phase of this hands-joined process for every project completed throughout the year. Given the limited time in music class, you will need to be judicious about which projects are shared in this manner.

An Example: Applying the Five Steps to General Music

In my own eighth grade general music class, I often began the year by asking the students what they wanted to learn about music. One year, students wanted to learn more about how instruments worked (Step #1). While the students and I then developed units derived from this student interest, we did not explicitly follow DeMink-Carthew and DeMink's (2016) suggestions. However, imagine that we did follow the steps outlined above and began by generating a series of "I Wonder" statements (Step #2) such as "I wonder why my mom's *erhu* only has two strings" or "I wonder how you can make a flute out of the bamboo in my yard." Together, we might discuss possible projects and eventually decide that part of the class wants to build invented instruments while the other wants to research the invention and development of specific instruments. Then, I would differentiate and work with each group to co-plan (Step #3) the project's rubric and later provide them with an appropriate graphic organizer to continue planning independently. In order to facilitate the inquiry (Step #4), each group would have a designated workspace as well as their own peer review and teacher check-in schedule posted in the classroom. Finally, authentic sharing (Step #5) might take various forms, such as convening a panel of local historical experts to evaluate the research projects or a visit to the local elementary to share the invented instruments with kindergarteners. Alternatively, both groups might collectively organize a gallery walk and formal presentation for parents and family members.

Rethinking the Genre/Musician Research Project by Joining Hands

Adopting an approach to project-based learning that joins hands does not mean you must throw out your existing projects; rather, you may simply need to rethink something you already do. Almost any project might be turned into a hands-joined project. The degree to which the hands-joined, collaborative elements are emphasized may change with each particular project or with each group of students.

One of the most common projects I hear described by middle level general music teachers is some variation on a research project and presentation either about a composer or a musical genre (see Activity Idea 4.1). Since genre or musician research projects are so common in middle level general music, this assignment might be an ideal place to start when thinking about hands-joined learning. Jessica, Hannah, Holly, Alexis, Abby, and Eric all do a variation on this project, but none of them described their projects to me in a way that suggested the implementation of the hands-joined steps delineated above. Abby is the only teacher who, through the creation of the composer's cell phone as the final project assignment, marginally integrates students' perspectives into the project, although the assignment itself remains teacher-directed. Below, I suggest five simple changes that might help make this common research project more hands-joined.

- Suggestion #1: Determine Student Knowledge and Interests
- Suggestion #2: Provide a Menu of Projects Based on Student Interests
- Suggestion #3: Allow for Unexpected Student-Initiated Topics
- Suggestion #4: Provide Tools to Guide Student Work
- Suggestion #5: Monitor Progress through Peer Review

Activity Idea 4.1

Genre/Musician Research Project

Suggested Grade Level:

- 5th & 6th

Primary National Core Arts Standard:

- MU:Re7: "Perceive and analyze artistic work" (SEADAE, 2014c, p. 7). Select the appropriate grade level standard.
- MU:Cn11.0: "Demonstrate understanding of relationships between music and the other arts, other disciplines, varied contexts, and daily life" (SEADAE, 2014c, p. 10).

Modified from Activities Developed by:

- Jessica, Hannah, Holly, Alexis, Abby, & Eric

Description:

In this activity, students individually research a genre or musician and then present their research to the class as a poster, PowerPoint, or other form of visual display. In addition to researching facts, students should listen to and select an appropriate musical example to share and explain during their presentation. For example, Abby has students research Western classical composers and then imagine what this composer would have on his/her cell phone including contacts, playlists, apps, and invented text message conversations that convey important historical information. Based on their research, Abby's students have invented text conversations about the composer's death, identified babysitting apps because the composer had a lot of kids, and other creative interpretations of the assignment parameters.

Suggestion #1: Determine Student Knowledge and Interests

When students research and share about a musician or genre that interests them, their perspectives are valued, and they feel like they have contributed to the musical knowledge of their peers and perhaps even their teacher. Instead of assuming what students already know, you might begin by asking the students two personal reflection questions:

1 What music or musicians are your favorite?
2 What more would you like to know about this music or these musicians?

Then, students' answers to the questions above might be transformed into the class-created inquiry questions.

Alternatively, you might try an activity Alexis does with her students, particularly when she is unsure whether her students can name multiple musical genres:

> We start off with a brainstorm. I give them a minute and they come up with as many genres as they can think of [working with a partner]. The kids read [their lists] out loud. If they say country music, but another pair [of students] has also written out country music, they have to cross that off [their lists]. [The group] left with the most [genres] at the end, they "win" the brainstorm [and get a piece of candy or other small prize]. It just goes to show them that there are lots and lots of genres out there, and so, we'll talk about [many of those genres].
>
> —Alexis

Once all of the well-known genres are eliminated, you might make a list on the board of the remaining genres. Then, ask the students what questions they have about the genres listed on the board or allow them some time to do exploratory research online before settling on a topic.

Suggestion #2: Provide a Menu of Projects Based on Student Interests

Teachers who know their students well can easily take the inquiry questions or topics generated by the students and develop a "menu" of project choices—poster, PowerPoint, fake social media account, etc.—each with its own rubric and instruction sheet. Although students are not deciding on their final product completely autonomously, they are also not required to complete the same project as everyone else in the class. Thus, a menu of project choices provides students with choice regarding how they want to demonstrate their learning at the end of the project. Theoretically, this menu of projects could be easily modified from year to year based on students' inquiry questions. In addition, while students will produce different end products, they should all be able to use the same scaffolding tools (see Suggestion #4 below) because all projects will still need the same planning steps and have the same research requirements.

Suggestion #3: Allow for Unexpected Student-Initiated Topics

One way that the genre or musician research project becomes more hands-joined is to encourage students who ask permission to explore genres and musicians not typically considered part of "school" music. For example, students in Alexis' class are not limited to either

Western classical genres or American popular music and thus many of her Latinx students choose to complete projects on a traditional Mexican or South American genre. Other students choose more unusual genres. For example, one student did a project on lullabies while another student completed a death metal project. Since most death metal recordings are not appropriate for school, the student found a death metal version of "Let it Go" from Disney's *Frozen* to share with the class. In Alexis' project guidelines, she requires each student to give a presentation on their genre and to share one musical example for their classmates to respond to in writing. Typically, Alexis only allows students to play the audio of the song—in order to strengthen music listening skills and also to avoid imagery that might not be appropriate for school—but in the case of this student's project, she chose to share the video with the students:

> I'm watching this one, I'm cracking up at my desk, and the kids are like, what is so funny? Well, it's because this band had put their [death metal] sound over the images of Elsa actually singing ["Let it Go"] in the movie [Frozen]. So I'm like, okay finish writing what you're writing, and then we're all going to watch this together, because this is just too funny. It was so hilarious to hear this death metal sound and see Elsa [singing]. So, it's interesting the things that [the students] come up with [when allowed to work independently].
>
> —Alexis

This death metal project, and the subsequent collective class enjoyment, was only possible because Alexis allowed her students to choose their genre and she was open to unexpected and unusual choices.

Suggestion #4: Provide Tools and Familiar Support to Guide Student Work

Many young adolescents struggle with how to plan a large project because as elementary students they were rarely asked to complete large projects without adult supervision. When given only the project instructions and rubric, many young adolescents will feel overwhelmed and quickly abandon the project. However, if you provide the students with tools to scaffold their work and employ familiar supports or expectations used in other classes, students will have a greater chance of success.

Here, I provide two different graphic organizers that might aid young adolescents in working independently on the genre research project. Although these examples focus on the genre research project, they are easily adaptable to the musician research project or a project on another topic altogether. In the initial planning stage of this project, Teacher Resource 4.1 guides students in thinking through their project beginning with the selection of an "I Wonder" statement before beginning their research. The guided research worksheet, Teacher Resource 4.2, helps the students learn the specific facts they should research about their genre and guides them to keep track of their sources.

Teacher Resource 4.1

Hands-Joined Co-Planning Graphic Organizer: "Genre Research Project"

Essential Question: How can I learn more about what makes a specific genre unique?

Standards:

- MU:Re7: "Perceive and analyze artistic work" (SEADAE, 2014c, p. 7). Select the appropriate grade level standard.
- MU:Cn11.0: "Demonstrate understanding of relationships between music and the other arts, other disciplines, varied contexts, and daily life" (SEADAE, 2014c, p. 10).

Objectives:

- I can demonstrate six important facts about my chosen musical genre through a project that helps my peers learn and meets the "excellent" level on the rubric.
- After listening to four songs from my genre, I can describe my chosen genre using five musical vocabulary words that are appropriate to all four songs.

My guiding question (Choose an "I wonder" question from the question bank created by the class. This will be the question that guides your project.)	**I want to investigate this guiding question because. . .**
I will research the _________ musical genre (Write the name of the musical genre below.)	**I want to research this musical genre because. . .**
My final project will be a __________. (PowerPoint, presentation, fakebook or other social media page, cell phone, movie trailer, etc. If you are having trouble, review the posted list of possible options.)	**I will do the following things to complete my project** (Try to be specific as you list the steps.)
In order to complete my project, I need __________. (Try to think of all the supplies you need for both your research and to complete your final project.)	**I think this project will meet the requirements on the rubric because. . .** (Use the rubric provided to specify how your project will meet the criteria.)

Teacher Resource 4.2

Research Guide: "Genre Research Project"

Essential Question: How can I learn more about what makes a specific genre unique?

Standards:

- MU:Re7: "Perceive and analyze artistic work" (SEADAE, 2014c, p. 7). Select the appropriate grade level standard.
- MU:Cn11.0: "Demonstrate understanding of relationships between music and the other arts, other disciplines, varied contexts, and daily life" (SEADAE, 2014c, p. 10).

Objectives:

- I can demonstrate six important facts about my chosen musical genre through a project that helps my peers learn and meets the "excellent" level on the rubric.
- After listening to four songs from my genre, I can describe my chosen genre using five musical vocabulary words that are appropriate to all four songs.

BEGIN YOUR RESEARCH

Answer the questions below as you complete your research	**For each answer you find, write the bibliography for where you found your information. *(Simplified MLA format below or change for your school's expectations.)***
My chosen genre is:	Bibliography template: **BOOK:** Last Name, First Name. *Title of Book*. City of Publication, Publisher, Publication Date. **WEBSITE:** Name of Creator (if available). *Name of Site*. YEAR (if available), URL.
1. What are three famous songs that fit within your genre?	Source where you found #1
2. Who are three famous musicians/groups known for performing music within your genre?	Source where you found #2
3. When did your genre first begin OR when was your genre most popular?	Source where you found #3
4. What musical instruments (if any) are most associated with your genre?	Source where you found #4
5. One question I have about my genre is. . . **The answer to my question is. . .**	Source where you found #5
6. A second question I have about my genre is. . . **The answer to my question is. . .**	Source where you found #6

MUSICAL LISTENING	
I will listen to these four songs from my genre. (List the song title and artist.) 1. 2. 3. 4.	**The five best musical vocabulary words to describe song #1 are. . .**
The five best musical vocabulary words to describe song #2 are. . .	**The five best musical vocabulary words to describe song #3 are. . .**
The five best musical vocabulary words to describe song #4 are. . .	**After listening to my four songs, the five musical vocabulary words that I think best describe my genre are. . .**
I will share the following song with the class. . .	**I have chosen this song to share with the class because. . .**

Middle level learners are just beginning to conduct independent library or internet research and thus they need guidance and consistency. School librarians are usually willing to create a cart of books on a particular topic for you to use in the library or keep in your classroom during the course of the project. If students have already completed their graphic organizer, you will know their chosen genres and thus can provide a list to the librarian. If conducting this research online, a list of approved websites with clickable links posted on the school's learning management system will help students focus their research on reputable sources. I also recommend checking with your students' language arts and social studies teachers to find out their typical expectations for research projects, such as citation style. Once you know what other teachers in your school expect of your students, you can reinforce familiar expectations.

Suggestion #5: Monitor Progress through Peer Review

The addition of peer feedback is an excellent way to make a genre or musician research project more hands-joined. The extended multi-day nature of this project means that sometimes students lose sight of the ultimate goal. A peer review day allows students to mentally regroup, to provide feedback to someone else, and, in doing so, gain new insights into their own work. Middle level researchers Michael M. Grant and Robert Branch (2005) observed that when students received project feedback from peers, they stretched their own capacities and improved their projects.

A peer review day might begin with a whole class discussion about the goals of the project and a review of the checklist or rubric for the project. Then, once everyone agrees on how the project will be evaluated, students can use the official rubric/checklist or a modified one to evaluate the progress of their partner. Alternatively, in discussing the project goals as a class, the teacher can guide the students to create a quick checklist that each student can then use to give their partner feedback. Adding a peer review day to an existing project is a simple way to ensure that midway through the project all students are reminded of the project's purpose.

Performing Music as Joining Hands

In many ways, musical performance is synonymous with music education. The preparation of ensembles for concerts, parades, contests, football games, and other *public* performances is one major way music educators receive recognition and support from administrators, parents, and the larger community. Performing in large ensembles, chamber groups, and as a soloist, comprise a significant portion of the preservice music education curriculum where the reasoning is that the higher the quality of a music teacher's performance skill, the better he/she will be at building those skills in others. While this reasoning is incomplete and perhaps contestable, the reality remains: musical skills in performing are highly prized components of music education. Perhaps you, like many music teachers, joined the profession in order to lead your own ensembles and share your passion for music with future generations. These are laudable goals, and in an ensemble setting, clearly the performing standards play a major role. However, in general music, particularly at the middle level, it is necessary to look at the performing standards through a slightly different lens.

Artistic Process: Performing

The 2014 National Core Arts Standards shifted thinking in US music education from the dichotomy of singing or playing instruments (as stated in the 1994 Standards) to a consideration of six performance-related process components: (1) select, (2) analyze, (3) interpret, (4) rehearse, (5) evaluate & refine, and (6) present. According to Erin Zaffini (2018) who served on the committee to write the Standards, the performing standards shift the focus from teacher-directed to student-directed performing:

> Typically, when preparing a piece of music to perform in our classes, music teachers make most or all of the decisions. As teachers, we select the music, analyze it, interpret it, and share our interpretations with students and rehearse, evaluate, and refine the music so that we can ultimately perform it. The new standards not only keep all of these steps in the forefront of *Performing* but also call on our students [to] partake in all of this work themselves. When you give the students the responsibility of doing this themselves, they are experiencing the process of performing as authentically as possible, the way a professional musician would. (p. 58)

In essence, the performing standards still want students to perform a variety of repertoire using both instruments and their voices, but suggest that students collaborate with their teachers in building their autonomous music performance skills. This is joining hands in performance.

Young adolescents are mature enough to thoughtfully consider musical selections, learn how to analyze, at least partially, the repertoire chosen, and consider specific interpretations of the chosen repertoire, to name just a few abilities. Young adolescents may also desire to work hard to create the best product possible, through evaluation and refinement of their performances and out of an innate concern for how their work will be perceived by others.

Why Perform If Not in Concert?

If you are not required to prepare your general music classes for public performance, what is the relevance of performance and the performing standards in your middle level general music classroom? In middle level general music, the word performance loses its association with polished public displays of music making and rather focuses on collective and individual music-making intended to help students understand music and improve skills. It is important to remember that throughout the world music-making is a social endeavor, what music education philosophers David Elliott and Marissa Silverman (2015) call a praxial approach to music-making done in community. For the majority of adults around the world, informal engagement with music takes some form of collaborative music-making such as singing the National Anthem at a sporting event, playing a guitar around a campfire, teaching children folk, cultural, or religious melodies, singing or playing an instrument in a house of worship, or jamming with friends at a party. Though students in middle level general music may never perform with their classmates in front of an audience, engagement in music learning involves collaborative *performance* or music-making within the classroom in order to inspire future musical journeys.

A Brief Word about Singing in Middle Level General Music

There is a (mis)perception expressed by some music teachers that general music is focused on singing. Historically, general music has singing at the center of the curriculum. Elementary music classes, regardless of pedagogical approach espoused by the teacher, feature students learning to sing dozens of songs each school year. Likewise, many music teachers have approached their middle level general music classrooms through singing. Of course, singing is something nearly every human is capable of doing, with varying levels of skill, and thus an important part of a comprehensive music curriculum. However, any general music class that focuses on only *one* aspect of performance (whether singing or playing an instrument) without incorporating other aspects of musical knowledge, such as listening or composing, is not meeting democratic principle #5. A whole semester focused on only singing or only guitar performance, while valid music learning, would fall outside of this definition of general music.

Many music teachers struggle to integrate singing into the middle level general music classroom because of students' perceptions about singing (Lucas, 2011; Sweet, 2010) and of the impact of students' adolescent development on their voice. By joining hands in general music class, student perspectives are valued and included within the curriculum. Consequently, students' perspectives on their voice change, along with any other singing perceptions they may hold, need to be acknowledged and integrated into the curriculum if there is any hope of students using their voices in class. Validating these experiences will help to cultivate a safe classroom space where students feel comfortable singing.

Encouraging young adolescents to sing in middle level general music may be challenging, but there are numerous strategies you might try in order to integrate your students' perspectives and work together.[3] First, you can simply admit to students that you know they might feel uncomfortable singing and ask them to share when they feel comfortable using their voices in a musical way. Perhaps they like to sing along to their favorite songs, but not to unfamiliar music. If this is the case, you might then ask the students to suggest songs that the class could perform with their voices and build the singing portion of your curriculum around students' suggestions. Green (2008) and her collaborating teachers were surprised by how willing students were to sing when they chose the repertoire themselves. Second, techniques like singing together, singing while drumming or playing guitar or ukulele, and chanting or rapping can encourage students to use their voices with less pressure. When students are playing guitars or ukuleles in general music classes, they will often sing along with the play-along video or the teacher without prompting if they are already familiar with the song. Third, ask students to create and perform original lyrics either for new compositions or for parodies of familiar songs. While their vocal performance might not meet our ideal of quality singing, the students are using their instrument to discover how it works as they experience this period of physical development and vocal register shifting.

Lesson: Ukulele or Guitar Performance Game

Eric has developed this series of lessons (see Lesson Sequence 4.1) as part of the ukulele portion of his sixth grade curriculum. Here, the lesson is listed for eighth graders because of the featured performance standard (MU:Pr5.1.8.a) that asks eighth grade students to judge for themselves when a musical performance is ready to be presented. This eighth grade standard specifies that students themselves should independently develop the criteria to assess their performances, presumably based on prior learning. The same lesson sequence might be done with earlier grades, but the teacher and/or teacher and students together would need to establish a set of criteria or a rubric at the outset of the lesson sequence in order to guide students in assessing their performance level. Eric's sixth grade students are an example of how grade levels specified in the Standards are not always applicable to a student population.

For this lesson sequence, Eric has completed significant pre-class planning in order to establish a game-like atmosphere with his students. The goal of the game is for students to earn, through adequate ukulele performance, 75 points (see Teacher Resources 4.3 & 4.4). This lesson sequence is active and purposeful because all students understand the learning goal or outcome (achieving 75 points through good performance) and are working in a hands-joined way in order to achieve it. In addition, because they are required to evaluate their own performances to determine whether they are ready for teacher review, students must use prior musical knowledge to assess their own performance abilities. Eric describes how he developed this somewhat novel approach to developing performance skills in his general music class:

> I went to a conference ... and I saw a session using ukulele play-along videos that this teacher had been making. So, I found out about these play-along [videos] and I tried one out and it worked great with the entire class, but at the same time ... it was still too basic for some of [my students]. As I was researching on YouTube, I found that there were a whole bunch of these play-along videos, so what I did was I curated them into playlists of different levels of difficulty [in order to create] a game of the ukulele curriculum.... Immediately the engagement switched over to a hundred percent.
>
> I invited my Principal [to visit class] and he looked around and said, "this is amazing, every single student was looking at their laptop playing whatever song they want and learning how to play the ukulele that way."
>
> [In this activity they are] learning the chords, learning how to move [on the fretboard, and] getting the dexterity. I subscribed to all the [YouTube] channels I could [in order] to add to my list [of songs]. I was able to come up with stipulations for the really advanced students: once you get to two hundred points then you do level-4 [song] with [a] strumming pattern, you can start [reviewing other students'] playing tests and awarding points. I was getting overwhelmed and inundated running back and forth to the students to help them [and] to get the playing checks. When [students] were ready [to be reviewed] they'd just come up [to the SMARTboard], type their name on the list at the bottom, [and wait their turn]. Once it got rolling it became this well-oiled machine. I just was able to sit back and watch my advanced students go around and check and award points and they loved that—being the keeper of the points. And students that needed help, I was able to spend time with them and help them. It just totally changed my ukulele curriculum.
>
> —Eric

While Eric did not plan the game-like lesson sequence in collaboration with his students, there are two important hands-joined features of this performance-focused game. First, Eric allows students to select the songs they would like to play (from his curated list), moving at their own pace, and choosing an ability level they feel is appropriate. This allows each student to integrate his/her own perspective and choices into the curriculum and thus find internal learning motivation. Second, students are required throughout the lesson sequence to self-assess their own musical performance in order to determine whether or not their individual performance is ready for teacher/peer review. This self-assessment means that each student is learning autonomously, thus cultivating in students the ability to continue musical learning once they leave the classroom. In these ways, Eric and his students have joined hands in order to create an active and purposeful learning environment focused on performance.

Lesson Sequence 4.1

Ukulele or Guitar Performance Game

Basic Lesson Information

Suggested Grade Level:

- 8th

Prior Knowledge:

- Students have learned the basics of how to play the chosen instrument.
- Students can play at least two chords.
- Students have used play-along videos as a whole class.

Approximate Number of 45-Minute Periods:

- 5-10

Essential Question:

- How do I know when I am ready to perform?

Materials:

- Ukuleles or guitars for individual student use (the same idea might be used with other instruments if play-along videos are available or created).
- Ukulele or guitar play-along videos curated into levels by the teacher and put into a YouTube channel or other online resource students can easily access. See Teacher Resource 4.3 for suggestions.
- iPads, Chromebooks, or other internet accessible devices (ideally one per student).
- Headphones
- Teacher Resource 4.4
- Point record for each class period (projected or posted on the classroom wall)

Modified from Lesson(s) Developed by:

- Eric

Primary National Core Arts Standard:

- MU:Pr5.1.8.a: "Identify and apply personally-developed criteria (such as demonstrating correct interpretation of notation, technical skill of performer, originality, emotional impact, variety, and interest) to rehearse, refine, and determine when music is ready to perform" (SEADAE, 2014c, p. 5).

Objective:

- Using a curated list of play-along videos, the students will be able to independently select and practice chordal accompaniments on ukulele or guitar and determine when they are ready to perform for the teacher with technical accuracy in order to earn at least 75 points in the game.

Formative Assessment(s)/Check-Ins:

- Daily point totals identify which students need additional support or challenge.

Summative Assessment(s):

- Successful completion of 75 points

Lesson Sequence

Day 1:

- Begin the class by reviewing the chords learned previously. Consider using a play-along video to review.
- Ask the students to "pair and share" their struggles thus far on the instrument.
- Ask for volunteers to share with the class.
- Based on responses: provide a mini-lesson review or group students and provide differentiated instruction based on student identified needs.
- Tell the students that they are going to continue building their skills through a game-like environment.
- Ask the students, "What criteria should we use to decide if a piece we are working on is ready to perform?" Students might suggest things like: not missing any chord changes, being able to get to the end of the song, etc. Generate a list of suggestions on the board. Guide the students to narrow the list, if necessary. Keep the list to post each day during the project as a reminder for the students.
- Pass out Teacher Resource 4.4 and explain that students can work alone or with a partner to learn to play songs in order to earn a grand total of 75 or more points.
- Show the students the point record and explain that their points will be displayed in the classroom so they can track their progress. The goal is to earn 75 points, but they can continue earning points after they reach 75.
- Distribute supplies or ensure students have access to devices, the curated play-along videos, and headphones.
- Allow class time for students to begin working independently.

Day 2–10 (or more):

- Remind the students of the rules and procedures for the game.
- Post the student generated list of criteria for when a piece is ready to perform.
- Prepare a sign-up list on the board so that when a student is ready to perform for points, he/she can write their name on the list rather than sit in the room with their hand raised not practicing.
- The teacher circulates the room listening to students who have listed their name on the board as ready to perform. If students are not prepared, send them back to keep working without yet earning points. Otherwise, document the points earned.
- Encourage the students to review the list of criteria for a performance-ready song before putting their name on the board to be reviewed.
- Wrap-up each class period by asking the students to review their point total.
- Finalize the project when all or nearly all students have reached the 75 point requirement. If students need an extension, consider offering them support afterschool or during lunch.

Possible Extensions or Additions:

- After students reach 200 points AND have played a Level 4 song with an interesting strumming pattern, they can become "helpers." Helpers are allowed to award points to classmates who are ready to perform or asked to work one-on-one with a peer who is struggling.
- Allow students to find a play-along video not on the teacher's curated list that he/she would like to learn. Ask the student to consider the number of chords and the difficulty of the chord changes. Then, ask the student to suggest a point value along with the reasoning for the point value. If you agree with the student's assessment, add the song to the curated playlist and allow the student to prepare it for points.

Framework Commentary

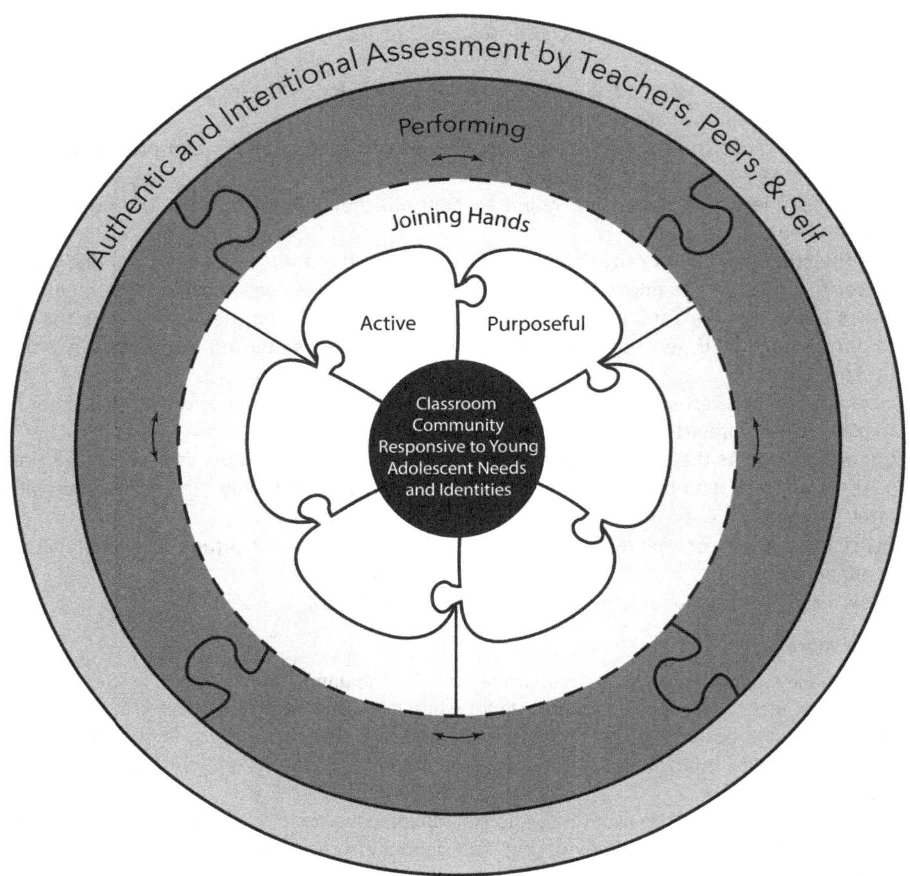

Joining Hands

This lesson is a strong example of *active* and *purposeful* learning because students are working at their own pace to achieve a specific learning goal: developing performance skills on the instrument, evaluating their performance against the performance criteria, and earning a specified number of points when successful. Providing choice often motivates young adolescents, engages them actively in the learning task, and requires them to actively listen or practice through significant hands-on and minds-on class time.

Artistic Process

The focus of this lesson is on developing skills in recognizing when a *performance* being prepared is ready to be shared publicly. While each student may learn different musical skills during the course of this project, each will learn the musical skills needed to accomplish performance of his/her chosen songs. Ultimately, because each student must learn at least one Level 2 song, all students should be able to perform a 3 or 4 chord song as a result of the lesson sequence and then easily transfer these new skills to future learning.

Authentic and Intentional Assessment

Authentic and intentional formative self-assessment is a critical component of this activity. Learning to self-assess during the practice process is an important and authentic skill that all musicians need. By the time they earn 75 points, the students will possess more refined skills in performance self-assessment.

Teacher Resource 4.3

Ukulele Performance Game Suggestions by Level

Excerpted from Eric's list

Level 1 (10 points each)

- "Surfin' USA"–The Beach Boys (G7, C, F)
- "The Dreidel Song" (C, G7)
- "London Bridge is Falling Down" (F, C)
- "Day-O (The Banana Boat Song)" (F, C7)
- "Gummy Bear Song" (C, Am, G)
- "Thunder"–Imagine Dragons (C, F, Am)

Level 2 (20 points each)

- "Shake It Off"–Taylor Swift (Am, C, G)
- "Try Everything"–Shakira (from *Zootopia*) (C, F, G)
- "Someone to Lava" (C, G7, F)
- "Let It Be"–The Beatles (C, G, Am, F)
- "The Cup Song"–Anna Kendrick (C, F, Am, G)
- "I'm Yours"–Jason Mraz (C, G, Am, F, D7)
- "Jolene"–Miley Cyrus (C, G, Am)
- "Jingle Bells" (C, F, G7)
- "You Are My Sunshine" (C, F, G)
- "Brave"–Sara Bareilles (C, F, G, Am)

Level 3 (30 points each)

- "I'm a Believer"–The Monkees (G, C, D, F)
- "Bad Moon Rising"–Creedence Clearwater Revival (D, G, A)
- "I Got a Feelin"–Black Eyed Peas (G, C, Em)
- "Hallelujah"–Rufus Wainwright (C, G, F, Am, E7)
- "Just Like Fire"–Pink (Em, C, G, Am)
- "Firework"–Katy Perry (G, Am, Em, C, D)
- "We Know the Way"–Lin-Manuel Miranda (from *Moana*) (A, D, E7)
- "Feliz Navidad" (Em, A7, D)
- "Believer"–Imagine Dragons (Am, F, E7, G)
- "Ghostbusters Theme"–Ray Parker, Jr. (A, G, D, Am, AmM7, Am7, D7)

Level 4 (50 points each)

- "Better When I'm Dancing"–Meghan Trainor (D, G, Em, A)
- "Somewhere Over the Rainbow"–Israel Kamakawiwo'ole (C, G, Am, F, Em, E7)
- "Cake By the Ocean"–DNCE (Em, Bm7, Am, C)
- "Sweet Caroline"–Neil Diamond (C, F, G, G7, Em, Am, Dm)
- "Story of My Life"–One Direction (A, Bm7, D, Em, G)
- "The Campfire Song Song"–Spongebob Squarepants (C, F, D7, G7, C7, Fm)
- "Game of Thrones Theme Song" (Cm, C, Gm, Bb, Fm, Ab, Eb, G)
- "All I Want for Christmas"–Mariah Carey (G, Em, C, D, E7, Eb, Am, B7)
- "Happy"–Pharrell Williams (G, C, D7, Eb, Dm)
- "So Much More"–Grace Vanderwaal (Dm, C, F, Bb, Gm)

Level 5 (75 points each)

- "A Whole New World" (from *Aladdin*) (D, Bm, A, Em, F#7, G, E7, Bbdim7, A7, F, Dm, C, Gm, Bb, G7, Edim7, Eb, C7)
- "Rubber Ducky" (from *Sesame Street*) (C, C#dim7, Dm7, G7, C7+5, F, Fm6, Am7, Em, B7, Cm)
- "Blackbird"–The Beatles (G, Am7, D, C, A7, D#dim, Em, Gaug, A9, Cm, D7, Gm7, Dm, F)
- "You've Got a Friend in Me"–Randy Newman (from *Toy Story*) (C, E7, Am, Cdim7, G7, D#dim, Dm, C7, F, D7, A7, B7, Em)

Teacher Resource 4.4

Ukulele or Guitar Performance Game Procedures (from Eric)

Select songs from the play along video playlists on the YouTube channel. There are five levels:

Level 1 = 10 points each

Level 2 = 20 points each

Level 3 = 30 points each

Level 4 = 50 points each

Level 5 = 75 points each

Your goal is to accumulate a total of **75 points**. At least one song must be a song from Level 2 or higher.

To earn points, you must play the entire song with the video for your teacher. All chord changes must be played correctly.

You can earn bonus points for any song by practicing different strumming patterns. Some videos give you an interesting strumming pattern to use for the song. You might also consider using a different strumming pattern for the verse than you use for the chorus of the song.

- One strum per chord = 0 bonus points
- Strumming on half notes = 2 bonus points
- Strumming on quarter notes = 3 bonus points
- Strumming on eighth notes = 5 bonus points
- Rhythmically interesting strumming pattern = 10 bonus points

Performing Lesson Suggestions for Differentiation

Several differentiation strategies are built into the game-like structure of Eric's lesson sequence. Innate in the design is individualized differentiation because each student can select the repertoire best suited to his/her own level of ability. This is perhaps one of the best features of this lesson sequence because young adolescents can make their own decisions about what level of song is best for them. Thus, a student who is struggling on the ukulele can work on an easy piece and eventually earn points while a student who desires a challenge can potentially spend the same amount of class time working on a much harder piece.

In addition, Eric has specifically designed differentiation for those students who are excelling. It is sometimes easy to forget that advanced students may need modified assignments in order to prevent boredom. Even if your middle level general music class does not include students enrolled in one of the ensembles, you may still have students in your class with significant musical knowledge because they have taken years of piano lessons, are studying guitar outside school, have learned a traditional cultural instrument in their family or community, or for some other reason. Additional bonus points are available for students who try advanced strumming patterns, and Eric has designed a leadership role for those students who reach the top levels of ability.

Although Eric did not describe modifications for those students with documented disabilities, innate in the game structure is one obvious modification. Students requiring learning modifications may not be able to reach the 75 points in the allotted class time. A simple modification is to set a more realistic point total based on the specific student's needs. Additional modifications related to reading and tactile ukulele and guitar issues are discussed below.

Ukulele/Guitar Notation Modification Suggestions

There are a number of differentiation strategies that can help those students who struggle in playing either the ukulele or guitar. For neurally diverse students with reading struggles, transferring guitar and ukulele notation to the instrument is often a challenge, as Lindsey describes:

> For students who have learning disabilities like dyslexia, I'll work on a different type of notation. I might color-code the notation, like different strings or different highlighters. I'll [also] flip the notation upside-down so that it's more of a mirror image.
>
> —Lindsey

The fact that tablature notation appears on the printed page upside-down from the strings of the instrument or that students must reverse the chord chart in order to understand where to put their hands can be confusing at first for most young adolescents.[4] For those who already struggle to decode the written page, this new form of "writing" can cause students to abandon the effort to play guitar or ukulele before they have begun.

Color-coding is one easy way to help with these notation challenges. One option is colored strings which are available online for both guitar and ukulele. While the colored strings are more expensive, having at least one instrument with colored strings can be a useful investment. Once the student has the instrument with colored strings, you simply need colored markers or a color printer to mark the student's tablature notation or chord charts with the same colors. Similarly, if students find it difficult to understand the numbering of various frets, number stickers in various colors can be purchased at any arts and crafts store. These stickers can be placed under the strings on a student's fretboard in order to help the student remember where to place his/her hand for various exercises. Similarly, Abby used two different colors of the small flag post-it strips that are often used to mark text in books as a tool to mark fret two and four when she taught simple melodies to her self-contained special education music class.

Ukulele/Guitar Physicality Modification Suggestions

Lindsey and Abby have both taught guitar to students who have specific physical or tactile challenges and have developed some simple and successful adaptations. Some students find that touching the vibrating string is too much physical sensation, but Abby found a simple solution:

> I had [these] little rubber finger cover things, that you use for turning pages. We used those for the kids who couldn't stand to touch the strings that hard, or they might not have the dexterity to even pinch that hard. And we spent like three days, just pushing on the strings trying to get a clear sound.
>
> –Abby

The rubber finger cover things Abby refers to are called "rubber finger tips." They look like sewing thimbles, but are made of rubber and come in various sizes and colors.

Lindsey has also used some other tools in order to make the guitar easier to play:

> For some students pressing on the strings is a tactile sensation that they can't handle or don't want to. [In that case] I'll do anything from a low modification of like they would just rather play the guitar incorrectly, like flat [on their laps] or using the hand position wrong. I just don't correct that because that's [the] adaptation they need. [Also] I'll tune the guitar to an open G chord and then they have like a little piece of PVC-like thing that [is] like a little claw that goes between your thumb and your finger. It will press down and then you can bar all the chords. [Using this,] you just move to whichever fret you [need] depending on the chromatic scale.
>
> –Lindsey

The PVC-like tool that Lindsey describes is most likely a "guitar barre" that can be strapped on to students' fingers and used to play bar chords (Bell, 2014). In his research adapting the guitar for a student with Downs Syndrome, Adam Bell (2014) also describes a tool called a "guitar buddy" which enables students to play the guitar or ukulele by pushing buttons. Of course, as the tools for adaptations become complex, they also become more expensive. The guitar buddy is the most expensive tool mentioned here. Knowledge of your school population will help you determine whether or not the cost of these more sophisticated tools is beneficial.

Making Listening Active and Purposeful: Listening Logs

When considering how to make middle level general music more active and purposeful, music listening activities that meet the responding standards are likely not at the top of the list. Performing and composing inherently have clearer hands-on elements than do responding activities. In the elementary general music curriculum, hands-on responding to music is evident in circle and line dances, movement activities with scarves, steady beat games, etc. When these hands-on activities are taught correctly, students can take the musical embodiment they experienced in the dance or game and begin to cognitively understand musical form, dynamics, or steady beat.

Many music teachers consider the commonly used elementary general music listening activities too childish for young adolescents while others have found successful solutions. Danielle, who teaches a K–8 general music curriculum with a great deal of listening, describes how she engages students in listening activities, often with drawing activities or conducting,

> I give them stuff so that when they're listening to music [they can focus]. I'm a doodler and I love puzzles. Nothing is just listening; there is always a concept; there is always a purpose, some way to integrate it. [Listening is] active because you're physically either using an instrument [such as a marker to draw] or conducting.
>
> —Danielle

In addition, as can be seen in Hannah's classroom vignette at the beginning of this chapter, some students will still embrace movement activities as a chance to act silly and child-like for a moment. Young adolescents do like to dance and move, provided that they are already comfortable with the type of movement you are asking them to complete. However, young adolescents will not complete movement activities where they risk embarrassing themselves in front of their peers. Knowing your students continues as a key theme because what works in one classroom community at one grade level may not work in another.

Danielle's and Hannah's efforts to make listening active and purposeful are supported by research in music education. In her dissertation research, Bush (2017) found that, following class periods where middle level learners sat still and passively listened to music, students reported disengagement from the lesson. In contrast, based on her research in middle level general music, Davis (2011) reported that middle level learners found "listening activities meaningful, provided they [were] presented in a way that allow[ed] students to be actively involved in the process, and provided that the music itself [was] seen as relevant" (p. 19). Passive listening to large portions of a piece of music is not what is intended by the responding standards; rather, students should be taught what to listen for and how to listen for a particular musical element.

Several teachers in this study use daily or weekly listening logs as a way to regularly integrate musical listening into their curriculum. These listening logs make listening to music active because students are listening and actively applying recently acquired musical knowledge (minds-on) in order to respond to the prompt (hands-on). The purpose of listening logs is clear: the student should listen and answer a question or otherwise respond. When the teacher and students work together to select the music or to develop the prompts used, the listening log becomes hands-joined (see Do-Now Activity 4.1 & Teacher Resource 4.5). Through teacher or student developed prompts, students can build their use of musical vocabulary while responding to nearly any genre of music.

Do-Now Activity 4.1
Listening Logs

Suggested Grade Level:

- 5th–8th

Approximate Length of Time:

- 10–15 minutes per class period

Materials:

- Listening Log (see Teacher Resource 4.5)
- Audio files

Primary National Core Arts Standard:

- MU:Re7: "Perceive and analyze artistic work" (SEADAE, 2014c, p. 7). Select the appropriate grade level standard.

Modified from Activities Developed by:

- Katie, Holly, Alexis, Danielle, Robert, & Stephanie

Description:

- The goal of a listening log or record is to develop purposeful, attentive listening. Prompts chosen give students a guide for listening actively to unfamiliar music and the ability to apply recently developed listening skills. Daily Do-Now practice with listening and responding to music builds students' skills and comfort with listening purposefully to both unfamiliar and familiar repertoire.
- Hands-joined possibilities include:
  - o Work with the students to develop the criteria for the listening log worksheet.
  - o Ask the students to provide song suggestions and then use these songs after they are screened for school-appropriate content. A song suggestion box in the classroom allows students to suggest songs throughout the year. Alexis asks students to suggest songs on the first day of class, and Eric regularly asks his students what artists he should be listening to. Every Monday, Alexis uses one of the student's song suggestions for their listening log.
- Provide students with several pages of listening journal prompts to put in their class notebook or folder and keep to a regular schedule for listening logs.
- Listen to the song at least twice; three times is best, but your students, class time, and listening selection length will dictate what is realistic.
- After listening, ask students to share and where appropriate provide context or additional details regarding the composition.
- Choose a variety of genres and/or align listening selections with other content being studied.

Teacher Resource 4.5

Listening Log Prompt Possibilities

Option #1

Date:

Song Title:

Instruments:

Vocal Style:

Dynamics:

Form:

Tempo:

Mood:

Topic:

Other:

Option #2

Date:

Song Title:

Choose one of the statements below to complete in a paragraph response to the song played. Be sure to use at least one music vocabulary word in your response.

1. The music made me feel __________ because
2. This music made me think of __________ because
3. I would like to hear this piece again because
4. My favorite instrument in this piece is __________ because
5. If I made a cartoon with this music, the cartoon would be about __________ because
6. I would use this music for a commercial advertising __________ because
7. I would use this music in a movie about __________ because

Option #3

Date:

Title:

Composer/Performer:

Genre/Musical Period:

What instruments/voices do you hear?

What tempo marking would you give the piece?

Largo *Adagio* *Andante* *Allegro* *Prestissimo*

What is the texture of the piece?

Monophony *Homophony* *Polyphony*

Describe the piece with at least two good adjectives.

Notes:

Modification Suggestions

Modify these listening logs for English Language Learners by providing the student's native language and English side-by-side or by providing visual prompt choices such as a turtle and rabbit for tempo or various emojis for mood.

Similarly, modify listening logs with visual prompt choices for students with reading challenges. Try to select images appropriate to the individual student's needs without making the listening log appear as though it is designed for a young elementary school student. Depending on the student's needs, limit the number of responses required for a particular listening log. For example, consider five listening activities in a row where the student only responds to tempo and mood and then two new prompts for the next five listening activities.

Extend the listening activity by having the students conduct, march, dance, draw, or follow a listening map in response to the music.

Opening listening activities or Do-Nows are a great way to introduce students to a wide variety of teacher- and student-chosen music and still practice important music responding skills. Once these skills are developed through regular practice, integration of a listening requirement into a larger assignment, such as the genre/musician research poster project (above), is simple because the students already know how to listen. Thus, music listening need not take an entire class period, can be productive time that settles the class, and can be practiced regularly throughout the entire middle level general music course.

Wrap-Up: Joining Hands

Joining hands in learning, as I have defined it here, integrates students' perspectives, requires active and purposeful learning that encourages students to construct their own understandings, and ensures collaboration between teacher and students. In collaborating with our students, the student to teacher relationship shifts as the teacher steps back and allows students more autonomy within the learning environment. While every minute of a middle level general music class will likely not meet the expectations of hands-joined learning outlined here, any steps toward making the classroom more active and purposeful will reap positive benefits for young adolescents, cultivate independent music learning, and improve motivation to learn. As you think about the young adolescents in your classroom, consider their evolving developmental needs and cultural identities and ask: where might joining hands serve my students well? How can I transform an existing project into a hand-joined project? What forms of scaffolding and support do my students need in order to be successful?

Notes

1 In another twentieth century music lesson, Hannah uses chromatic boomwhackers to teach students about 12-tone serialism.
2 Using purchased kits, recycled objects, or the shop/tech theater/visual art teacher as a resource, each student can build his/her own ukulele, tubano, or invented instrument to learn about sound production and later use it for performance or composition. Ukuleles can be made from kits or cigar boxes and tubanos from concrete form tubes.
3 For additional suggestions, see Frank Abrahams' (2005) chapter on singing in the book *Engaging Musical Practices: A Sourcebook for Middle School General Music*.
4 Thompson (2011) suggests the software Pro Guitar 6 because it easily translates guitar tablature into Western notation or the reverse, and allows teachers to print both guitar tablature and Western notation together.

5 Making Connections

Relevant and Integrative General Music Learning

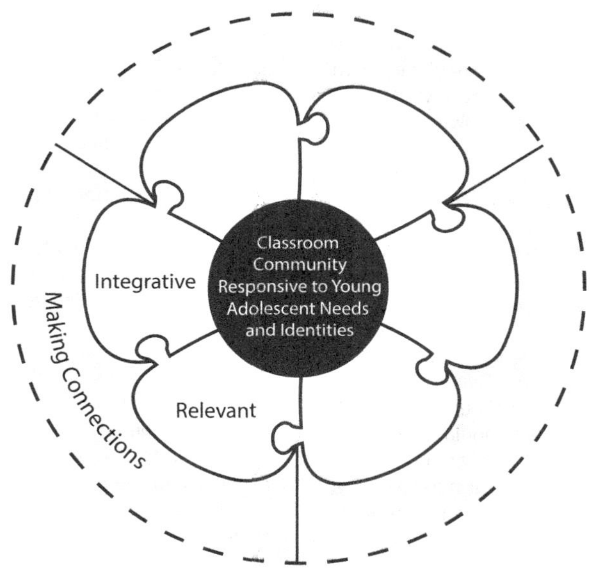

Democratic Principle #3: Helping Students Connect

What is the point of enrolling in a middle level general music class? How is this class relevant to me? How is music related to the subjects I like? These are some of the many questions young adolescents might ask when middle level general music appears on their course schedule. As music teachers, one of our roles is to model thinking that connects music learning to the rest of school and life outside school (democratic principle #3). When teachers model these connections through their curricular and pedagogical choices, young adolescents improve their ability to independently make connections and begin to find value in middle level general music class and interest in pursuing future musical experiences.

DOI: 10.4324/9781003124245-6

Tyler

All around Tyler's classroom, the students are working in pairs. Some students are seated at computers while others are standing face to face, holding sheets of paper, and taking turns rapping. The whiteboard at the front of the room says: Characteristics of a *Hamilton*-style Rap Battle:

1. Two people
2. Each person says their piece & later responds
3. Insult one another with clever lyrics
4. Make the audience say "ohhhh"
5. Include real quotes
6. Research to make it historically accurate

Next to the characteristics of a rap battle is a sheet of paper. The paper contains a list of famous figures from early American history beginning with explorers and extending through the Civil War. On this list, students have written their own names and identified their partner; thus, each pair of students has selected two famous figures for a rap battle.

In one corner of the room, Benjamin Franklin and Samuel Morse are battling over who has the best invention, while in another corner Abigail Adams and Sojourner Truth are in a heated debate over women's rights. As we listen in, we overhear students rapping about various moments in American history: the Salem witch trials, the Declaration of Independence, the best route to travel from Albany to Buffalo, NY, whether a family should move west, and how Native American tribes should be treated.

Two students approach Tyler as he moves around the classroom. One student hands Tyler a piece of paper and says, "we are having trouble."

Tyler glances down at the piece of paper and says, "what's the issue?"

"None of our lyrics fit the beat."

The second student points to a paragraph on the paper and says, "we want to use these quotes, but they aren't working."

"Remember how we talked about using only small parts of quotes? We want to use the words of the historical figures if we can, but we also need to focus on rhyme and meter. Instead of using the whole paragraph, let's look at the quote carefully. What are some important words or phrases in this quote? Can you go and highlight or circle the most important words? Once you've chosen some words or phrases, can you put those with your own words so that they fit the meter and the rhyme?"

"So, like, we don't have to use the whole quote?"

"That's right. Remember, we want your rap battle to be historically accurate and to use real quotes, but musically it needs to make sense. You need to be able to perform the rhythm and rhyme just like the rap battle from *Hamilton* that we watched last week."

Nicole

On the whiteboard, a single question is written in all capital letters: WHAT IS FORM? As we glance over the shoulder of a student in Nicole's classroom, we see a sun, a cat, a house, a rainbow, and an unfinished American flag outlined in dry erase marker on a handheld whiteboard. Glancing around the room, all students are drawing variations on the American flag.

"Ok," Nicole calls out, "please hold up your American flags. Look around. What do you notice?"

A student raises his hand, "they are all different."

"You're right, they are all a little different, but what's the same about them?"

"They all have stripes and stars," a student offers.

"That's right," Nicole responds. "What else?"

Another student suggests, "they are all rectangles."

"Yes! Ours were all different, but we had the overall big idea. We all know that the American flag is a rectangle and that it has stripes and stars. So how do these drawings connect to music? Music is not put together randomly. Just like the American flag or a rainbow, there are different parts that are put together to make music. What kinds of parts does music have?"

"Melody," one student offers. "Rhythm," says another. "A chorus and verse," offers a third.

"Ah," replies Nicole. "How do you know a song has a verse and chorus?"

"Well, they sound different," replies one student.

"And you can sing along to the chorus because it repeats later in the song," shares another.

"Ok, so I'm going to sing a little song for you," Nicole begins to sing a short two bar phrase on la. "Did everybody hear it? I'm going to sing it again. Can you sing it back to me?" She sings and all the students repeat the phrase. "Ok, this time, I'm going to make my song longer and I want you to raise your hand when you hear the part you know." After saying this, Nicole sings a short ABA improvisation using the original phrase as the A section.

After singing Nicole continues, "if you raised your hand at the beginning and the end, you're right." She writes two giant As on the board with a space in the middle and says, "If we label my original part A, what letter goes in the middle for the new part?"

"B" comes the reply from around the room.

"Exactly. What I just sang would be labeled ABA. We are identifying different sections or parts of a piece of music and labeling them. This begins to answer our question for this unit," she says pointing to the board, "what is form? We recognize the objects we drew because they have a specific form. Let's see if you can identify the form of some more musical examples by writing the letters on your whiteboard. Then we'll listen to "Fossils" from *Carnival of the Animals* that you'll remember from last year."

Making Connections

Most young adolescents enjoy music in some capacity. Yet for various reasons they have been turned off from *school* music. What is taught in elementary general music is extremely valuable for providing a musical foundation upon which any student can build regardless of their future musical pursuits. However, some students feel so disconnected from music class in elementary school—the reasons for this disconnection are wide ranging and individualized—that they believe middle level music will continue this trend of irrelevance.

As discussed in Chapter 4, constructivist pedagogy argues that through active engagement in the learning experience, students construct their own understandings of the topic under study (Wiggins, 2016). Thus, it is the student who is ultimately responsible for connecting what is learned in music class with previously learned music content, content in the disciplines, and personal experiences outside of school. However, young adolescents who are still developing their abilities to think abstractly cannot do this entirely independently. Young adolescents need guidance and a curricular experience that fosters connection making rather than one that forecloses connections through disciplinary insularity and memorization. Thus, young adolescents need experiences that allow them to engage in the principle being taught *and* to have the connections illuminated for them by the teacher or their peers while they build their skills. Through modeling, scaffolding, and active engagement in connection-making activities, young adolescents strengthen and hone their ability to think critically and creatively, two lifelong skills that are not cultivated in all learning environments.

At first glance, Tyler's and Nicole's lessons in the opening vignettes seem very different, but they share a common thread: an adoption of democratic principle #3. Both Tyler and Nicole are drawing on musical and non-musical content familiar to their students' everyday lives and content from other subject areas—although the social studies and language arts connections are stronger in Tyler's lesson than are the visual art connections in Nicole's. In both vignettes, the flexibility and comprehensiveness (democratic principle #5) of the general music curriculum enable these teachers to select widely different genres yet plan integrative and relevant connections that illuminate for students the connections between music learning and other areas of students' lives (Barrett, 2016).

Drawing on the two cross-disciplinary anchor standards (#10 and #11) specified in the 2014 US National Core Arts Standards, the authors of the music standards articulated two K-8 general music connecting standards that parallel our discussion in this chapter:

- MU:CN10.0: "Demonstrate how interests, knowledge, and skills relate to personal choices and intent when creating, performing, and responding to music" (SEADAE, 2014c, p. 9).
- MU:CN11.0: "Demonstrate understanding of relationships between music and the other arts, other disciplines, varied contexts, and daily life" (SEADAE, 2014c, p. 10).

Unlike the performing, responding, or creating standards, the connecting standards have no grade level details or sub-standards specified. According to three of the authors of the Standards, making connections is naturally situated within the other three artistic processes (Shuler et al., 2014). Thus, instead of writing detailed connecting standards, the authors chose to cross-reference grade level specific creating, performing, and responding standards that explicitly help students make connections.

I agree that connections between music, other subjects, history and culture, life beyond school, and personal experiences, are made primarily through musical experiences in performing, creating, and responding. However, because cognitive development occurs differently for each young adolescent and is influenced by experiences, we must endeavor to develop activities that model connective thinking so that students will develop competencies in doing likewise. Through experiences making connections, young adolescent brains are primed for lifelong abilities to think beyond disciplinary boundaries and are thus better prepared for work in any discipline.

Relevant Music Learning

Relevant music learning enables young adolescents to connect learning in middle level general music to personal experience and the world around them, now and in the future (MU:CN10.0). According to *This We Believe,*

> Curriculum is relevant when it allows students to pursue answers to questions they have about themselves, the content, and the world. When teachers help them to see the many connections that link various topics and subjects, students recognize the holistic nature of all knowledge.
>
> (NMSA, 2010, p. 22)

The musical content, knowledge, and skills selected for a middle level general music class should immediately draw young adolescents into the learning experience by making learning personal. In turn, what they produce musically should be influenced by their experiences.

The teachers participating in this book agree that relevant music learning is a priority for middle level general music. Lindsey and Holly point out that a relevant curriculum helps engage young adolescents, particularly those who are placed in rather than choose to enroll in middle level general music:

> I think that in middle school, especially, if you don't have a relevant curriculum the kids won't be engaged. You need to really show them: yes, this is why we're doing [this learning activity] and this is how it relates to [your] life. I think that's a big part of what makes [general music] successful in middle school.
>
> –Lindsey

> Half of these kids don't necessarily want to be in music. They're not there to be musicians. That's a lot of the reason [districts] stopped general music in fifth or fourth grade. [The argument was] the kids are going to go to choir or band [to get] music; everybody else, you're done [with music learning]. So, when you have the opportunity to have sixth, seventh, and eighth grade [general music] I think you have to find something that is relevant to them.
>
> –Holly

Relevant music learning not only helps students connect school music learning to their personal lives, but it also serves as a means to engage young adolescents in a curricular subject that may have previously held little or no interest.

Music educator Adam Kruse (2016) argues for an approach to relevant music learning based in four principles of hip-hop culture. Teachers integrating these four principles into music curriculum and pedagogy might cultivate a relevant and responsive music learning environment. According to Kruse, the four principles of a hip-hop classroom are:

1 Keep it Real: Be authentic to yourself, allow your students to be their authentic selves, and study music as authentically as possible within its cultural context.
2 Flip the Script: Do something different. Rethink and repurpose musical content and musical learning in new ways.
3 Make Some Noise: Regardless of the genre studied, make music, as opposed to only talking about music. Embrace unexpected musical creation and move away from the idea that there is one "right" way to perform or create music.
4 Stay Fresh: Keep abreast of new ideas in education and current trends in the music young adolescents prefer.

In Eric's lesson sequence featured in Chapter 4, we saw that he "flipped the script" in developing his game-style pedagogy and that his students were certainly "making some noise" while learning to play their ukuleles. Additionally, when discussing the relevant features of his curriculum, Eric talks about "keeping it real" and "staying fresh":

> Try everything. Keep your mind open [and] broaden your horizons. Some of the things that I do, [I do because of my experience.] I do West African drumming because I traveled to West Africa, to Ghana. I do the technology because I went and I found the technology program. I think [relevancy is about] just being flexible and being willing to try things that are outside your comfort zone, and to respond to what the students are doing, to kind of see what catches them, where their interests are, and how to roll with that. Talk to [the students]. Engage them in conversation. Ask them questions: what are you listening to? Who should I listen to?
>
> —Eric

In what ways are you making your general music class relevant to your students' personal lives, their lived experiences, and their cultural identities? What practices have you instituted that enable you to remain current with the latest musics and cultural experiences of your students? What new idea would you like to try or how would you like to change your pedagogical approach to make your classroom more relevant to your students?

Relevant Music Learning through Familiar Music

In an effort to diversify music education beyond Western classical music and appeal to young adolescents, many music educators advocate for the integration of current popular musics into the curriculum (see Dunbar-Hall & Wemyss, 2000; Green 2006; Isbell, 2007). Certainly, using popular musics in the general music classroom is one avenue for improving the relevancy of the general music curriculum, but it is not the only possibility. Relevant music learning moves beyond the simple dichotomy of Western Classical musics vs. popular musics. Any musical genre, artist, or song derived from your students' cultural identities (from elementary school, home, community, peers, popular culture, the media, etc.), about which they are familiar and have questions, might be used as a tool for helping students make personal connections to music learning.

While many teachers assume popular musics are familiar to all young adolescents, students' cultural identities and geographic locations matter. In some school communities, the musics most familiar to students may be the musics of students' religious practices or cultural backgrounds, while in other communities it might be musics used in TV, movies, or sports.

It is important to learn from your students' and not make assumptions about their experiences based on one facet of cultural identity. Jessica acknowledges that not all of the Latinx students in her school are of Mexican heritage. However, her use of mariachi music in the classroom opens a dialogue about the Latin American music genres listened to at home by many of her students, thus increasing the relevance of music learning.

> We have a high Hispanic population [at my school] so a lot of students are familiar with the mariachi music [covered in the curriculum]. [The students] might not know all the history of [mariachi], and they might not know who is one of the founders [of mariachi] or who was the person who [did X in the development of mariachi]. But they've heard it, or their grandparents might have listened to mariachi [at home]. [Sometimes they say,] "oh, we don't listen to mariachi, but we listen to [Cuban] cha-cha or [salsa or Puerto Rican reggaetón]."
>
> –Jessica

Jessica finds that beginning the course with mariachi music engages many of the students in her class and, in her words, "brings them in" to the music learning space. It is our responsibility as educators to know our specific students and the musics they "own" and thus bring with them to the classroom. Through this knowledge, we can seek out quality musical examples that facilitate specific learning goals, regardless of the genre.

There is no limit to the genres that might be used as relevant musics in middle level general music. Do not be afraid to listen to your students and try something new. For example, Nicole uses the videogame *Fortnight* as a tool for making music learning relevant to students who are reluctant to participate in general music.

> I really try and take into account how music is important in their lives. I'll have a kid that says, "I don't like music or guitar." And I'll say well, "how do you consume music, how is music important [to you]?" All I have to [say is], "does *Fortnight* use music?"
>
> –Nicole

Almost any videogame, including *Fortnight*, has music. In fact, many video games contain musical motifs for characters, settings, or events within the game. When faced with a recalcitrant student in general music, Nicole will suggest:

> Why don't you go create two *Fortnight* characters? But guess what, [your characters] need a theme song, go get that xylophone [to create their themes]. That really got the kids very interested.
>
> –Nicole

Thus, the musical concept of theme or character motif is taught through a videogame rather than an opera or symphonic work. The difference is that the connection is relevant and student interest and investment is dramatically altered because the musical concept is connected to familiar music over which students feel ownership.

While drawing on familiar musics can help personalize music learning, a few caveats are warranted. First, when teachers adopt students' music in the classroom, there is a risk that students will feel that "their" music is being turned into "school" music. Thus, teachers must be careful how and when students' musics are used in the classroom. Second, using familiar musics should not be done as a form of tokenism. Familiar musical examples should be used because they are critical to the lesson objective and illustrate an important musical concept, not simply so that students pay attention before moving on to the "real" music of the lesson. Finally, using familiar musics in the general music classroom should not forsake other genres when appropriate. Consider Katie's argument for when to use popular music using two contrasting examples:

> You can play a Gregorian Chant or you can play Justin Bieber. If you can teach the same thing from both of [those musics], you might as well do the Bieber because [the students are] going to get more out of it. Sometimes you can only teach [important musical knowledge] through Gregorian Chant [for example, so] then find a way to make it relevant. Let's talk about this and make it relevant to your life and what you hear on the radio, or what you're listening to while playing a video game, or what you hear in a TV commercial. Otherwise, [in music class] you're hearing things you've never heard of and will never hear again.
>
> —Katie

Katie is making her point effectively: If you want music learning to be relevant and are teaching a concept common to many musical forms, such as monophony or unison singing, why not use a musical genre or artist that students are comfortable discussing? However, if you are trying to teach a specific concept easily recognizable only in particular musical genres like Gregorian Chant, you should use that genre and help students find the relevancy in another way. When used carefully and intentionally, familiar musics are one avenue to help students make personal connections to music learning, illuminate important music content, and engage students in the middle level general music classroom. However, when used incorrectly, familiar musics also have the power to alienate students and weaken the music curriculum.

Making Music Relevant through Career Education

Another way to make middle level general music relevant is to help students understand the wide variety of future career possibilities available to them through music (Akos et al., 2011; Schafer & Rivera, 2016). Often young adolescents have questions about how the music they listen to is recorded, how the music videos they watch are produced, or how a particular artist becomes more popular than another. Recording engineers, managers, producers, composers, lyricists, music supervisors, instrumental repair persons, luthiers, DJs, backstage or front-of-house staffers, and music critics are just some of the many music-related careers students might find appealing if introduced to them as young adolescents. Many of the music standards can be achieved by exploring activities that mimic the job tasks of these and other music professionals.

By introducing students to the knowledge and skills needed to succeed in music-related careers, we might foster student interest in pursuing a career in music previously unknown to students. Tyler, in particular, has chosen this direction for his seventh grade general music class, which he describes as his "real world" year:

> I started trying to focus on how [music] is a career option, [that there is] real-world application of this stuff [you are learning in music]. [I try to show the students that music] could be a career for you even if you're not making the music. I mean, before I started teaching [after my rock career ended], when I was looking for a job, I cast the net pretty wide and one of [those job possibilities] was buying music for television stations. So, there are lots of careers where you can use your musicality, [but] where you're not actually making music. Seventh grade is my real-world year, because between hip-hop and film scoring, if any of my students are going to work in music, [there are lots of career options there]. Also, I'm going to add [an assignment about music in] video game design [next year].
>
> –Tyler

Prior to teaching, Tyler was an active performing rock musician, so he knows first-hand all of the many career possibilities in the music industry and beyond. Tyler's assignments enable students to participate in career related music tasks that may provide his young adolescents with a new future aspiration.

Career education has another possible point of connection when the local community is brought into the classroom through guest visits (whether in-person or online). In many locations, there are community members (including parents) who pursued careers related to music and are willing to share their knowledge with students. When young adolescents engage personally with community members who hold these careers, the possibility of doing something similar themselves becomes a concrete reality. Another option is to use *In-Tune Monthly*, a music learning magazine that occasionally highlights specific music careers in articles written at a level accessible to most young adolescents. While not as experiential as a guest presenter, the career highlights in *In-Tune Monthly* may be useful for helping students connect personally to music class through career exploration.

Integrative Music Learning

The intention of integrative music learning (MU:CN11.0) is to help students develop the ability to recognize and build on the intra- and inter-disciplinary connections innate in all musics (Barrett, 2016). According to John Dewey, disciplinary knowledge learned in isolation "is so disconnected from the rest of experience that it is not available under the actual conditions of life" (1938/1998, p. 43). Music permeates all aspects of life and is intertwined with other disciplines, and thus, integrative music learning illuminates those connections. However, in *most* schools serving fifth through eighth grade students, disciplinary boundaries imposed by schedules and classroom spaces still exist and serve to shape most of students' educational experience. While music has deep historical disciplinary practices, it is also an art form with wide-ranging connections to history, culture, other art forms, and a host of other subjects. Thus, it is essential that we help students make these cross-disciplinary connections.

Does Integrative Music Learning Address Non-Music Standards and Objectives?

A music teacher might ask: should I be addressing standards or objectives in the other subject(s) I am connecting to music? The short answer is: it depends. As music teachers, our first responsibility is to teaching musical content. In many learning environments, this means addressing the music standards and establishing music objectives aligned with those standards before considering content in other subject areas. In this section, I would like to describe four possible scenarios or variations on integrative music learning. My hope is that integrative learning will help students make explicit connections beyond the disciplinary boundaries of music.

- Variation #1: No Clear Connections, One Subject Dominates
- Variation #2: Thematic Connections Across Subjects
- Variation #3: Teacher Collaborations that Develop Connected Units
- Variation #4: Arts-Integrated Units

Variation #1: No Clear Connections, One Subject Dominates: If you have taught general music (particularly elementary) for any length of time, another teacher has probably asked you some variation on this question: could you teach my students a song about, for example, volcanos? In the case of volcanos, the song "Someone to Lava," contains specific science content that might reinforce volcanic content learned in science class. However, if a music teacher simply teaches this song to help the students identify important volcanic vocabulary, there is no clear curricular connection to music because the music teacher is not evaluating students' progress toward a musical standard or objective.

Alternatively, perhaps the science teacher instead asks for the students to learn a song about birds. In this scenario, the science teacher does not provide any more information, so the music teacher decides to teach the students to play and sing the Beatles "Blackbird" as part of the ukulele curriculum. In keeping with the ukulele curriculum, the music teacher decides to use this song to assess students' abilities to play and read a melody in tablature notation. Here the music teacher has developed a music lesson that addresses a music standard and objective, but the lesson has little or no connection to the bird-focused science curriculum.

Both examples above are perhaps extreme, but provide good illustrations of curricular choices that do not meet the definition of integrative music learning espoused here. While there is a loose connection between what is being taught in science and music, the connections are so vague that no student is going to experience deeper, integrative learning as a result. However, music teachers should not despair. In the first example, the addition of a music learning objective supporting the learning of "Someone to Lava," or in the second example, a specific conversation with the science teacher about the bird curriculum might suffice to modify these two examples so that students make connections between music and science learning.

Variation #2: Thematic Connections across Subjects: Some schools establish school-wide themes for the year or a semester. Then, each individual teacher develops lessons or units within his/her own subject, based on the theme. At Tyler's school, the eighth grade science and language arts curriculum begins with a study of New Orleans, a theme Tyler has built upon for his eighth grade general music curriculum,

> The first unit [of the year] coincides with science and English. They do a study for hurricane Katrina and so I do a unit, a style survey of music from New Orleans that is entirely student-run. I give [the students] a list of famous musicians, plus they can suggest one [if they want], and they all do mini-reports. [They are required to] talk about what they hear and what [the music] sounds like. I grade them on their use of academic language that they know from [previous years of] music class.
>
> –Tyler

In this unit, Tyler is building on the New Orleans theme established by the other teachers. The teachers are not collaborating to better integrate the three subjects, but rather using the same theme for their own subject-specific purposes. Tyler is not responsible for standards or objectives in the other subjects, but rather is reviewing musical vocabulary and connecting thematically to New Orleans through an investigation of music, genres, and musicians who have important connections to New Orleans. Any direct connections to science or language arts made in music class would likely be unplanned connections students make independently.

Unless music teachers seek out additional information about what students are learning in other subjects (and this is recommended), the cross-curricular connections will likely rely on a student sharing, "we learned about this in history." The thematic approach is a useful variation on integrative music learning, but may not lead to fruitful connections within music class if young adolescents are not adequately prepared to make these connections. Music teachers using a thematic approach must guide students in these connections by modeling cross-curricular thinking and asking questions that lead to students' independent connection-making.

Variation #3: Teacher Collaborations that Yield Connected Units: One year, I saw that the visual art teacher had sixth grade students making animal-inspired plaster masks using their own faces. When I asked her about the project, she told me that the students were asked to reflect on their outward and inward personalities and then design both the inside and the outside of the mask to reflect this self-understanding in creative animal form. As we talked, I realized that this personal reflection and the mask design might align nicely with our study of musical theme and motif. The next year, the visual art teacher and I collaborated on a combined music and visual art unit where, as the students developed their masks, they also investigated musical themes, considered how various sounds evoke particular feelings, discussed how themes or motifs were used to portray characters in musical storytelling, and eventually composed a musical theme to represent either the inner or outer part of their mask. From a musical perspective, composing themes for the masks they were creating in visual art, helped to make students' understanding of musical themes more concrete.

In this variation on integrative music learning, two teachers collaborate to design what might be called parallel units in each subject. The collaborating teachers work together to develop separate yet deeply related units of study that occur at the same time in the school year. Ideally, the final assessments, like the masks and musical themes, are discipline specific, but connected in some way. For collaborations of this nature to succeed, teachers should be aware of what students are learning in the other subject and communicate regularly about students' progress and understanding. Teachers working on these kinds of projects will bring in content, for example vocabulary or other concepts, from the other subject, knowing that this material has already been taught by the collaborating teacher. These authentic connections are designed to enliven both subject areas and build students' interests and engagement in the overall study.

Variation #4: Arts Integrated Units: In order for integrative music learning to move to the level of arts integration, the lesson or unit must address standards and objectives in *both* subjects equally (Silverstein & Layne, 2010). For example, in planning for the coming school year, the music teacher and social studies teacher decide to collaborate on an arts-integrated unit about the Civil Rights Movement. The two teachers work together to identify music and social studies standards to be addressed in co-taught lessons that unite music and social studies content. They agree on a final assessment, a composition portfolio complete with drafts and a final product, where students compose an original ballad about the life of an historical figure from the Civil Rights Movement. Embedded in the assessment are expectations that allow students to demonstrate both music and social studies knowledge and skills simultaneously. These arts-integrated units require significant pre-planning and are often more common when teachers partner with external organizations, such as Robert's ongoing composition partnership with the local university.[1] In some cases, music teachers possess significant experience and knowledge in another subject area and thus might use their "lateral knowledge" in another discipline to develop an arts-integrated unit independently (Barrett, 2016, p. 176).

Integrative Music Learning and the Interdisciplinary Team

In many middle level schools, the term "interdisciplinary teams" is used to describe how smaller communities within the larger school are created by grouping teachers and providing shared team planning within the schedule (Arhar, 2013; Glover & Zwemke, 2016). According to a 2009 study, 72% of surveyed middle level schools used an interdisciplinary team model to organize the school community (McEwin & Greene, 2011). In addition to monitoring student progress and supporting students' social and emotional needs (Arhar, 2013), one major goal of interdisciplinary teams is to foster cross-curricular unit planning, although this outcome is not always achieved (Beane, 1993). Theoretically, interdisciplinary teams should provide teachers with an opportunity to discuss the curricular content and work together to make connections across the disciplines.

One frustration for many arts teachers is exclusion from an interdisciplinary grade-level team due to the school schedule. When interdisciplinary teams are given common or shared planning time within the daily schedule, the students still have to be taught by a teacher of some subject. As a result, when the sixth grade team meets, the sixth grade students are typically attending music, visual art, physical education, or other "elective" courses (Beane, 1993; Hamann, 2007). Despite the many integrative possibilities of middle level general music, music educators are often not privy to the cross-curricular planning of the teachers of the "big four" subjects.

If you are not part of an interdisciplinary team that involves the language arts, math, science, and social studies teachers, do not despair. You can still initiate conversations with teachers on the grade level team(s) by visiting their classrooms, meeting them at lunch or after school, or showing an interest in their student work displays. I once overheard a seventh grade science teacher talking about how students built musical instruments for their final assessment during a science unit on sound. After some discussion, I built on the science teacher's initial idea by developing a simultaneous unit (variation #3 above) where students explored how instruments create sounds and how different notation systems work. Ultimately, the students applied knowledge from both subjects to succeed in the final assessments for each class: the creation of the instrument in science and the invention of a new notation system and the performance of an original composition on their invented instrument in general music.

If you teach only one grade level of general music, I encourage you to participate in grade level conversations. This will provide you with insight into the curricular content covered in the other subject areas as well as new insights into the successes and challenges faced by individual students. While you may be unable to participate in an interdisciplinary unit designed by the team, you may be inspired to design a new general music unit connected to a topic you were unaware was covered in another subject.

Making Connections by Applying Historical Thinking in General Music

The ultimate goal of learning within a discipline is to think and act like those who work within the particular discipline. In music, we teach students to perform so that they can think and act like performing musicians. Sometimes, we also teach students to compose so that they can think and act like composers. As music teachers, we might also teach students to think and act like musicologists and ethnomusicologists. These musician-scholars focus broadly on researching and understanding the historical and cultural contexts of music (be they local, remote, historical, modern, art, folk, or popular), and thus musicology and ethnomusicology are critically important for music learning that focuses on making connections.

World Music Pedagogy advocates for teaching students to listen, perform, and improvise or compose while simultaneously integrating and contextualizing the historical and cultural contexts surrounding the music genre's creation or performance (Campbell, 2004, 2016).

This approach to general music is an excellent tool for diversifying the general music curriculum as it teaches students about diverse musical cultures through embodiment. Extending those ideas, what I advocate for here is teaching students to conduct the observational and inference-driven work of musicologists and ethnomusicologists by applying the principles of "historical thinking" (Wineburg, 2001, 2007) to general music learning. I believe that using the principles of historical thinking in general music will scaffold connection-making and enable students to become better observers and analyzers of any new musical genre they encounter.

The historical thinking approach to teaching history "involves interpreting and analyzing historical artifacts and primary sources and constructing and critiquing narratives about the past" (Waring & Robinson, 2010, p. 22). Thus, students who are learning to be historians examine primary and secondary sources, such as diaries, newspaper articles, letters, and photographs, to develop an understanding about a particular time and place. These students are encouraged to review historical documents critically and to ask questions about what they see or read in order to better understand the creator and his/her context or perspective. This form of authentic learning through the engagement in tasks completed by real-life historians requires students to use critical thinking skills to analyze, synthesize, and interpret historical evidence (Claravall & Irey, 2020).

Five Steps for Historical Thinking in Music

Here, I apply the principles of historical thinking to learning in general music. Instead of simply telling the students about a composer's life, when a piece was written, or the cultural traditions surrounding a musical selection, teachers develop historical thinking activities that enable students to establish these details for themselves through techniques of observation, questioning, and further investigation.

My approach to historical thinking in music begins with artifacts (including musical notation, instruments, audio or video recordings, historical documents, photographs, song lyrics, etc.) the music teacher selects for study. The music teacher then asks the students to examine these items critically, perhaps using a graphic organizer, group work, or whole class discussion. The five steps for historical thinking in music are:

- Step 1: Students observe the musical artifact and document their observations.
- Step 2: Students make assumptions or inferences based on their observations.
- Step 3: Students identify questions they have based on their observations.
- Step 4: With the help of the teacher, students identify the resources they need to answer their questions.
- Step 5: Repeat Steps 1–4 with new musical artifacts, musical activities, or other learning experiences.

For the sake of illustration, let us consider a lesson that introduces students to a new musical instrument and thus begins a study of the related musical culture.

In the first three steps, the students look closely at the new musical instrument and proceed through a brief interrogation of the object. In step one, the teacher asks the students to look closely at the instrument and to describe what they see. These descriptions should be as detailed as possible and documented in writing. In step two, the teacher asks the students to make assumptions or educated guesses based on what they see. For example, a student might say, "I see beads on the outside of the instrument, I assume those beads make noise." The teacher might then list all of the students' assumptions on the board. In step three, the music teacher asks students what questions they have about the instrument based on their observations and assumptions. The teacher should guide the students to identify questions that can verify or falsify the students' assumptions. Although I have described these three steps as a conversation between the teacher and the whole class, these steps might also be completed by students individually, in small groups, or as a series of "centers" organized around the room.

In the fourth and fifth step, teachers and students collaborate to determine how best to answer the questions students have identified. In step four, the students and teacher decide together what materials, resources, or activities they need to complete in order to answer the identified questions. Lessons involving performing, responding, and creating may serve as possible answers to the students' questions. In step five, once the teacher and students develop a plan, the process begins again with additional artifacts or other resources that reveal more information. Since time is limited in middle level general music, this step cannot continue indefinitely. The music teacher may need to provide students with additional information to answer some of their questions.

Using Historical Thinking in Music to Develop Skills in Lyrical Analysis

While many forms of musical artifacts might be examined through the lens of historical thinking, song lyrics in particular are an important textual source of historical and cultural knowledge (Wineburg, 2001). Like other historical texts, song lyrics often tell the story of a particular person or event and can reveal important context clues about the perspective of the lyricist or composer. Consider the context of Pink's 2006 "Dear Mr. President," a rebuke of President George W. Bush and his policies, or Bruce Springsteen's 2002 "The Rising," a response to the 9/11 US terrorist attacks. In both cases, the year in which the song was composed, as well as the lyrical content, provide important details about the historical context and the perspectives of the performers and composers.

Many young adolescents are drawn to a song because of the catchy hook or memorable beat, but may need guidance in developing their ear to attune to the lyrics. Providing the lyrics in writing, asking the students to analyze the lyrics as if they are poetry, and then listening to the song while following the lyric sheet can guide young adolescents in focusing their listening skills on the lyrics in a form of attentive listening (Campbell, 2005). Teacher Resource 5.1 is a graphic organizer similar to a KWL chart and is useful when applying historical thinking in music to lyrical analysis. Instead of KWL (**K**now, **W**ant to Know, **L**earn), the chart focuses on **K**now, **A**ssume, and **Q**uestion (KAQ), the first three steps in applying historical thinking to music. In this graphic organizer, the students move through the KAQ process three times: first by examining the lyrics in written form, second by listening, and third by thinking about the performers or composers, perhaps based on what they already know or using information the teacher provides. After completing the three levels of the graphic organizer, the students will be ready for Step 4 of the historical thinking in music process either individually or as a whole class.

Teacher Resource 5.1

Historical Thinking in Music KAQ Chart

	KNOW (evidence)	ASSUME (infer)	QUESTION (research or learn)
LYRICS	What is the message/ main idea of the lyrics?	What do you *think* the music will sound like? What point of view do you *think* the lyrics are trying to convey? OR What do you *think* is the purpose of this song based on the lyrics?	What questions do you have about the lyrics?
LISTENING	What musical elements do you hear in the song? How does listening to the song change your understanding of the lyrics?	What do you *assume* about the song's message or purpose?	What questions do you have after hearing the song?
PERFORMERS OR COMPOSERS	What do you know about the beliefs, perspectives, or experiences of the performers or composers?	What do you *assume* about the beliefs, perspectives or experiences of the performers or composers?	What questions would you like to ask the performers or composers about their beliefs, perspectives, or experiences?

Of course, lyrical analysis in middle level general music is limited to those songs available in English or with easily accessible English translations. If you teach in a school where a large population of students speak and read a language other than English, consider involving those students in lyrical analysis of a folk or popular selection in their native language. This will involve all students but allow students with diverse language backgrounds to take a leadership role in the classroom. For those musical genres without lyrics or for which no English translations are available, Teacher Resource 5.1 might be modified so that instead of beginning with lyrics, the process begins by watching a performance video of the selected song on silence. The KAQ prompting questions for the silent video watching would remain similar for the A and Q sections of the graphic organizer. For the K section, students would document what they observe or see in the video rather than what they analyze by reading the lyrics.

Rethinking Introducing a New Music Culture through Historical Thinking in Music

Many of the teachers in this book described approaches whereby they introduced several new musical genres by providing a general overview of the historical, geographical, cultural, and social details. One such approach is described in Activity Idea 5.1, "Passport around the World." Jessica and Nicole use this approach to structure their middle level general music courses and Nicole even provides her students with a "passport" in which to collect course materials as they "travel." As Nicole's students traverse the globe musically, they are introduced to a new musical instrument through which they explore specific performance genres and the accompanying culture. Nicole's curriculum has a quick, survey-like structure as she has only twenty class periods in her sixth grade general music rotation:

> I call it around the world in twenty days. Using the instruments, we just try and learn as much as we can about different places and different cultures. Ukulele is really easy for Hawaiian [culture, and] the drums are really easy for African music. I have Native American flutes, [and with] guitar we do American rock and roll. [I use] xylophones and we take the bars on and off and do all kinds of different modes and scales and songs with those. So I think about: where [geographically] do I want to go and what is the [musical] concept I want to teach [based on] where [we] go [in our "travels"].
>
> –Nicole

Although Jessica and her students also explore music cultures from around the world, they do not switch instruments, but rather focus entirely on the guitar. Jessica has chosen music genres and accompanying cultures in which the guitar plays a prominent role:

> We start with the folk music of Mexico, mariachi. Then we take a trip to Spain for the flamenco music and [spend] time … learning about the dancing and the clapping and the singing and how they all come together to create this really great tradition and heritage of Spain. Then, by that time, [the students] have basic finger-picking techniques and they know a few chords. And then we hop over to Ireland and we end up with American folk and popular music. This year I did a little bit of an extension, kind of teaching them a bit about American music history.
>
> –Jessica

In both Jessica and Nicole's approaches, cultural and historical contexts are integrated into performing and responding to particular music cultures. However, both teachers admit that they could do more improvisation and composition in their musical travels. The inclusion of improvisation and composition exercises would enable Jessica and Nicole to address the creating standards and allow students to apply their understanding of musical concepts to their own creations.

Activity Idea 5.1
Passport around the World

Suggested Grade Level:

- 5th & 6th

Primary National Core Arts Standard:

- MU:Pr4.1 or MU:Pr4.2: "Select, analyze, and interpret artistic work for presentation" (SEADAE, 2014c, p. 4). Select the appropriate grade level standard.
- MU:Cn11.0: "Demonstrate understanding of relationships between music and the other arts, other disciplines, varied contexts, and daily life" (SEADAE, 2014c, p. 10).

Modified from Activities Developed By:

- Jessica & Nicole

Description:

Provide the students with a folder or notebook designed like a passport. Build the guitar, piano, ukulele, singing, and/or listening curriculum around an exploration of various musical cultures. "Visit" a musical culture for several class periods and focus on learning to play/sing culturally appropriate rhythms, melodies, etc. Augment this performance focus with listening, geography instruction, and discussion of instruments, famous musicians, and/or the appropriation of folk melodies. During each musical culture "visit," students will collect artifacts (listening logs, notes, maps, songs to perform, etc.) in their passport before traveling to the next location. Consider beginning your travels with the cultures represented in your classroom community. Asking parents or other community members to visit class as culture bearers allows students to experience local musicians and involves parents in the classroom.

Imagine that you teach a twenty-day rotation class like Nicole's and that you want to use a variation on Passport Around the World to structure your curriculum, whether focused on world musics, Western music history, or some other connecting theme. You might consider beginning the twenty-day rotation with an historical thinking in music exercise that introduces students to the various musical cultures you intend to address. Divide the students into groups and provide each group with a piece of chart paper, a marker, and a listening example (each group would receive a different musical culture you intend to study). Have the students divide the chart paper into four quadrants: (1) describe what you hear; (2) hypothesize about what you hear; (3) identify questions you have; and (4) list ways you can answer your questions. Working in groups, have the students listen to the music and fill in each quadrant on their chart paper, thus proceeding through the first four steps of historical thinking in music. Then, collect the students' responses and develop the remaining days of the curriculum ensuring that students' questions are answered and some of their suggestions for how to answer particular questions are incorporated into the learning environment. Additional hands-joined activities, such as those described in Chapter 4, might be added depending on the time constraints and the suggestions provided by the students.

When an historical thinking in music activity like the one described above is incorporated into the beginning of a middle level general music course (whether about world musics or entirely different genres), the teacher receives valuable information about how students work collaboratively, what they already know, and what they would like to learn. This is a simple way to ensure that the remaining curriculum is relevant to the students in your classroom and that you are modeling integrative connections that your students will understand. The goal is that through historical thinking in music activities students see connections modeled, develop their own connections, and understand how what they are learning in music is connected to their lives, to other subjects, and to history and culture.

Responding to Music as Making Connections

Given modern technologies for music listening, the act of "listening" to music is nearly ubiquitous. While constant music listening may be the norm for your young adolescents, it should not be assumed that these students know *how* to listen to music or are experienced at listening attentively. Young adolescents need guided practice in how to listen and respond to various musical genres.[2] When students receive developmentally appropriate instruction in listening and responding to music, they hone their abilities as educated consumers of music, those likely to seek out future music listening opportunities. As music teachers, we must remember that responding to music skills are not only developed through isolated music listening exercises, but also through listening that requires students to respond to and assess their own creations or those of their classmates during performance or composition tasks.

Artistic Process: Responding

The 2014 US National Core Arts Standards identify four process components for responding: (1) select, (2) analyze, (3) interpret, and (4) evaluate (SEADAE, 2014c). In all four responding process components, students are also asked to make relevant and integrative connections appropriate to the music being studied. The fifth grade responding standards provide an example of the relationship between responding and connecting:

- SELECT–MU:RE7.1.5a: "Demonstrate and explain, citing evidence, how selected music connects to and is influenced by specific interests, experiences, purposes, or contexts" (SEADAE, 2014c, p. 7).

- ANALYZE–MU:RE7.2.5a: "Demonstrate and explain, citing evidence, how responses to music are informed by the structure, the use of the elements of music, and context (such as social, cultural, and historical)" (SEADAE, 2014c, p 7).
- INTERPRET–MU:RE8.1.5a: "Demonstrate and explain how the expressive qualities (such as dynamics, tempo, timbre, and articulation) are used in performers' and personal interpretations to reflect expressive intent" (SEADAE, 2014c, p. 8).
- EVALUATE–MU:RE9.1.4a: "Evaluate musical works and performances, applying established criteria, and explain appropriateness to the context, citing evidence from the elements of music" (SEADAE, 2014c, p. 8).

In each of the standards listed above, musical context is emphasized. The standards for the "select" and "interpret" process components both reference interests and interpretations, suggesting the importance of relevant and personal connections. Moreover, the "analyze" and "evaluate" process components focus on the integrative connections found in the social, historical, and cultural contexts of music. Thus, students must be taught how to listen and what to listen for, both musical elements and the historical or cultural cues that give music meaning.

Lesson: Responding to Protest Music

Over the course of nine weeks, Holly's seventh grade general music class examines American popular music beginning with early blues, jazz, and 1950s rock 'n roll through to 1990s rock, pop, and rap. Two or three days of Holly's nine-week unit focus on protest music. The featured lesson sequence presented below (see Lesson Sequence 5.1 and Teacher Resources 5.2 & 5.3) is developed from Holly's lessons on protest music. The lesson sequence is written for sixth grade in alignment with applicable responding standards.

Holly explains that her American popular music unit focuses on developing listening skills while connecting history and culture. Through her experience with her students, Holly has identified that her students struggle with music listening. She says they do not know what to listen for in their own music or in the music she is introducing. As she works to make the American popular music unit integrative and relevant, Holly focuses on teaching students to listen for specific musical ideas in each genre and to listen across genres for similarities and influences as American popular music develops.

Connecting the Past and Present through Relevant Music Learning

In Holly's current school, she discovered that many of her students were unaware of the origins of American popular music despite experience and interest in particular genres. She describes this as the impetus for her curriculum:

> [My students'] parents listen to rap music or hip-hop and [thus the students] listen to rap or hip-hop music. I'd say out of four hundred kids in one school, I'll get ten who will be like, oh yeah, I've heard of that person. I thought okay, you don't know who the founding fathers of American music are? So that's my basic reasoning. [The students] don't know where their music comes from, and I don't think we teach enough of American music.
>
> –Holly

In addition, Holly discovered that her students were completely unaware of the intradisciplinary or intra-musical connections that exist between historical and current popular genres. Thus, she works to help students make connections between early American popular music and today in the hope that they will make more informed listening choices in the future.

> For me, [middle school] is a great time to [expose students to American popular music] because this is when they're getting older, they get their own phones, and they can choose [their own music]. Not that they're all of a sudden big jazz music fans. [But] I did have a kid come back [and told me], "I got a Beatles album this summer. My mom took me to an album shop, and she got me a Beatles record, and look at this," he opens his coat and he's got a Beatles shirt on. I get some kids who [say], "oh that's my grandma's, she listens to that music!" I even had a parent email me one time and [say, "my kid] came home and they were talking about this [music], and I was just so surprised." So that's when I started sending out my newsletter saying this is what we're going to cover, so if you know this stuff ask your kiddo about it.
>
> –Holly

One example of this historical and modern connection making is when she introduces Ray Charles and his influence on American popular music. Holly plays the Ray Charles song "I've Got a Woman" for the students and tells the students they will recognize it. The students are doubtful, but she says, "as soon as [I] start [the song], it never fails, the second [Charles sings] 'she gives you money,' they [all shout] 'This is from 'Gold Digger!'''[3] The "Gold Digger" example is relevant because Holly knows her particular students, their experiences, and their musical preferences and uses this knowledge to engage them in understanding earlier American popular music.

Connecting the Past and Present through Integrative Music Learning

Holly's unit on American popular music is also integrative as she weaves historical context and social studies knowledge into the discussion of various American popular music genres. In teaching protest music, the historical connections have become particularly important. As Holly explains, many of her students do not understand why anyone would protest a war, nor do they understand the historical significance of the draft:

> I do talk about historical events [related to 1960s protest music]. And [the students] are like, "why are they protesting war?" Half these kids [ask,] "what is the draft?" When I said all the [college] kids were drafted, [the students looked puzzled and asked,] "what does that mean?" So, there is a lot of historical cross-curricular stuff that happens.
>
> –Holly

Once students understand the historical context of the draft and the conflict in Vietnam, they can better listen to and analyze the protest music Holly shares. A lack of historical knowledge would make the lyrics of 1960s protest songs meaningless, much like a lack of knowledge about current events and social issues would make modern protest music equally meaningless.

Using Protest Songs "of the Moment" to Deepen Lyrical Analysis Skills

As they finish the protest music section of the unit, Holly asks students to go home, find a current protest song, and bring it in to share with the class. The students are required to listen to the song, analyze the lyrics, and be prepared to explain to their friends what is being protested:

> [The students] come up with great stuff, like Pink's, "Dear Mr. President," John Legend's "Glory," the Black Eyed Peas, "Where is the Love," [or] Macklemore and Ryan Lewis' "Same Love." And [when their classmates share the song, other students say,] "oh, I knew that song, but I never realized it was a protest song." Then I'll say to the student who brought it in, "Well, why is this a protest song? Your friend says they didn't realize it was, [please explain]." It probably only takes ten minutes of that next class period to go through the songs that they [bring in], but it brings in my point of constantly trying to relate today and yesterday.
>
> —Holly

In keeping with Holly's emphasis on connecting the protest music of yesterday and today, Day 5 of Lesson Sequence 5.1 asks teachers to modify the lesson based on the most current and relevant protest movement. If I were to teach Holly's protest music lesson sequence, I might choose Miguel's "Now," a song protesting immigration detention centers. Alternatively, I might choose H.E.R.'s "I Can't Breathe" or Lauryn Hill's "Black Rage," songs about the Black experience in the United States. On several occasions, I have used the Black Eyed Peas' "Where Is the Love" for lyrical analysis and discussion of protest through song. While "Where is the Love" was originally written in 2003, updates to this song were released in 2016 and 2020. As a music listener, I am also particularly moved by the messages of Macklemore & Ryan Lewis' "Same Love," Mickey Guyton's "What Are You Gonna Tell Her," Lady Gaga's "Born this Way," and Maren Morris' "Better Than We Found It" and might choose to incorporate these songs into Lesson Sequence 5.1 below, depending on my student population.

Perhaps you wonder why I have not provided you with a "classroom approved" list of protest songs. Since both popular culture and protest movements are continually evolving, any list printed in this book would immediately be out of date. I encourage you to select songs that you feel are "of the moment" and relevant to your students and their community.

Non-Violent Responses to Injustice through Protest Music

Perhaps one of the best lessons we can teach young adolescents is that artists have a platform to respond musically to injustices they see in their lives and worlds. While the topics may change, popular artists across the decades have used their music as a platform for speaking out in protest. It is essential that young adolescents learn how to peacefully stand-up for what they perceive as wrong and unjust. Music is one possible avenue for peaceful protest.

Young adolescents have questions about the injustices they see in the news and the injustices they experience in their own lives. Protest music gives students a forum to explore what it means to stand-up, speak-out, and respond to their world, a deeply relevant way of learning. It is our responsibility as music educators to help young adolescents find their voice in this way.

Lesson Sequence 5.1
Responding to Protest Music

Basic Lesson Information

Suggested Grade Level(s):

- 6th

Prior Knowledge:

- Students have studied other genres of music and/or studied music specific to various decades in the history of American popular music.
- Students have developed music listening skills through listening logs or other in-class activities and can identify various musical elements (instruments, tempo, dynamics, form, etc.) to support genre and mood identification.

Approximate Number of 45-Minute Periods:

- 8-10

Essential Question:

- How can I improve my understanding or interpretation of a song through critical listening?

Materials:

- Audio Recordings and Lyric Sheets for:
  - Bob Dylan "Masters of War"
  - Pete Seeger "Bring 'Em Home"
  - Jimmy Cliff "Vietnam"
  - Edwin Starr "War"
  - Marvin Gaye "What's Going On"
  - Phil Ochs "What are you Fighting For"
  - Joan Baez "Saigon Bride"
  - Creedence Clearwater Revival "Fortunate Son"
  - Bob Dylan "Blowin' in the Wind"
  - Nina Simone "Backlash Blues"
- Musical notation for "We Shall Overcome" for teacher use (if needed)
- Copies of Langston Hughes' poem "The Backlash Blues"
- Teacher Resource 5.2
- Final assignment sheet (if desired)

Modified from Lesson(s) Developed by:

- Holly

Primary National Core Arts Standards:

- MU:Re8.1.6.a: "Describe a personal interpretation of how creators' and performers' application of the elements of music and expressive qualities, within genres and cultural and historical context, convey expressive intent" (SEADAE, 2014c, p. 8).
- MU:Re9.1.6.a: "Apply teacher-provided criteria to evaluate musical works or performances" (SEADAE, 2014c, p. 8).

Objective:

- Given class listening exercises and discussions about protest songs of the 1960s, the students will be able to work collaboratively to develop a set of criteria for evaluating protest songs and use this criterion to evaluate their own protest songs and those of their classmates.

Formative Assessment(s)/Check-Ins:

- Completion of Teacher Resource 5.2 (Days 1-5)
- Exit slips (Days 6-9)

Summative Assessment(s):

- Each student will submit completed rubrics for all of the original protest songs presented in class.

Lesson Sequence

Day 1:

- Teach the students to sing the first verse of "We Shall Overcome" by rote.
- Ask the students what it means to "overcome." Discuss why an individual or a group of people might need to "overcome." Connect overcoming to protesting an injustice and why someone would need to do so.
- Have the students pair and share to create a list of "injustices" in their lives and then create a class list.
- Choose one of the suggestions for protest and ask the students to brainstorm ways that they might protest or ways they have seen other people protest the selected topic. Lead the conversation to the idea that music can be used as a form of protest.
- Ask the students if they know any songs that are protest songs and if so, what is being protested. If appropriate, listen to one of the student's suggestions in the moment of class or use the suggested song in an upcoming lesson.
- Tell the students that in the 1960s, many popular musicians were writing protest music. Ask the students if they know what historically was going on in the 1960s. In this lesson, focus the students' attention on the war in Vietnam, the protests by young people, and the draft. You might want to give the students something to read or simply summarize some historical basics for the students.
- Complete Teacher Resource 5.2 for Bob Dylan's "Masters of War" through multiple listenings, discussion, and lyrical analysis.
- Ask the students to suggest ways they might use classroom resources to find out more about Dylan and this song in order to prepare them for the next day's activity.
- Repeat the preceding two bullets for Pete Seeger's "Bring 'Em Home." In particular, lead a discussion about the lyrics of the chorus and the power of this protest statement.
- End class with a recap and a review of "We Shall Overcome"

Day 2-3

- Begin with a review of the previous class.
- Ask the students to divide themselves evenly into eight groups. Have each group draw one of the following songs: "Vietnam," "War," "What's Going On," "What are You Fighting For," "Saigon Bride," "Fortunate Son," or "Blowin' in the Wind." Provide the students with recordings or links to YouTube as well as lyric sheets.
- Tell the students that their task is to listen to their song at least two times and then use their listening and internet research skills to complete Teacher Resource 5.2 as a group. Tell the students that their group will need to share what they have learned with the rest of the class at the end of the next class.
- Allow work time for two class periods.
- At the end of Day 3, have each group share what they learned and play their song for the class. Provide additional details (if necessary) and wrap-up class by discussing what injustice(s) the writers of these songs were trying to overcome.

Day 4

- Review with the students what they have learned thus far about protest music and the war in Vietnam.
- Provide the students with some historical context about the home-front during the war in Vietnam. Help the students understand that while the war in Vietnam was happening and United States citizens were protesting the war, another important historical movement was happening at the same time: The Civil Rights Movement.
- Ask the students what they know about the Civil Rights Movement from social studies. You might want to show the students some images from the Civil Rights Movement to help remind them.
- Tell the students that while African American young men were drafted into the military the same as white men, their families were experiencing inequality and injustice at home due to segregation policies in the southern states.
- Tell the students that "We Shall Overcome" was considered the anthem for the Civil Rights Movement and it was almost always sung at any protest or march.
- Consider showing the students an historical video of a Civil Rights protest in which the song is being sung.
- Tell the students that one unique thing about "We Shall Overcome" is that the words were often changed to fit the particular occasion. As the verse they know finished, a leader would call out the next line, such as "we shall all be free," "we'll walk hand in hand," etc. and then the group would sing those words as an additional verse. While some verses were regularly sung, there was also a tradition of creating new verses to fit the particular occasion.
- Ask the students for suggestions for new verses for "We Shall Overcome" and consider testing out some of these verses as a class.
- Distribute copies of Langston Hughes' poem "The Backlash Blues."
- Ask the students to discuss the words and meaning of the poem with a partner.
- Listen to Nina Simone's "Backlash Blues."
- Compare and contrast the song to the poem and complete Teacher Resource 5.2.
- Discuss how "Backlash Blues" is both a protest song for the war in Vietnam and the Civil Rights Movement.
- Wrap-up class with a review or question/answer time.

Day 5

- Tell the students that protest music wasn't just written in the 1960s. While the topics are different, American popular musicians have chosen to use their skills as musicians to protest current events throughout history.
- Select a current event and related protest song to discuss and analyze using Teacher Resource 5.2.
- Ask the students to review their completed worksheets and identify what they think are the important characteristics of all protest songs.
- As a whole class, create a list of protest song characteristics and vote, if necessary, to come to a consensus as a class.
- Use the class list of characteristics to create a three-level rubric. Work as a class to develop the Level-3 criteria and then have students work in small groups to develop the criteria for one additional cell (see Chapter 7).

- Tell the students that for the final project, they are going to work with a partner or small group of their choice to compose a protest song on a topic of importance to them. Composition parameters will vary based on the students' abilities and prior knowledge, but students should strive to meet the criteria established in the rubric created for the evaluation of protest music. Some possibilities include:
    - Composing new lyrics to a familiar song
    - Writing lyrics in poetic form
    - Composing an entirely new song using a specified chord structure
    - Writing one new verse to a familiar song used by the whole class
- The most democratic approach would be to provide students with broad expectations and allow each group to decide how to meet the expectations in a manner most relevant to the skills and abilities of the group members.
- Tell the students that next class you will provide them with a copy of the rubric they just created and that they should use this rubric as a guide for their protest song composition.
- Allow the students to spend the remainder of class forming groups and getting started on their project.

Day 6-9 (as needed)

- Begin the sixth class by distributing the rubric created previously. Ask the students to listen to an unfamiliar protest song and evaluate it on the rubric. Ask the students if they have any questions about using the rubric.
- Remind the students of the project goals and allow groups to begin working.
- Circulate the room, helping students as needed.
- Encourage groups to share ideas with each other and get feedback on drafts of their songs. Remind the students that they can give feedback to one another using the rubric the class created.
- End each class with a group exit slip addressing progress and any challenges faced. The exit slips will enable you to provide support during the next class, prepare a mini-lesson for all students, and/or determine an appropriate time for sharing songs.

Day 10 (approx.)

- On the final day, ask for volunteers to share their compositions with the class.
- Listening students should evaluate the presented protest song using the class rubric.
- End with a final discussion about the power of protest songs.

Possible Extensions or Additions:

- Work with the social studies or language arts teacher to make the final project more integrated. Students might work on their lyrics as a poetry study in language arts or the social studies teacher might suggest that students focus their protest songs on a particular historical period being studied. While these collaborations might limit student autonomy and choice, they would provide additional connections across the curriculum.
- Ask the students if they would like to turn their protest songs into music videos to raise awareness about their protest topic. These videos can easily be shot and edited using cellphones, iPads, or other devices. Work with the school media center or other district resource to publicly share these videos.

Framework Commentary

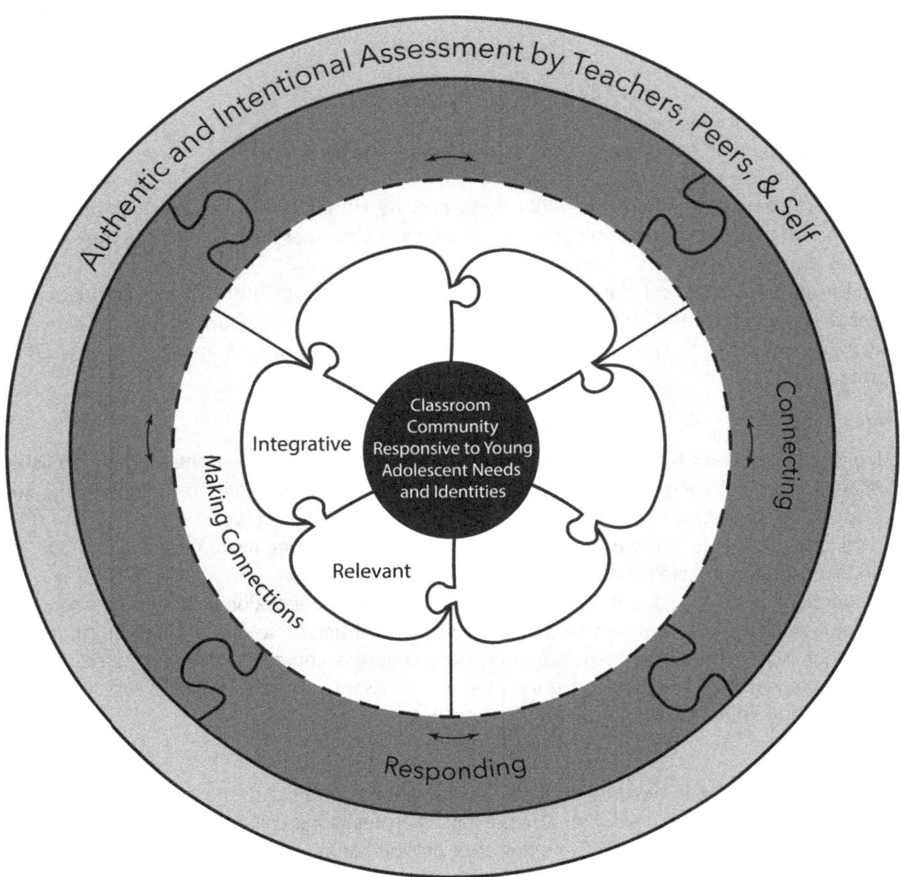

Making Connections

This lesson sequence is a good example of how musical content might be taught in middle school general music in order to support middle level learners' ability to make connections to their own lives and to content learned in other subjects. The *integration* of the war in Vietnam, the Civil Rights Movement, and poetic analysis connect music learning, particularly responding skills, directly to social studies and language arts. In addition, the discussion of injustice in their own lives, the integration of modern protest songs, and the final composition all serve to make music learning *relevant* to the young adolescents' own experiences.

Artistic Processes

This lesson sequence focuses primarily on skills in *responding* to music: listening, lyrical analysis, and evaluating other's compositions. Although responding is the focus of this lesson sequence, the historical lens used throughout also addresses *connecting* through the integration of protest music analysis and the injustices experienced by Americans historically and in modern life. While students compose their own protest song, the focus of this lesson sequence is not on *creating* skills or the compositional process.

Intentional and Authentic Assessment

During the completion and sharing of the final project, students are building skills in *self- and peer-assessment* (see Chapter 7). The predetermined criteria created by the class makes this assessment *intentional* and the fact that the assessment mimics the work of musicians makes it *authentic*.

Teacher Resource 5.2
Responding to Protest Music Worksheet

Song Title:

Song Performers:

Step 1: Listening	Step 2: Lyrical Analysis	Step 3: Research	Step 4: Hypothesize
What is the genre?	What is the message or subject of the lyrics?	When was this song written or recorded?	What do you think this song is protesting? Give at least one piece of evidence from Step 1, 2, or 3 to support your answer.
What to do hear in the music that supports your genre choice?	What words or phrases support your chosen message or subject?	What historical context might be influencing why this song was written?	
What is the mood of the song?	What injustices are identified in this song?	What other information can you find about the artists' purpose in writing/recording this song?	
What do you hear in the music that supports your mood choice?	What words or phrases support your identified injustices?	Was this song ever performed at a specific protest event?	

Teacher Resource 5.3

Online Resources to Support Responding to Protest Music Lesson Sequence

(All links are designed for teacher use and are accurate at time of publication)

- The Gilder Lehrman Institute of American History
  https://ap.gilderlehrman.org/period/8

- PBS American Experience
  https://www.pbs.org/wgbh/americanexperience/

- Library of Congress, Music in the Civil Rights Movement
  https://www.loc.gov/collections/civil-rights-history-project/articles-and-essays/music-in-the-civil-rights-movement/

- Smithsonian Folkways Recordings
  https://folkways.si.edu/

- TeachRock, Book 3: Transformation
  https://teachrock.org/book/transformation-2

- Time Magazine, "Why the Vietnam War Produced Such Iconic Music"
  https://time.com/4949617/music-vietnam-war/

- United States Foreign Policy History & Resource Guide
  http://peacehistory-usfp.org/protest-music-vietnam-war/

Responding Lesson Suggestions for Differentiation

While it is important to help all young adolescents develop skills in responding to music, students with diverse needs may face challenges in developing listening and responding skills. Listening is a primarily auditory endeavor, yet the principles of Universal Design for Learning suggest that all curriculum planning should provide for multiple modalities for engagement, representation, and action within a particular learning activity (CAST, 2018). Thus, as teachers, we must consider how the auditory activity of music listening can be represented visually or tactilely (as examples). While I cannot provide details on all of the possible differentiation solutions, I would like to point out a few easy modifications for the lesson sequence above.

First, for students with challenges reading English, whether because they are English Language Learners (ELLs) or are challenged with reading in some other way, lyrical analysis may be difficult. Lyrical analysis requires reading a lot of words presented poetically as well as an understanding of metaphors and literary allusions. Whenever possible, provide ELL students with translations or pictographic representations of the lyrics. Alternatively, allow students to use a dictionary, a universal translator, or Google Translate. For students with a reading challenge, you might reduce the length of the passage or excerpt specific words or phrases so that the student can achieve analytic success within the time limits.

Second, some students, particularly those on the Autism Spectrum (Morris, 2009) have sensitivity to certain musical sounds, particularly loud sounds or sounds on specific frequencies. These students should be allowed to wear earplugs or headphones during listening activities (as well as during composition and performance activities, if needed). Some students find auditory relief when allowed to sit/stand on a square of thick carpet or if they position themselves in a certain part of the room away from the classroom speakers. Some teachers have also reported that allowing students to stand in the hallway during music listening activities has enabled students to listen along with their classmates, but at a distance that reduces the musical stimuli.

Third, responding to music can be difficult for students with hearing impairments. It is important to understand the nature of a student's hearing loss and whether the device he/she uses can be programmed to improve the music listening. The two primary ways that students with hearing loss engage in music listening are through tactile or visual stimuli. Students with hearing impairments might find success in listening activities if they sit close to the speakers, if the speakers are placed on the floor and they are allowed to remove their shoes to feel the vibrations, or when given an inflated balloon to hold in front of the speaker in order to feel the vibrations (McDowell, 2010). In addition, any resource that provides a visual representation of the music selected for listening can aid those with hearing loss. According to deaf educator and researcher Julia Silvestri and colleagues, "technology that transforms music into colors and shapes that visually correspond to sound's basic elements: intensity (volume) and frequency (pitch) ... [are] widely accessible through smartphone and tablet applications [such as] *Absorbed, Audiogasm, Decibel 10, GarageBand, Gravitarium,* and *insTuner*" (Silvestri et al., 2018, p. 3).

Finally, analyzing the lyrics of protest music may be an emotional trigger for students. When you introduce the lesson sequence, be sure to prepare students for the experience. Let the students know that they can leave the room (following class procedures) if they begin to feel too emotional about what the class is discussing. If a student experiences an emotional trigger during class, follow-up with that student to learn more, let them know you care, and (when needed) bring the student to the attention of the counselor and other relevant school personnel.

Making Composition Relevant and Integrative: Speed Compositions or Improvisations

While the compositional process is a valuable one for developing creative musicians, it is also time-consuming. It is understandable that composition may not be a priority in middle level general music due to the time constraints imposed by the school schedule. However, I believe this is a mistake. The experience of composition and improvisation often illuminates important musical understandings as young adolescents begin to make their own connections within and beyond music. In addition, a single composition project can also easily assess standards and objectives in other areas of music as well.

Do-Now Activity 5.1

Speed Compositions or Improvisations

Suggested Grade Level:

- 5th–8th

Approximate Length of Time:

- 10–15 minutes per class period

Materials:

- No materials necessary, but you might want classroom instruments, computers, visual prompts, etc.

Primary National Core Arts Standard:

- MU:Cr1: "Generate and conceptualize artistic ideas and work" (SEADAE, 2014c, p. 1). Select the grade appropriate level standard.

Modified from Activity Developed by:

- Tyler

Description:

- "Speed compositions" are individual or group quick composition or improvisation activities that can be used at any point in class, but might be useful as an opening "do-now" activity. Speed compositions should only take about 10 minutes.
- The most democratic way to conduct speed compositions is to:
  - Have students suggest musical styles, inspiration ideas, etc. to inspire compositions.
  - Allow students to choose the instruments or other sound-producing objects for their compositions.
  - Allow students to use invented or traditional notation to document (if desired) speed compositions. Given the shortened timeframe for these speed compositions, notation should not prohibit student participation.
- Create a section in the students' notebook or folder for documenting speed compositions.
- Keep to a regular schedule for speed compositions.
- Incorporate recently learned musical knowledge or skills into the compositional prompt.
- Progressively increase the difficulty of the speed composition prompt.
- Allow students to share their speed compositions with the class only as they feel comfortable.
- Where appropriate, develop a particular speed composition prompt into a larger project.

Teacher Resource 5.4

Speed Composition or Improvisation Prompt Suggestions

1. Provide a one or two measure rhythmic or melodic A section and ask students to create a B section.
2. Play a short excerpt of the rhythmic track from a familiar song and ask the students to generate a new melodic line, an accent rhythm, or chanted/rapped lyrics.
3. Ask students to write new lyrics to the chorus of a familiar song on a specified topic (try a newspaper headline or an upcoming school event as the prompt).
4. Play a repeating back-beat and have students work in groups to create a short rap (consider specifying the topic, drawing on everyday experiences such as the weather, emotions, food, or holidays).
5. Have students use iPads, online software (such as drumbit.app), or classroom furniture/body percussion to create a 2-measure drumbeat to be used for a specific purpose (i.e., dancing, relaxing, working out, studying, etc.)
6. Have students work in groups to generate a bass line, harmony, or rhythmic accompaniment for a song learned previously in class.
7. Ask students to create a variation for a familiar melody used as the theme.
8. Display a work of art, photograph, online image, etc., and ask students to respond musically to the inspiration.
9. Ask students to improvise a short melody over a familiar chordal pattern (i.e., I-V-vi-IV or 12-bar blues)
10. Draw upon a character found in a novel from English class or a historical figure or event studied in social studies as the inspiration for a quick composition. The same might be done with a concept taught in math or science.

Tyler, he has found that sometimes his students struggle with long-term compositional projects:

> My old model was based on compositional [projects where] as you're learning the [new musical skills/knowledge] you're applying them directly to your composition. Your final composition grows as you learn. But I've seen over the years that I don't think that that's how preteens and early teenagers work. They tend to be "zip-zip, I'm done." If they don't see the bigger picture or if they don't know what they're shooting for, then it's not as likely to add up.... The process was so drawn-out. When I started making them do speed composing, I [got] even better results.
>
> –Tyler

Inspired by Tyler's notion of "speed compositions," Do-Now 5.1 is designed to help students make connections through quick, challenging composition or improvisation prompts that allow students to explore the world of composition or improvisation and concretely apply newly learned knowledge to a creative endeavor. Sometimes, young adolescents enjoy the challenge of moving quickly through a project without the stress of doing things exactly right or needing to fully understand what to do. The low-risk nature of a speed composition or improvisation activity can help young adolescents be creative and quickly create something new without the need to critique or over-analyze their work.

A few speed composition prompt ideas are provided in Teacher Resource 5.4, but there is no limit to the kind of prompts that might be used for speed compositions. Prompts that connect to a topic taught in another class, everyday events like summer vacation, or a current event within the school or the greater community, are great ways to help make these low-risk speed compositions or improvisations integrative and relevant. In addition, incorporating a musical concept or genre taught in the previous class into the speed composition prompt can serve as a form of application and review.

While speed compositions or improvisations serve a specific connection-making and musical growth purpose, they should not be considered a replacement for experiencing the complete compositional process. Rather, speed compositions are one way to generate initial ideas that might later be expanded into a larger project or to reinforce and apply important knowledge learned previously.

Wrap-Up: Making Connections

In emphasizing connection-making in general music, music teachers increase the likelihood that young adolescents see the purpose in taking a general music class. Explicit relevant and integrative connections can help to motivate students previously uninterested in school music learning. When students learn, through modeling and experience, to connect music learning to life outside the walls of the music classroom, they begin to see how music might be part of their life in the future. As you reflect on your own middle level general music classroom, where are you making strong connections to your students' personal experiences or learning outside of the music classroom? What is one lesson or unit you already teach where you might improve the relevant or integrative connections? Have you assumed that your students can make connections on their own or do you model connected thinking for your students? Is there one strategy or curricular example presented here that you would like to try as you work to improve your ability to help students make connections?

Notes

1 The book *Sound Ways of Knowing: Music in the Interdisciplinary Classroom* (Barrett, McCoy, & Veblen, 1997) is a useful resource for those beginning to develop integrated music curricula.
2 Campbell's (2005) three-phase pedagogy for music listening is a useful tool for guiding students to develop listening skills.
3 I acknowledge that both "I've Got a Woman" and "Gold Digger" contain lyrical messages of misogyny and are inappropriate for school. Holly does not play the full songs in her classroom, but rather focuses students' listening on the opening riffs.

6 Stretching Limits

Exploratory and Challenging General Music Learning

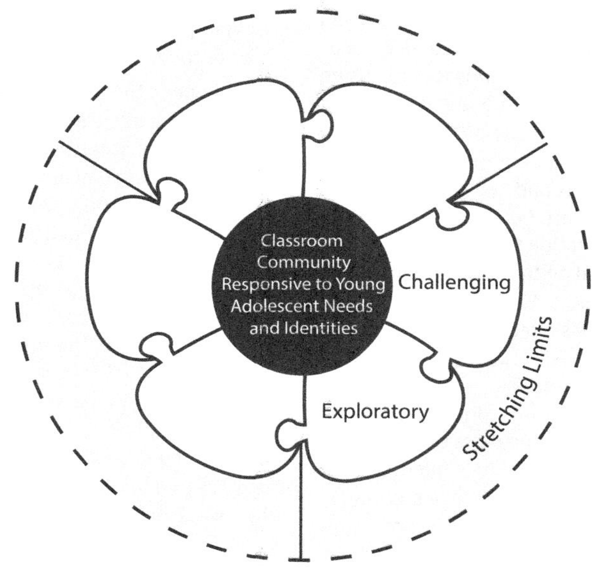

Democratic Principle #4: Encouraging Student Growth

To be inspired to pursue lifelong musical experiences of their choosing, all middle level students need to explore unfamiliar musics and music-making activities and be challenged beyond their current musical abilities. Of course, very few students will become professional musicians. However, all can be challenged and encouraged to explore their musical potential, develop as independent learners, and discover possible future musical selves. In this way, middle level general music teachers strive to meet democratic principle #4 through the encouragement of student growth both within the classroom and beyond. Cultivating student growth through scaffolded exploration and challenge is "stretching limits."

DOI: 10.4324/9781003124245-7

Robert	Katie
Around the classroom are posters titled, "The Basic Melody Recipe," "An Ostinato Recipe," and "Accompaniment Recipe." Each poster displays a list of simple compositional rules designed to remind the students of basic principles learned earlier in the year.	We have arrived at Katie's classroom before the bell rings to find the classroom arranged in five different pods, each with identical sets of musical instruments. Guitars, keyboards, drum sets, and upright basses sit mutely anticipating the arrival of students. On the SMARTboard are the following instructions:

Robert

Around the classroom are posters titled, "The Basic Melody Recipe," "An Ostinato Recipe," and "Accompaniment Recipe." Each poster displays a list of simple compositional rules designed to remind the students of basic principles learned earlier in the year.

Scattered throughout the room, students are working alone or in small groups. Some students sit on the floor with what look like stuffed animals, cardboard boxes and aluminum foil, and other odd materials. Two boys are holding a microbit processor[1] connected to a Star Wars figurine from which appears to be emanating a repeated four-beat ostinato. Nearby, a student working alone is carefully outlining the shape of a violin onto a piece of cardboard. Other students sit at computers using music composition software or Scratch, a basic code writing software. A few students are using USB cables to connect their computers to microbit processors that are the same size as their hands.

At the front of the classroom, Robert and three students are gathered around the teacher's desk. Robert and one student are both playing trumpets and sightreading the notation for a duet two female students have composed on their laptop. When they stop playing, Robert turns to the composers and says, pointing to the "Basic Melody Recipe" poster on the classroom wall, "what part of the melody recipe do you think you forgot?"

The two students think for a moment and then one says, "in the middle, the two parts were both too complicated, so it sounded bad. The higher part had too many leaps, and Jason couldn't play it easily."

"That's right," Robert responds, "do you know what you need to change?" The composers nod yes.

"What are you going to do once you correct your composition?" Robert asks.

Silent until now, the second composer says, "we are going to make backpacks for two of our old cabbage patch dolls. We'll put the microprocessors in the backpacks so that the dolls can sing the parts of the duet when they are near each other. We already figured out how to use the radio waves to make our microbits recognize each other, but we still have to code all of our music into Scratch."

"That sounds like fun! Will the dolls sing anything when they are alone?" In response, the two girls look at each other and shrug. "Well, keep thinking about it. I'm sure you'll come up with something great!"

The girls collect their laptop and return to their seats as Robert turns to Jason who is putting away his trumpet. "Now, Jason, let's take a look at this musical Twister game you and your group are building."

Katie

We have arrived at Katie's classroom before the bell rings to find the classroom arranged in five different pods, each with identical sets of musical instruments. Guitars, keyboards, drum sets, and upright basses sit mutely anticipating the arrival of students. On the SMARTboard are the following instructions:

1. Please collect your folder and find your group.
2. Review your "Writing a Song" instruction sheet.
3. Your group should have finished the chorus of your song last class. Review your chorus as a group.
4. Read the instructions for "Part 3: Music for the Verse" and begin testing out musical possibilities as a group.
5. Before you leave today, please decide on your chord pattern for the verse AND decide who will write the lyrics for each verse.

Katie opens the classroom door as the bell rings. Suddenly, the silence is broken by students who enter the room, greet their friends, drop their bags, and pick up instruments. Some students stop to read the SMARTboard while others walk directly to an instrument without noticing the instructions. By the time the tardy bell rings, all students have joined a group and a jumble of four chord pop-song choruses are being performed.

As we circulate the room, we look over the shoulders of the students to read their song drafts. One group is writing a song called "Rewind"[2] which is about going back in time, another group appears to be writing a song about their backpacks, while the lyrics of a third group feature the school janitor. When we arrive at their space, the fourth group is discussing the lyrics of their verses which currently look like the directions for a recipe: "roll out your puff pastry to start/spread your jam on your pastry/put all the ingredients in your cart/apricot tart." As students in this group suggest additional lyrics, one member says, "Let's sing the chorus again so we remember," and they begin singing: "apricot tart/apricot tart/put all the ingredients in your cart." This group is not the only group focused on food. The fifth group has written the following chorus:

> "Ice cream is so good, I like to eat it in a bowl
> I could eat it everyday, yes I could.
> Oh, ice cream, yeah, yeah,
> You make me whole."

This group has also written G-C-G-D at the top of their notes to indicate their new verse chord progression. As we pass, ideas about ice cream are shouted out by the group members: "vanilla," "chocolate," "strawberry," "cones," "sprinkles," "it's cold," "while watching TV," and on they continue.

Stretching Limits

Each middle level student has certain interests and talents that are well-honed, as well as those that are undiscovered. Consider the student who plays competitive soccer. He or she has well-honed athletic abilities (and hopefully interests), but may have never had a chance to see whether he/she has an affinity for acting on stage or writing computer code. General music is one of the many middle level curricular offerings that provides an opportunity for students to explore and try-on a wide range of abilities, skills, and interests. Encouraging student growth means creating and maintaining a learning environment in which each individual student is appropriately supported in their endeavors to stretch beyond what they believe possible about themselves.

In stretching students' limits, teachers must cultivate a classroom community where stretching oneself is both possible and comfortable. First, this requires a positive and safe classroom community like the one discussed in Chapter 3. Second, it requires that teachers provide the right form of support or scaffolding to enable each student to succeed. Lev Vygotsky's (1978) social constructivist learning theory asserts that optimal success as a learner is possible when a "more knowledgeable expert" (teacher, parent, or peer) provides the right amount of scaffolding to help a learner move from what he/she can do alone to what he/she is attempting to accomplish. The space between what a learner can accomplish independently and what he/she can do with the help of provided scaffolding is called the Zone of Proximal Development (Vygotsky, 1978), a space that is critically important for young adolescents to navigate in order to stretch their own limits. As young adolescents grow through this stretching process, the scaffolding evolves to help them continually improve their abilities. Thus, learning focused on stretching limits must involve regular evaluation by and collaboration with the teacher and must be differentiated to meet each student's individual learning needs (Shabani et al., 2010). Through this process of stretching limits, the young adolescent moves along the pathway to independent musicianship, a key goal of middle level general music. As a middle level general music teacher, finding the "sweet spot" between differentiated supports and student musical independence is key to stretching limits.

Exploratory Music Learning

Exploratory music learning refers to a curricular and pedagogical approach whereby students are given the opportunity to engage with and explore a variety of musics and music learning skills. When given proper support by the teacher, this exploration enables students to develop themselves as learners and more well-rounded individuals. Middle level general music that is exploratory may take many different forms, but students are empowered, through their experiences in the music classroom, to discover new ways of being musical. For example, in Katie's opening vignette, her students are exploring the professional work of composers and lyricists and trying on these roles to see if they fit. Katie explains further:

> I think exploration is important because this is really the main opportunity we have as teachers to introduce kids to new things with a somewhat open mind.
>
> —Katie

And Lindsey agrees with this emphasis on exploration as an important developmental feature of music learning for young adolescents:

> I think [the] purpose [of exploration] in middle school is to help students find their giftedness areas. So, I think that that is part of why I choose things [that expose students musically].
>
> –Lindsey

Thus, exploratory music learning supports young adolescent development and furthers the approach of middle level general music put forward in this book–that this course should help inspire students to continue musical learning beyond the timeframe of the class.

Using Exploration to Stretch beyond Relevant Music

One way to think about exploratory music learning is to consider exploration as a counterbalance to relevant music learning as discussed in Chapter 5. While it is important that students see how what they are learning in school is connected to their "real lives," it is equally important to push students to explore musical knowledge and skills beyond their comfort zone. The scaffolding you provide, perhaps through setting the context or connecting to previously learned content, will help to facilitate young adolescents' exploration of unfamiliar musical experiences. Although covering different musical content, this exploratory approach is taken by both Jessica and Alexis:

> [In my guitar class,] I try to provide the students with material that they are not necessarily experienced with or might not have had any experience with. So, I try to allow them to explore different cultures and learn about different styles of music.
>
> –Jessica

> They're doing things that they're not used to doing–they're rapping a children's book, they're building an instrument, they're having to create a poster–they're exploring things that they've never thought about in music before.
>
> –Alexis

Young adolescents may, through exposure in your class, find a musical genre, artist, or other aspect of music that they care deeply about. Thus, the choices you make in your middle level general music classroom need to provide a balance of relevancy and exploration.

I cannot provide a single definitive list of what to consider an "unfamiliar" musical experience. What is unfamiliar to one group of students may not be unfamiliar to students in a different school community. For example, in many schools across the country, introducing students to music from India, for example, a raga or Bhangra, would be considered an exploratory experience designed to stretch students. However, in some school districts near where I work in central New Jersey, traditional or popular musics from India would be familiar to many students given the large Indian-American population in the community.

Recall that the fifth democratic principle stated in Chapter 1 emphasized the importance of including comprehensive and diverse musical experiences in the middle level general music classroom. It is impossible to even consider "covering" all aspects of music within the time-frame of a middle level general music class. However, I challenge all teachers to consider their planned curriculum in light of the following questions:

- Does your curriculum content meet democratic principle #5?
- Does your curriculum content provide students with an opportunity to explore unfamiliar content?
- What is the balance of exploration and exposure to new content, and delving deeper into content that is already familiar and relevant to students?

Moving from "Exploratory" to an Attitude of Exploration

In many middle level schools, the label "exploratory" or "exploratories" is given to general music (along with other subjects such as visual art, drama, technology, and family and consumer sciences, among others). Courses classified as exploratory are typically short-term course offerings through which students rotate during the course of the school year. In many middle level schools, a six- or nine-week "wheel" schedule is common for these courses. One objection to short-term "exploratory" courses is that "general music classes, once intended to foster the sequential acquisition of comprehension and skill, become self-contained and sometimes unrelated segments of learning and instruction" (Stauffer & Saunders, 1992, p. 8). Certainly, a student who enrolls in a short-term general music class scheduled at the end of seventh grade will have difficulty remembering the musical content learned during a similar short-term course taken at the beginning of sixth grade. Sequential learning is certainly less vibrant under these circumstances; however, it is the responsibility of the music teacher to adopt an attitude of exploration within middle level general music without "watering down" the musical content. This does require the music teacher to be selective and intentional in choosing the musical content and the scaffolding needed for students to grow, if only incrementally, their independent musicianship.

Abby and Nicole have adopted this exploratory attitude despite their difference in approach. Abby's goal is to expose students to a variety of musical ideas so that the students can consider whether they would like to learn more at a later time, either through a more advanced class offered at her school, music lessons outside school, or future informal music learning.

> [General music is] exploratory mostly because we're delving into everything, not really going for mastery but just like finding if we can do these things and if we can, is it worth pursuing more later?
>
> –Abby

This does not mean that Abby's general music class is less academic or less musical than another class. It simply means that she emphasizes exposure to unfamiliar musical experiences over in-depth understanding of only one form of musical knowledge. Similarly, Nicole approaches her middle level general music course as a tour of world musics through which students sequentially build music fundamentals while exploring a variety of musical performance skills.

> [My class is exploratory through] world music cultures and using new instruments. It's very rare that I'll get a kid who will just say, "I hate this, I don't want to be here." They might not like African drumming, it's too loud, or they may not like Native American flutes because it reminds them too much of a recorder. I always say, "you know what, if you're not having fun on the drums, let's just focus on what you're learning on it, rather than the instrument you're on."
>
> –Nicole

Nicole's hope is that, regardless of the musical instrument being used, the students will develop music fundamentals, such as rhythm and melody, as they explore new musical cultures.

Exposure to wide-ranging musical experiences through musical exploration does not preclude the importance of sequential music learning experiences. Certainly, students need the opportunity to develop their musical knowledge and skills in a systematic matter. Some music teachers choose to emphasize the sequential development of music listening skills, others emphasize Western musical notation, while still others choose composition skills or an understanding of form as the sequential thread. Regardless of the approach taken, middle level general music can be simultaneously exploratory and musically substantive.

Challenging Music Learning

Challenging music learning in general music can take many forms. Whether or not a particular musical experience is challenging to an individual student will depend on factors including the musical content selected by the teacher, the scaffolding or support provided within the general music classroom, and the individual abilities of the students enrolled.

One potential misperception of challenging music learning is that general music cannot be challenging because its very nature is *general*. However, just because general music provides comprehensive and diverse musical experiences for *all* does not preclude those learning experiences from being challenging.

All middle level general music teachers can have high expectations and can set tasks for students that require students' application of their developing musical knowledge to novel situations. Both Lindsey and Holly agree:

> I think that yes, [my class is] challenging, but it's not challenging to the exclusion of all students being able to do it. [I] like *all* students being able to [be successful]. Other teachers [sometimes say,] oh this is just fun, you don't do anything hard in [music]. [But my students and I know] it's hard what [we're] doing ... we're not just doing nothing.
>
> –Lindsey

> I do think it's challenging because its stuff they've never learned before. It takes [some students] three weeks to tell the difference between dynamics and tempo. They still say, "what's tempo again?" So, [I] keep [doing] listening twice a week.
>
> –Holly

Challenging Music Learning for ALL Students

The diversity found within your school community will likely be reflected in your middle level general music classroom. Hence, what one student may find challenging, another may find easy. It is critical that all students find something to challenge them within the middle level general music curriculum, but that the appropriate supports are provided so that all students can also be successful.

Upon hearing the term challenging, some teachers immediately exclude their general music class from this label because they equate the idea of challenging to a gifted and talented program, as Alexis did at first:

> When I think challenging, I think the gifted program. My class is definitely not geared towards that. I'm sure for some kids it is challenging, and I think I ask kids to do things that maybe are a little bit outside of their comfort zones sometimes. [My students] had to take children's book and they had to rap the children's book [using a backbeat they found online]. That was really challenging for some of the kids because some of them can't keep rhythm. [Other students] were able to rap it, but then we went into the library during the Kindergarten library time and they had to rap it in front of Kindergartners, and that was challenging for them because it was in front of these little kids. So, in that way my class is challenging, but I don't know that it's academically challenging.
>
> —Alexis

It is interesting to observe Alexis' thinking here. At first, she thinks that her course is not challenging because it is not designed specifically for those students identified as gifted and talented by the school district. However, as she considers it more, she realizes that there are many ways in which the things she does in her curriculum stretch the limits of her students' abilities or comfort levels. At the same time, Alexis is still struggling with the idea of the word challenging being applied to a class she considers "non-academic." Alexis is not alone in her thinking. Many music teachers do not see general music as an academic or challenging course for a host of reasons. However, the question we must ask ourselves is: am I challenging my students to stretch themselves through the content, activities, or projects I have developed?

Very few middle level general music classes will be like Robert's (in the opening vignette), which enrolls a high number of students labeled by the school as "gifted and talented." To be clear, students enrolled in Robert's general music class must also be enrolled in another music class offered by the school, but his general music class is not limited to students labeled gifted and talented. Regardless of the student population Robert serves, it is his attitude toward his curriculum and his students that makes his class challenging:

> The curriculum is challenging by nature, but also because it allows itself to be as challenging as the kids want to make it. So, it's really adjustable.
>
> —Robert

Robert's curriculum is inherently differentiated because of imbedded student choice. His flexibility with his students' individual interpretations of a given assignment allows students to challenge themselves as they see fit and/or feel capable. He also points out that while many of his students are considered gifted and talented by the school, these advanced cognitive abilities often also come with emotional and social hurdles that provide a different kind of challenge:

> [Many of my students] have an emotional level not matching their cognitive level. The ability to work well with others and in teams is very challenging for a subset of those students, which is why I try my hardest to vary the type of teams. Then of course [I also] deal with the issues of perfectionism and the paralysis at a certain point in their project. [The students say,] "I can't do this anymore because I'm worried I'm going to ruin it."
>
> –Robert

A middle level curriculum that includes choice and some structured independence is likely to challenge some students in one way and other students in an entirely different way. This is hopefully achieved by considering the many different ways a particular assignment or activity might stretch your specific students' limits in the classroom. It is important to remember that challenging music content is not the exclusive right of those who are the highest performers in the school. In fact, challenging students who are often not challenged in school may alleviate behavior issues before they even emerge.

Suggestions for Differentiation through Challenge

Given the inherent diversity in young adolescent development, differentiation is needed in general music even if your classroom serves no students with documented disabilities or advanced learning needs. Of course, it is important to review and carefully prepare appropriate resources for students with documented disabilities. However, differentiation that cultivates a challenging learning environment does not stop once you have fulfilled your obligation and met a student's IEP or 504 expectations. Students' prior musical experiences, cultural identities, and developmental stage all impact what musical learning circumstances might challenge them. Thus, it is essential that middle level general music teachers embed differentiation into every aspect of the general music class.

There are many approaches to take in differentiating a middle level general music class to challenge all students. Below are a few suggestions:

- When learning a new musical instrument, allow time for each student to independently explore the instrument or improvise based on a newly introduced concept.
- Ask for volunteers who would like to share their work who feel they understand and are willing to help their peers.
- When assigning a project, provide students with choices, some more difficult than others.
- Create an "enrichment" area of the room featuring advanced musical activities related to the topic being studied. Ensure that students know they are allowed to access the enrichment area once they have completed assigned work.
- Always have manipulatives, posters, or other supports available for those students who need them.
- If you give students a simple worksheet to practice a particular skill, create three levels of the worksheet and distribute the appropriate level to the students based on their abilities.

- If you are working on musical skills on an instrument, have a "reward" or "challenge" instrument available at the front of the room (such as an electric guitar, drum set, the teacher's piano, etc.). When students are demonstrating high quality abilities or are working hard, ask them if they want to use the special instrument on the next exercise.
- Be open to students' ideas about modifying a particular assignment or project. Sometimes student derived ideas are the best way for students to challenge themselves.

Stretching Limits: Cultivating Independent Music Learners

A key aspect of stretching limits, particularly when exploration and challenge are combined, is that stretching limits moves young adolescents along the Zone of Proximal Development toward independence as learners. The more frequently young adolescents are given a chance to test out their abilities without direct adult supervision, the more confidence they will gain as independent musical learners. One way to cultivate independent music learning is through student-directed, discovery-based learning. In this approach to music learning, students are challenged to explore a musical topic through trial and error and as a result, discover something new for themselves. Discovery learning enables students to stretch themselves and learn independently rather than relying on the music teacher as the source of all musical knowledge and decision-making (Bruner, 1960).

By modeling and encouraging independent discovery within the general music classroom, Eric and Tyler both cultivate a climate in which all students can see themselves as music learners absent of a teacher:

> I think there is a lot of room in my curriculum for students to discover and to learn through discovery. There is a lot of opportunity to make mistakes and then to fix those mistakes. There is a lot of responsibility placed on the students to do the learning, which may be the first time that they've experienced that. For many students that can be very challenging, especially in contrast to the "core" subjects that are very much based on testing [at my school]. I think I make a point to make [my class] more of an exploratory discovery-based thing.
>
> –Eric

> I'm using the Kodály model for the way that I teach. So, I'm almost never telling [the students] the answers to anything. I'm only ever asking questions that help them get to the answers. So, it's exploratory inherently in my teaching style. I also want to model that curiosity. I'm always bringing in [music or musical ideas] I'm working on or stuff that I've noticed on YouTube [or] Sound Cloud. I'm trying to model the musician I want them to be.
>
> –Tyler

In my seventh grade general music class, I wanted students to think about the purposes of musical notation, but without being tied to their prior knowledge (or lack thereof) of Western musical notation. Thus, I set up a series of stations around the room with unusual, but easily accessible musical instruments (crystal water glasses, a thumb piano, various sized hand drums, homemade shakers, etc.). Each station also had a small whiteboard and a dry erase marker. I wrote the three steps of the activity on the board:

1 Determine how to play the instrument.
2 Create a symbol system with a key or legend so that another group can understand how to play the instrument.
3 Create a short composition using the key/legend created.

In groups, students worked at one of the stations while I provided support as needed. Once all groups were done, each group rotated to a new station. At the new station, the students were responsible for interpreting (without asking their classmates) the symbol system and composition of the previous group. Once they understood the symbol system, they were to practice the composition so that they could play it for the class.

Once the activity was completed, we discussed the experience. Through the discussion, students indicated that they had discovered important aspects of musical notation, such as the importance of indicating duration or the need to be clear about exactly when something is played. When a group played another group's composition incorrectly, the conversation between the two groups helped to clarify the weaknesses of the invented notation or a misinterpretation of the symbols. Inevitably, this discovery-based approach helped students well-versed in Western musical notation to move beyond their reliance on standard notation while it emboldened those who struggled with traditional notation because they were finally able to "read" music. This lesson typically moved into an invented instrument project, but it could easily move into a unit on non-Western musical notation, guitar tablature, Western musical notation, or any other topic focused on the dissemination of music through written or oral means.

Discovery-based experiences cultivate independent learners because they challenge students to explore and discover something new for themselves and therefore construct their understanding. Personal experience through knowledge application, rather than the teacher, is the source of the answer. Teachers carefully scaffold the activity and then allow students to explore independently and develop their own conclusions. This does not mean that every student will learn the exact same thing in a given lesson, but in this way, the curriculum naturally differentiates based on each student's prior musical understandings. Each student will make his/her own progress toward better understanding of the topic.

Stretching Limits through Informal Music Learning

British music education researcher Lucy Green (2002) developed informal music learning pedagogy from her research with popular musicians. In this research, Green investigated how popular musicians learn to play their instruments and to compose original music. She found that popular musicians did not learn through the traditional approaches used in the Western paradigm such as musical notation, private lessons, etc., but rather learned from experimenting on their instruments, listening to recordings, figuring things out independently, or asking peers for help. According to Green, "it has been a central part of musical ideology from rock to hiphop, soul to reggae, that the music is a direct, unmediated and authentic expression of feeling, untrammeled by the dictates of convention, and arising naturally from the 'soul' of the musicians" (2006, p. 106). In essence, popular musicians perform their thoughts and feelings and improve their musicianship in informal ways that bear little resemblance to formalized music learning in classrooms.

Informal music learning is an approach to music education that combines stretching limits with hands-joined learning. The students completing informal music learning projects are given decision-making power and autonomy. Through discovery, students participating in informal music learning projects gain insight into how the popular music they consume is initially created. In many approaches to informal music learning, teachers have an almost invisible role once the parameters of the assignment are established.

Exploration and Challenge in Informal Music Learning

Green (2008) developed a curricular application of her research with popular musicians for the formal music classroom whereby students form bands and create a cover song by ear. She tested this approach with British music classes serving primarily 13- and 14-year-olds. Informal music learning is often quite successful in seventh and eighth grade because these students often have the maturity and experience to work independently in small groups. However, whether informal music learning is successful in a given middle level general music class will rely primarily on the readiness of the specific students enrolled because much of the typical scaffolding provided by teachers is withheld.

Green (2006) identified five aspects of an informal music learning classroom environment that are key to success:

1 Students choose the repertoire.
2 Students learn to play their chosen repertoire through listening and copying, what is sometimes called creating "cover" songs.
3 Students learn in self-selected groups with their friends and adults provide minimal guidance.
4 Students learn in "personal, often haphazard ways" (p. 107).
5 Students integrate "listening, playing, singing, improvising, and composing" naturally into the learning experience (p. 107).

To accomplish these five aspects of informal music learning, music teachers must be willing to design a learning environment where students take the lead in determining what and how they learn. This is not to say that the classroom environment has no structure, but rather that the students are working in groups toward the performance or composition goal set by the teacher. For example, the goal might be to prepare a cover song performance of a song of their choosing, but the instrumentation and all other musical decisions are left to the students. These five aspects naturally challenge students and cultivate an exploratory climate within the music classroom.

Katie's Adaptation of Informal Music Learning

There are a number of ways that informal music learning has been adapted by music teachers. Activity Idea 6.1, the "Band Project," briefly describes the approaches used by Katie, Lindsey, and Eric in their general music classes. Each of these approaches integrates formal and informal music learning experiences in order to ensure student success, an approach advocated by Green (2008).

Activity Idea 6.1

Band Project (Cover Song or Original Composition)

Suggested Grade Level:

- 7th & 8th

Primary National Core Arts Standard:

- MU:Pr6: "Convey meaning through the presentation of artistic work" (SEADAE, 2014c, p. 6). Select the appropriate grade level standard.
- MU:Cr3: "Refine and complete artistic work" (SEADAE, 2014c, p. 2). Select the appropriate grade level standard.

Modified from Activities Developed By:

- Katie, Lindsey, & Eric

Description:

Allow the students to form groups or "bands." Using available musical instruments, student's own instruments, and/or technological instruments, ask the students to work together to prepare a cover of a song of their choice (see Green, 2008). Creating a cover song requires repeated listening and collaboration to make musical choices that the students are capable of performing. Alternatively, have the students work together in their band to compose and prepare to present an original song in verse-chorus form. Consider applying students' knowledge of genres and require each band to select a genre "identity" in which to perform or compose. The band project might also be extended into a music video project whereby students must also design the video for their cover song or original composition.

Katie's general music band project is one adaptation of the student band formation component of Green's (2008) informal music learning. Katie's approach is perhaps more teacher-directed than the informal music learning advocated for by Green (2008) because she begins with more formal instruction and then moves students to informal music learning. Katie's approach also shares some similarities to the approach advocated for by the Modern Band movement supported by the non-profit, Little Kids Rock. Here, Katie describes the eighth grade general music curriculum that she developed:

> [In] the first unit [in eighth grade] ... we spend four days rotating through piano—which they have some experience on from seventh grade—guitar, double bass (we have five double basses) and drum set. So, the whole class does that instrument together, whatever it is. At the end of the fourth day, they rank the instruments and everybody gets assigned one. I usually manage to give everybody their first or second choice, and then they have like three or four days where they have to learn the basics on that instrument. So, if you're playing double bass, you have to be able to pluck a C-major scale; if you're doing guitar or piano, you have to play a song from the song book—it can be slow, but you have to be able to play the chords for it, in time; and if you're playing drums you have to be able to do a rock beat and a swing beat for eight measures each. So, like, pretty easy things if you like really sat down and worked on it, you could probably do it in one class, but I usually give them three or four. And they're working in like-instrument groups, so if there's one kid who's awesome at drums they can help the other three kids.
>
> Then when they pass that basic proficiency level, they get put into bands. I've rigged it so that there's four drummers, four bass players, and at least four pianists and guitarists. So, everybody has one of each, and usually two of something, depending on what the popular instrument was that quarter. And, then their first assignment in their band is to play a song from the song book as a band. Then, this year the last part of class was that they had to write an original song in their band and perform it.
>
> —Katie

In her adaptation of Green's Informal Music Learning, Katie moves between informal and formal music learning strategies in order to scaffold her students' experiences while also providing room for freedom and creativity. Katie ends the term with the original song writing project featured in the opening vignette; the featured lyrics were written by Katie's eighth grade students. As Katie's students move through the entire term in middle level general music, they are continually asked to stretch themselves in multiple ways: through exploration of musical instruments, the challenge of working together as a band, exploration of musical sound to create a cover song, and eventually the challenge of composing an entirely new song.

Rethinking Digital Technologies in Music

Digital technologies in the educational context, defined as "digital tools, strategies, and resources used to improve teaching, learning, and creative inquiry," have the potential to enhance the curriculum in middle level general music (Bishop et al., 2018, original italicized). Digital technologies include, but are not limited to, computers, tablets, MIDI-capable devices, audio and video files, websites, apps, etc. In some schools, implementation of online learning management systems or 1:1 laptops have simply resulted in students completing traditional tasks, such as submitting assignments or having class discussions, virtually rather than on paper (Bishop & Downes, 2013). However, this limits the potential of digital technologies. The use of digital technologies in the classroom should be innovatively implemented by the teacher so that students can engage with content in ways impossible in the absence of such tools (Bishop & Downes, 2013). Just like the phonograph enabled students to hear professional musicians that were previously inaccessible, digital technologies should enable students to advance their musical skills and complete musical tasks they are unable to do without the technology. The technology itself should provide a form of scaffolding to advance a young adolescent's musicality.

In the Spring of 2020, the world of teaching and learning changed abruptly and dramatically when schools across the globe were unexpectedly thrust into remote teaching environments with little or no advanced preparation. In many cases, digital technologies were implemented and used by teachers without adequate professional development—a barrier also reported by New York and Tennessee middle level teachers in a 2015-2016 survey (Brinthaupt et al., 2020). While many teachers across the globe rose to the challenge and altered their teaching and learning environments in innovative ways, many other teachers simply used the digital technologies at their disposal to disseminate instructions and collect written work. Despite over 60% of young adolescents, regardless of race, gender, or socioeconomic status, reporting access to a smartphone, a desktop or laptop computer, and daily internet usage (Lenhart, 2015), many students struggled during remote learning to complete basic computer tasks such as uploading assignments. Future research in the wake of the remote learning instigated by the pandemic will likely reveal ways in which the educational conversation around digital technologies has changed, and new inequities between those who have access to digital technologies at home and school and those who do not. My hope is that music educators will return to the definition of digital technologies espoused here and endeavor to use these tools to innovate teaching, learning, and creation in order to scaffold young adolescents' developing musical independence.

The Artistic Processes: Stretching beyond Existing Abilities with Digital Technologies

A key reason to use digital technologies in middle level general music stems from the definition of digital technologies discussed above—these tools enable students to take their learning farther, to scaffold students to success beyond their current abilities.[3] Digital technologies enable middle level students with limited musical knowledge and skills to express their musical ideas without prior knowledge of how to sing, perform on an instrument, or notate music. For example, while students enrolled in middle level general music may not have the Western theory abilities to notate their compositional ideas, digital technologies allow them to capture, review, and potentially revise their compositional ideas.

There are numerous ways that digital technologies might enable middle level general music to meet not just the creating standards, but also the performing, responding, and connecting standards (see Teacher Resource 6.1). Depending on the digital technology resources available to your school community, you could easily meet any standard using a digital technology (if that is your desire). In addition, if you are interested in conducting a unit on movie music, music videos, or other media arts projects that integrate music, I encourage you to investigate the 2014 US National Core Arts Standards for Media Arts. These standards are specifically designed to be useful across the arts disciplines and may help strengthen your argument with administrators for completing digital technology interdisciplinary arts projects in general music.

Teacher Resource 6.1

Digital Technology Recommendations for the Artistic Processes

---

Creating

- NotateMe (computer notation of handwritten scores)
- See Teacher Resource 6.3

Performing

- Modern Band (popular music teaching videos and resources from Little Kids Rock)
- Monster Musician (practicing app designed to improve music reading)
- SchoolTube (video sharing similar to YouTube, but safer as it is just for schools)
- SmartMusic (practice tools)
- SoundCloud (sharing audio recordings)
- Solfeg.io (performing tracks)
- ToneSavvy (aural skills and theory)
- The Shed (music theory and other resources)
- YouTube (video sharing, play along videos, instrument tutorials, etc.)

Responding & Connecting

- Grammy Foundation (educational videos)
- Jazz Academy at Lincoln Center (audio recordings and other resources)
- Musical Instrument Museum (virtual field trips)
- New York Philharmonic (*Young People's Concerts* online videos)
- NPR Tiny Desk Concerts (video performances by artists across genres)
- PBS Education (music and social studies materials)
- Rock and Roll Hall of Fame (videos and teaching resources)
- Silk Road Project (world music audio & video)
- Smithsonian Folkways Recordings (audio, interactive features, and lessons)
- The Metropolitan Opera (performance and behind the scenes videos)
- The Social Distancing Festival (live and prerecorded videos across genres)

Lesson: Composing Melodies and Rhythms with Digital Technologies

Lesson Sequence 6.1 is an adaptation of a unit Jackie conducts in her technology-focused sixth, seventh, and eighth grade general music classes. The rotation schedule instituted by Jackie's school district has students attending general music for about three weeks early in the school year and then returning later in the school year for another session of about three weeks. In the first session of the school year, Jackie typically focuses on basic piano keyboard skills because her school has piano keyboards, and in the second session, she focuses on music technology for composition. Jackie has chosen the music technology unit in part because of the importance of technology skills and because this unit stretches students' limits both through exploration and challenge:

> I want kids to be able to explore. I want them to be able to do this stuff on their own. I want them to fail and figure out how they can come up with the right answer. I've built this curriculum so that it would get progressively challenging as they go [through the different websites]. When they get to SoundTrap, that [is] probably the most challenging aspect of [the unit].
>
> –Jackie

In Jackie's class, students use four digital technologies, all websites–Chrome Song Maker, Isle of Tune, Incredibox, and SoundTrap–to complete composition projects. In modifying this lesson from the unit Jackie shared, I have incorporated additional digital technology ideas shared by several of the other teachers (see Teacher Resources 6.2 & 6.3). Most teachers featured in this book complete only one digital technology composition project with their students, but Jackie does several in a sequence of projects that progress in difficulty.

In the lesson sequence below, students are developing and applying their understanding of melodies and rhythmic ostinatos to a series of composition projects completed through the exploration of several digital technologies. The lesson sequence below is written for fifth grade, but could be adapted for the upper grades by incorporating more sophisticated musical expectations in alignment with the standards or might be used as-is for upper grade students without previous experience.

In this lesson sequence, Jackie allows each student to move at his/her own pace through careful teacher monitoring and a series of mini-lessons introducing each new technology.

> Basically, I did a brief overview on [the four] assignments and a talk about melody [in the opening lesson]. Then the next class period we would go a little more into depth to Chrome Song Maker [the first assignment Jackie gives]. I'd give them a couple of days to work through that [assignment]. As soon as it seemed that a lot of kids were turning in assignments [on Google Classroom, maybe] sixty or seventy percent [of students are] turning in assignments, then I know I can [introduce] the next assignment.
>
> –Jackie

Jackie's students know the "final" due date for all of the assigned projects and are allowed to keep working on any assignment that has been introduced until they are satisfied with their result. Jackie endeavors to give students regular feedback and allows them to revise as they have time. Unlike the optional revision in Jackie's classroom, in the lesson sequence below, critique and revision are a required part of the process designed to improve students' composition skills, stretch them with the challenging process of revision, build their final portfolio, and meet the standard.

Lesson Sequence 6.1

Composing Melodies and Rhythms with Digital Technologies

Basic Lesson Information

Suggested Grade Level(s):

- 5th

Prior Knowledge:

- Students can describe the difference between a melody and an accompaniment.
- Students have listened to and critiqued performances.
- Students have experience using digital technologies in school.
- Students have experience revising their work in other subjects.

Approximate Number of 45-Minute Periods:

- 8-12

Essential Question:

- Why is revision an important part of the creative process?

Materials:

- Computers or other internet connected devices for each student
- Headphones
- Teacher created handout or webpage with links and instructions
- Classroom instruments
- Peer Review Check Sheet (developed as a class during Day 1)
- Teacher Resource 6.2 (optional)

Modified from Lesson(s) Developed by:

- Jackie, Robert, & Abby

Primary National Core Arts Standard:

- MU:Cr3.1.5.a: "Evaluate, refine, and document revisions to personal music, applying teacher-provided and collaboratively developed criteria and feedback, and explain rationale for changes" (SEADAE, 2014c, p. 2).

Objective:

- While proceeding through a series of composition exercises using digital technologies, the students will be able to use collaboratively developed criteria to evaluate their own and peers' melodic and rhythmic compositions in order to revise and finalize compositions added to a portfolio of work.

Formative Assessment(s)/Check-ins:

- Peer Review Check Sheets
- Teacher review and feedback on mini-compositions as students submit their work.

Summative Assessment(s):

- Final submission of the portfolio containing drafts, feedback, revisions, and a reflection.

Lesson Sequence

Day 1:

- Open class with a "guess the tune" game. Play, hum, whistle, or sing in solfege familiar melodies. Ask the students to guess the name of the melody.
- After the guessing game, ask the students how they were able to recognize the familiar songs.
- Lead the students in a discussion that identifies key characteristics of a good melody and create a list on the board. These characteristics might include, but are not limited to:
  - o Moving primarily step-wise
  - o Using skips wisely and sparingly
  - o Beginning and ending on do or la (as appropriate)
  - o Possibly repeating rhythms, but providing some variation
  - o Silence (rests) are important
  - o Easy to sing or play on an instrument
  - o Easy to remember
  - o You like to listen to it
  - o Robert reminds his students: K.I.S.S. - Keep It Simple, Silly!
- Return to one or more of the melodies from the guessing game. Ask the students how they could use their bodies to make the song more interesting. Students might suggest creating a stomping pattern, beatboxing, tapping their desks, clapping, etc.
- Divide the class into groups. Let each group select a familiar melody, such as a nursery rhyme or other song familiar to everyone in the group. Ask each group to prepare a rhythmic accompaniment for the familiar melody. Tell them that they have about five minutes to create a rhythmic accompaniment and need to be able to perform the rhythmic accompaniment along with the melody. Ask each group to share.
- Lead the students in a discussion about the qualities of a good rhythmic accompaniment and create a list on the board.
- Introduce or review the term ostinato. Help the students understand how an ostinato can be useful in developing a strong rhythmic accompaniment.
- Ask the students how they might use the characteristics of a good melody and characteristics of a good rhythmic accompaniment to evaluate a composition they have never heard before. Ask the students how they might evaluate their own compositions or a friend's composition using these criteria.
- Tell the students that for the next few days they will work independently on several mini-composition projects using different websites/apps. Depending on your students' needs, introduce each website/app to the students as a whole group. Some students will prefer to explore on their own, but only you can determine whether your students are technologically savvy enough to do so without teacher instruction.
- Explain to the students that they will be keeping a portfolio of mini-compositions created during this project. For each composition they will have a draft, feedback from the teacher, and a revision. For at least two mini-compositions, they will also have a peer review and a revision. Tell the students that they can choose their peer reviewer and that they can choose which mini-composition gets peer reviewed.
- Explain to the students that you will use the criteria they developed at the beginning of class (written on the board) to create a Peer Review Check Sheet that you will give them in next class.
- Show the students how they will share their assignments with each other and the teacher (presumably through the school's learning management system).
- Provide the students with a list of the websites/apps they will use during the projects and allow students to use the remainder of class to explore without having to specifically work on any particular assignment.
- Explain to the students that next class they will get the assignment sheets and will be allowed to work at their own pace.

Day 2-10 (as necessary)

- Create an electronic or paper assignment sheet (or series of assignment sheets) for each mini-composition activity you would like the students to complete (see Teacher Resource 6.3)
  - Include in the assignment sheets a reflection requirement that asks the students to review all drafts and final compositions and reflect upon their learning in a written response.
  - You might provide Teacher Resource 6.2 or develop another planning resource based on assignments chosen.
- Remind the students that they will be able to work at their own pace on each activity, but that they need to remember to save drafts for peer/teacher review and they need to produce and save final versions after review. Remind students how to save their work using the school learning management system.
- Tell students that while they are waiting for peer or teacher feedback, they can move on to the next activity and return later to revise.
- Each of these activities should take the students 1-3 days to complete and each activity should progress slightly in difficulty and required length of time. Teacher Resource 6.3 lists project possibilities in order of difficulty.
- When completed, students should submit their entire portfolio of work to the teacher for evaluation.

Possible Extensions or Additions:

- Move the composition task from electronic form to live performance. Have the students work in groups to develop a melodic composition and rhythmic accompaniment using their bodies and classroom instruments. Consider standard or invented notation.
- Consider arranging a presentation, display, or online forum where students' portfolios and/or completed compositions are shared with peers, teachers, and/or parents. Allow each student to curate his/her own work, choosing compositions and providing notes to help visitors comprehend the work.

Framework Commentary

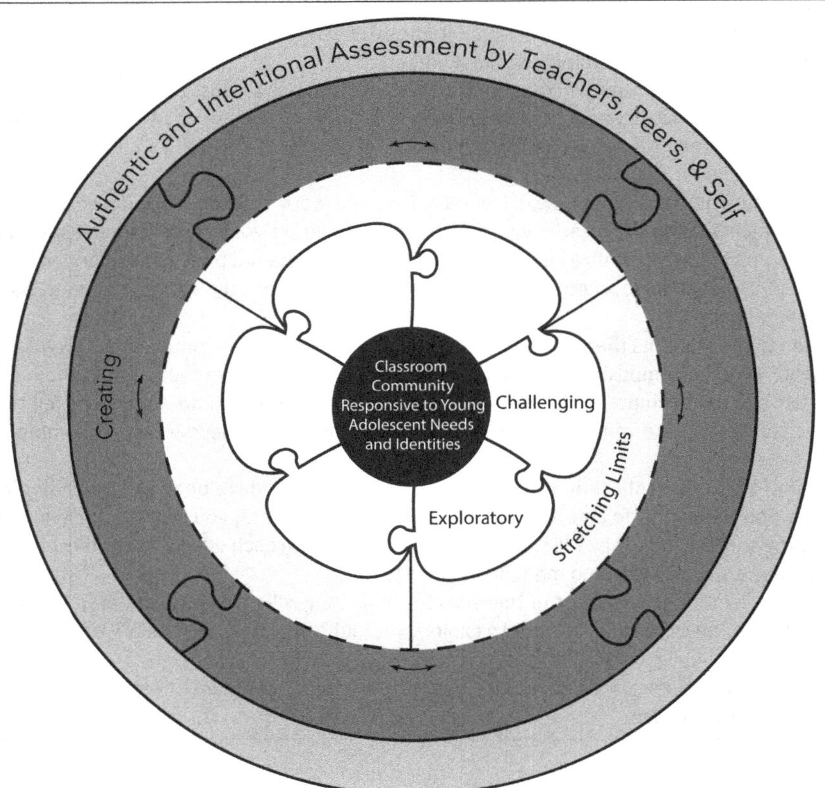

Stretching Limits

The focus of this lesson sequence is on student growth through *exploration* of composition and progressively engaging with more *challenging* projects. In particular, this lesson sequence is challenging because of the application of the melodic and rhythmic criteria both to their own work and to the work of other students. The use of multiple online software programs means that students explore music and see it visualized in multiple ways. While one online software may not help a student understand melody, the use of several different software products will let the students "see" melodies and rhythms represented various ways. The same kind of mini-composition projects could be done with mallets, rhythm instruments, invented instruments, piano keyboards, guitars, etc. Students with a strong musical background may find these mini-composition exercises too simple. Sometimes these students find the limits or possibilities of the software challenging and can be allowed to make refinements using the advanced features in the software. In other cases, in order to challenge advanced students, the teacher might need to develop a bonus or challenge assignment that is either added on to one of the mini-assignments or as an additional assignment given to those students who need it.

Artistic Processes

The focus of this lesson sequence is on *creating*, specifically evaluating and refining skills in composing melodies and rhythmic accompaniments. However, because emphasis is placed on the process of receiving feedback and revising, students are also using skills in *responding* to evaluate both their own and their peer's work.

Authentic and Intentional Assessments

The portfolio assessment embedded in this lesson sequence allows students to engage *authentically* with the creative process through drafting, receiving feedback, revising, and reflecting on their work. Through this process, this assessment *intentionally* focuses on the development of *authentic* composition and music listening skills. As part of this lesson sequence, students are *self-evaluating* and receiving formative feedback from both their *teacher* and *peers* (see Chapter 7).

Teacher Resource 6.2

Melodic Composition Planning Worksheet with Student Selected Musical Form (from Abby)

STEP 1: Create Four Different 4 Beat Rhythm Patterns

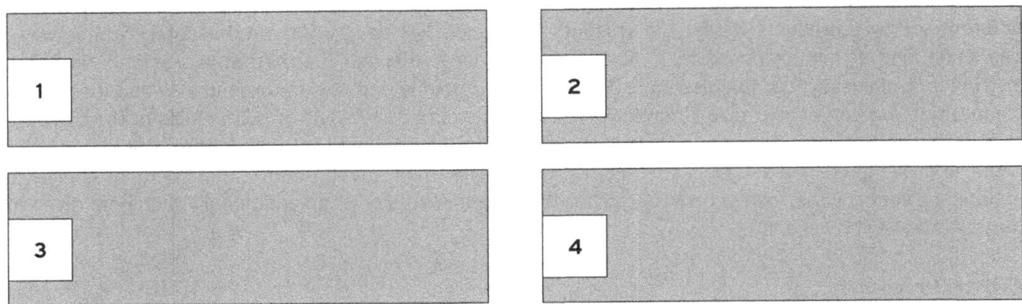

STEP 2: Choose the Form for Your Composition

You must compose 12 measures of melody, but you can decide how to divide up those 12 measures to give your composition form. Circle your option below. If you want to compose something beyond these options, please ask.

AB–6 measures in each section
AB–8 measures in one section and 4 measures in the other section
ABA–4 measures in each section
ABACA–2 measures in A section and 3 measures in B and C sections

STEP 3: Plan Your Composition's Rhythm

1. Label the rows of large grey boxes with your chosen form (for example: if you've chosen the first AB form option above, use the margin to mark line 1 and 2 as A and lines 3 and 4 as B. Use brackets if your form doesn't match the rows of boxes)
2. Use the small white boxes to choose one of your four rhythm patterns above for each box. Remember that all A sections should match.
3. Write out the rhythms for all of your measures.

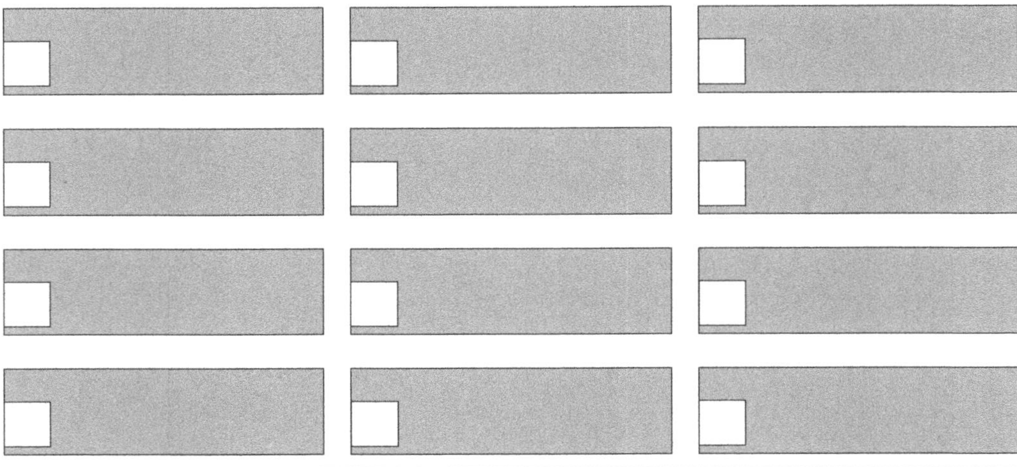

STEP 4: Compose the Melody for Your Composition using the Rhythm above

Teacher Resource 6.3

Digital Technology Possibilities for Lesson Sequence 6.1

Incredibox.com

- Students can choose one of four free options using the "demo" feature.
- Have the students create a beat-boxing ostinato that mixes rhythmic and melodic sounds. Note: a traditional melodic line is not possible with this software.
- If desired, require that the students create a recording of a specified length that is in ABA format. To do this, students either need to use the "solo" function or plan which parts of their ostinato to silence or add during a portion of their recording.

Chrome Song Maker (musiclab.chromeexperiments.com/Song-Maker/)

- This software allows students to see steps, skips, and rhythmic duration of their melody and rhythmic accompaniment in a colored block-like format.
- Chrome Music Lab has other visualizations of melody and rhythm similar to Chrome Song Maker.

Beep Box (https://beepbox.co)

- This online software allows students to create melodies that sound like the music in early video games such as Super Mario Brothers.
- Use the "easy" scale setting for pentatonic, the "normal" scale setting for a major or minor scale, or the "expert" scale setting for chromatic. Add rhythmic accompaniment by changing the instruments.
- Have students compose a theme for an existing video game character or develop a new video game character (drawing, description of abilities, and overall game purpose/theme). Characters can be animated and music can be added to the visual at moovly.com/students or animaker.com.

Classroom Keyboards

- Students can program instrument sounds in order to record a rhythmic accompaniment that plays on repeat while they compose and play an original melody. Teacher Resource 6.2 might help guide students in melodic planning.

Noteflight.com

- Free accounts are available for this online software, a basic Western notation software similar to Finale or Sibelius, where students can compose melodies and rhythmic/harmonic accompaniments orchestrated using many instrument options.

DAW platform such as Abelton Live, Garage Band, SoundTrap, Soundation, Mixcraft, etc.

- In developing a melody and rhythmic accompaniment in a DAW, allow students to select a preferred musical form and instrumentation.
- In Garage Band, students can set the lengths of different sections within the app, thus allowing them to easily create an ABA composition (for example). If using Garage Band on iPads, students can use pre-created loops and compose their own melodies, rhythmic, or harmonic accompaniments using the virtual "instruments" built into the app.

Makey Makey Boards (makeymakey.com)

- Talk to the science or technology teacher in your school. They may have Makey Makey boards available. Eric uses these boards for an instrument creation project similar to Robert's "microbit" activity featured in the opening vignette.
- Use Scratch.com to write basic computer code so that students can turn their Makey Makey board into a musical instrument. (There are many online video examples of how to do this.)

Movie Trailer or Music Video Creation

- Use a video creation software (such as iMovie) to have students create a movie trailer or music video for an original composition created using one of the above technologies.
- iMovie has a built-in movie trailer function or biteable.com has similar functions.

Consider other online software or apps (such as *Isle of Tune*) as accessible in your school district.

Digital Technology Suggestions for Access and Differentiation

While digital technologies can provide powerful differentiation and individualized scaffolding for diverse learners, access to these resources varies dramatically. Given that school districts across the country have differing access to laptops, iPad carts, computer labs, and internet access, I have endeavored in this chapter to focus on those resources that are, at the time of writing, freely accessible. For most of these free websites, it is essential that students can use their school email address to create and verify an account as this enables them to save their work. Be sure that you know your district's rules about school email addresses as some school districts allow only older grade levels to have access to email. You may need to talk to your school IT professional to get a specific website released for use in the classroom. You may also need to provide basic support in the computer skills young adolescents should already know, and to problem-solve issues with the IT department.

Additionally, I encourage you to investigate the platforms and resources your school already uses. For example, if your school uses Google Classroom as its learning management system, ask your IT professional to load the "Flat" extension which will provide your students with access to a music notation software. Similar to other Western notation software, the Flat extension also allows for real-time collaboration between users. If you are in a school where the access to digital tools is limited to a single computer lab that is always fully scheduled, I encourage you to investigate possible resources that can be borrowed from another facility in your district, request special permission for students to use their smartphones or other home devices, or reimagine one of the composition assignments using those non-digital resources available to you. Do not overlook resources already in your classroom, like your SMARTboard or teacher laptop. There are still things you can do with a little imagination. For example, you can use a single computer to create an enrichment or reward station for students to use independently when they have completed work or performed exceptionally well.

There are numerous ways that the lesson sequence above might be differentiated to accommodate different levels of ability in your middle level general music classroom, many of which have been discussed previously. Innate in this lesson sequence is the ability for students to move at their own pace and to explore each digital technology independently. Allowing students to choose from a "menu" of assignments enables them to select those assignments they most want to complete, rather than requiring everyone to complete the same assignment. Consider creating a "challenge" or "simplified" version of each assignment sheet and distribute these instructions to students who might need these modifications. Another option is to partner students who might struggle to complete these assignments independently. To accommodate students with a language barrier, consider creating screenshot videos of the instructions. Given the flexibility of the lesson sequence, there are many different ways you might differentiate based on the needs in your classroom.

Teacher Resource 6.4
Digital Technologies for Differentiation

- AirVox (a gesture-controlled app for iOS)
- Beemz App (a touch app that can also be connected to a non-touch device)
- FigureNotes (a color and shape matching system for learning music notation)
- Korg padKontrol or nanoPAD (drum pads played through touching various buttons)
- Skoog (a programmable squishy box that works by pushing large co ored buttons)
- Soundbeam (a touch free sensor device)

There are numerous digital technologies available that enable music creation by those students who, for various physical or cognitive reasons, are unable to succeed using the digital technologies recommended in the lesson sequence. While these adaptive digital technologies will require monetary resources to purchase, these technologies will make your middle level general music classroom more accessible to all students in your school community. The Makey Makey and microbit boards discussed in Teacher Resource 6.3 can easily be programmed by the teacher so that students can create music simply by touching an object, such as a piece of fruit, connected to the board. Teacher Resource 6.4 lists a few additional adaptive digital technologies for music making. The websites for these digital technologies provide demonstration videos so that you can decide which tools are best for the students you serve.

Making Performance Exploratory and Challenging: Circle Improvisations

Musical independence develops slowly through small, low-risk decision-making during performance activities. One way to do this is through a quick Do-Now Circle Improvisation activity (see Do-Now Activity 6.1) that was well liked by my seventh grade students. This activity became so popular in my class that students who were always late to class began arriving early to "claim" their preferred instrument or ask if it was their turn to be leader.

Circle Improvisations explore skills in performance, listening, and improvisation simultaneously and challenge students to develop musical independence and leadership. Circle Improvisations begin with a leader (the teacher at first, but later the students) setting the parameters and the steady beat in groups of 3 or 4 (or other meters as desired). Then, each student adds an ostinato that uses one or more of the beats. The goal is to repeat the ostinato on the correct beats for the duration of the improvisation. For example, if the leader sets a slow 4-beat steady beat, the first student to add a rhythm might add two eighth notes on beat two and a quarter note on beat four. This student would continually perform two eighth notes on beat two and a quarter note on beat four as other students join the improvisation. Accurately repeating the ostinato is part of the listening and performing challenge for most young adolescents. After listening to the first student's ostinato, the next student might add four sixteenth notes on beat one followed by three quarter rests, and so on around the circle. The objective (and challenge) is for each student to listen before adding something new so that the improvisation builds and grows with each new ostinato. Often students get a musical idea in their head and fail to listen to those who add their ostinato first. Thus, they are not listening and responding in the moment to what they hear.

Depending on your students' abilities, some scaffolding will be needed to ensure early success, but as the students improve, the scaffolding can be slowly removed. For example, the first few teacher-led attempts may take some significant class time, but once the students have the basic idea, Circle Improvisations can easily be used as the Do-Now opening 10-minute activity of class. Similarly, the teacher may need to guide the students in developing a set of class "rules" or scaffolding guidance for the Circle Improvisations, but once the students understand the basics, they can explore what happens musically when they "break" one of the established rules and evaluate whether the rule stands or can be modified.

Circle Improvisations also challenge young adolescents to explore their leadership skills. My students were eager for their turn as leader because the leader set the focus of the Circle Improvisation and tested new ideas that built on the previous attempts. For example, in keeping with the basic instructions, students first added new ostinatos clockwise or counter-clockwise

Do-Now Activity 6.1
Circle Improvisations

Suggested Grade Level:

- 5th–8th

Approximate Length of Time:

- 10–15 minutes per class period

Materials:

- Student bodies and/or classroom set of hand drums/rhythm sticks

Primary National Core Arts Standard:

- MU:Pr4: "Select, analyze, and interpret artistic work for presentation" (SEADAE, 2014c, p. 4). Select the appropriate grade level standard most appropriate (MU:Pr4.3 suggested).

Modified from Activity Developed by:

- Stephanie

Description:

- Sit or stand in a circle. The leader sets a steady beat by counting and clapping 1, 2, 3, 4 (or another meter). Moving around the circle, one student at a time adds a new ostinato using only some of the beats. The goal is for all students to add to the improvisation and continue performing so that a groove is developed. Once the class can successfully develop a groove, the teacher can suggest changes such as crescendo, decrescendo, or change in tempo. With each attempt, ask the students to reflect on how they did and what they would like to improve for their next attempt.
- The most democratic way to conduct the improvisation circle is to:
  - Have students develop the "rules" for the improvisation circle and modify the rules as necessary. Student rules might include: listen carefully, don't play all the time, make your ostinato simple, use loud/soft sounds, etc.
  - Have rotating student leaders set the beat.
  - Allow students to, collaboratively or through the student leader, set the day's musical goal. For example: fade-in and fade-out, move backwards around the circle, improvise based on a concept or idea (i.e., a thunderstorm), etc.
  - Allow the students to make their own connections within and beyond music class as inspiration for the day's improvisation.
  - Incorporate other instruments or technologies based on student desires.

around the circle, but later chose other patterns of adding ostinatos and/or removing ostinatos in order to listen to the results. In addition, leaders first played a simple steady beat with a specific count, but later performed more complicated rhythms that also served to establish a steady beat for the improvisation. My students made these modifications themselves, without my guidance, as they explored musical possibilities and continued to challenge one another and stretch the limits of possibility in this activity. Circle improvisations provide space for student-directed musical performance where every student is challenged, experiences leadership, and stretches his/her own limits in independent music-making.

Wrap-Up: Stretching Limits

Stretching limits in middle level general music encourages student growth and develops young adolescents' musical independence. As middle level general music teachers, it is essential that we recognize the importance of stretching all students' limits, not just those young adolescents with prior musical knowledge, skills, or abilities. I have highlighted how a differentiated approach to middle level general music facilitates students' exploration of their own musicality and challenges them to engage with new and ever more difficult musical experiences. Discovery learning, informal music learning, and digital technologies are all naturally differentiated and enable each student to stretch his/her own limits within the parameters of the assignment.

Stretching students' limits is incremental. Not every activity will stretch each individual student's musical abilities. However, careful consideration of your individual students' needs will enable you to work toward providing the appropriate scaffolding that moves every student closer to musical independence. As you think about your middle level general music class, consider whether your curriculum and pedagogy seeks to address the needs of all students in your classroom. Is your class too easy for some students or is it too hard for other students? Do you allow your students to explore music, but also challenge them in their musical growth? How might you integrate one suggestion in this chapter to improve the way your middle level general music class stretches students' limits and guides them toward musical independence?

Notes

1 A simple Single Board Computer that can be easily programmed.
2 All song titles and lyrics referenced here were provided by Katie from her students' work.
3 Professional development in digital technologies can be obtained through TI:ME. Professional development for differentiation-focused digital technologies can be obtained through the NA*f*ME Children with Exceptionalities Special Research Interest Group.

PART 3

Assessment on and through the Fertile Ground Framework

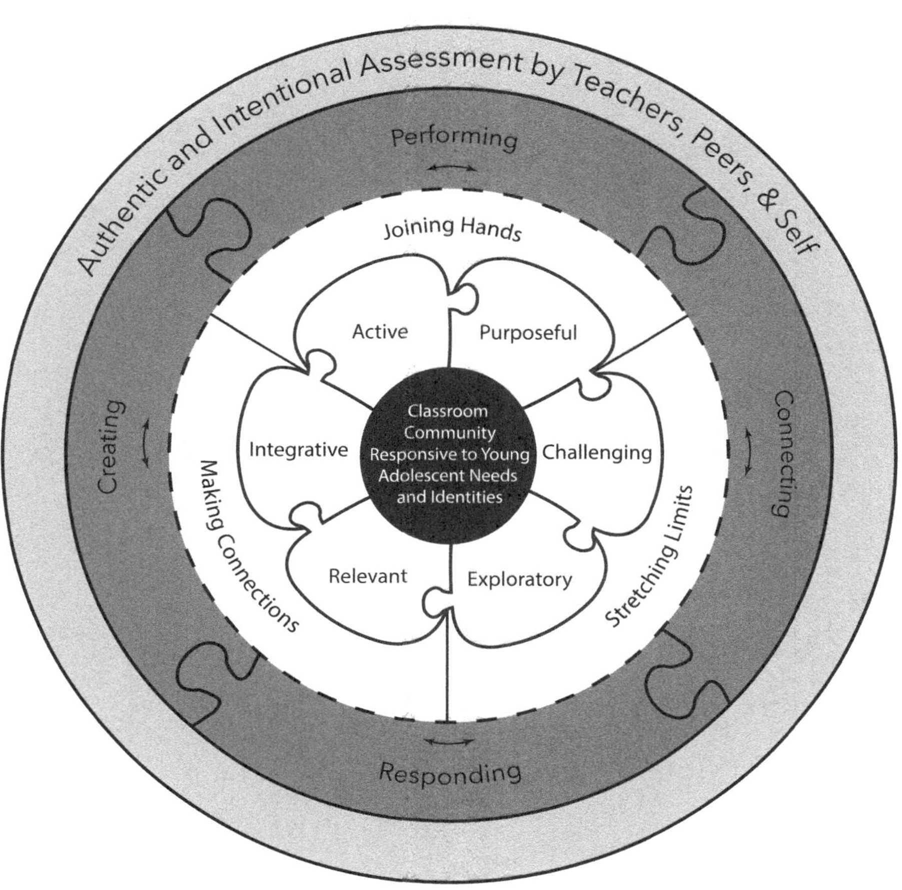

In Part 3—Chapter 7 and the Conclusion—our focus moves to the outer ring of the Fertile Ground Framework: the authentic and intentional assessment of student learning by the teacher, peers, and self. While Part 3 of this book focuses on assessment, assessment has been integrated into the discussions, materials, and reflection questions throughout this book. Chapter 7 focuses on the collaborative creation of assessments that allow all members of the classroom community to evaluate growth while acknowledging the administrative expectations or restrictions music teachers might face. Because the musical content in middle level general music should be diverse and comprehensive (democratic principle #5), so too must the assessments and those responsible for evaluating work. The Conclusion extends the idea of assessment to focus on evaluating ourselves as teachers through self-reflection within the Fertile Ground Framework.

7 Authentic and Intentional Assessment by Teacher, Peers, and Self

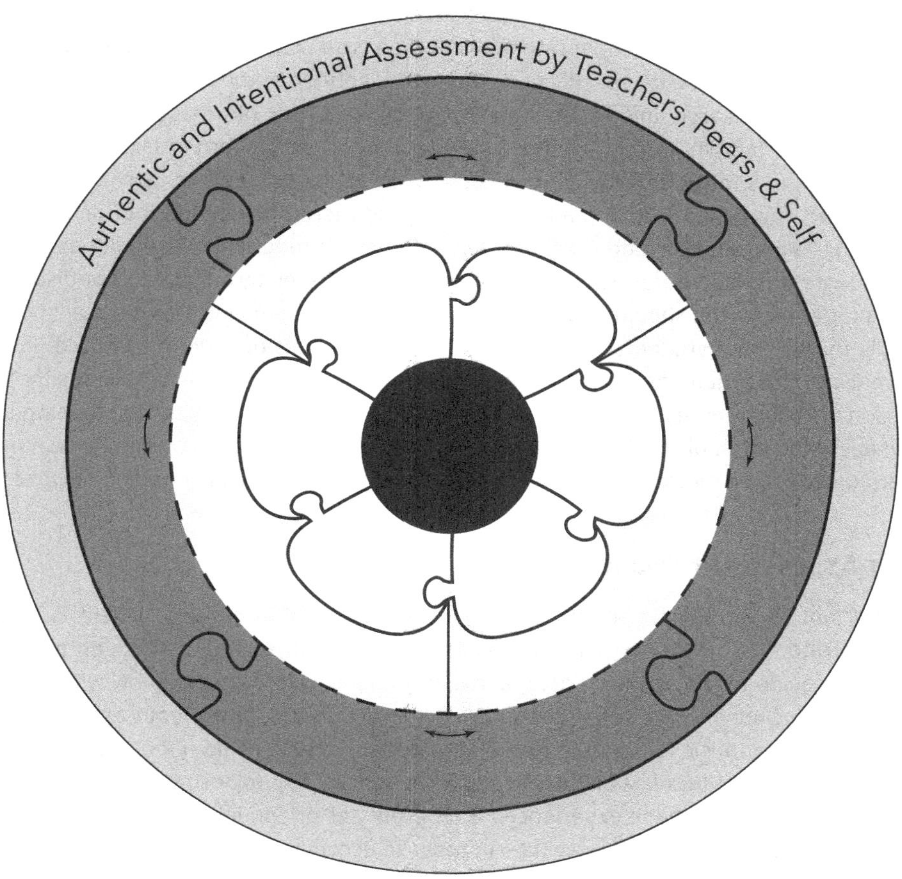

Democratic Principle #4: Encouraging Student Growth

Assessment should guide all aspects of your planning. It is the ongoing process of assessing students' progress toward achieving an objective or standard that holds all other planning, teaching, and learning together as a cohesive whole. Represented as a solid ring on the outside of the Framework diagram, authentic and intentional assessment by teacher, peers, and self visually

DOI: 10.4324/9781003124245-8

represents an enclosing of the puzzle pieces that shape the inner rings of the Framework. Once enclosed by the assessment ring, the other portions of the Framework diagram are united into a cohesive whole. Without authentic and intentional assessment, the hard work completed in rethinking middle level general music with students at the center will be for naught.

When we engage young adolescents in their own learning, we must be transparent about what is being learned, why it is being learned, and how students' learning will be judged. Young adolescents need multiple opportunities to demonstrate their knowledge and second chances when they struggle with a concept. By varying the ways in which we assess students and by ensuring that students receive regular feedback (from the teacher, their peers, and through self-reflection), we ensure that they understand their progress and can set their own goals for further learning and growth. These ideas regarding varied assessment forms and regular feedback from multiple evaluators are emphasized in both the US National Core Arts Standards and *This We Believe*. Neither document emphasizes standardized assessments nor assessment required for district data-collection; rather they emphasize assessments that enable students to demonstrate growth toward specific competencies identified at the outset of a lesson on unit.

As part of my research, middle level general music teachers often ask me some variation on the question: "but what exactly are the students *supposed* to learn in middle level general music?" If you as a music teacher do not know what students ought to learn in middle level general music, you cannot develop a learning goal and therefore will find it difficult to design assessments and evaluate student growth. My argument throughout this book has been that when students' musical futures lie outside the ensembles offered by our schools or districts, the musical content selected should respect this decision and seek to cultivate musical knowledge and skills that prepare students for future musical experiences outside of standard ensemble music making. This argument extends to the choices we make about the assessments that guide our lesson planning. There is no singular answer to what students are supposed to learn in middle level general music other than this: young adolescents should learn that there are multiple and varied ways to be musical and that they, as individuals, are capable of being musical.

Facing Assessment Realities

It is important to be realistic about how middle level general music assessment is impacted by administrators at our schools. The reality is that many US school districts do not provide a curriculum guide for middle level general music, administrators do not know what should or should not be included in the content, and the administrative dictates about grading and data may not fit general music learning. If these administrative realities do not apply to your situation, consider yourself lucky. My research suggests you are the minority. Each of the thirteen teachers featured in this book experienced a different set of administrative expectations and requirements that they needed to navigate in order to accomplish their assessment goals. Here are just some of the administrative expectations the music teachers in this book faced:

- The school's use (or not) of a learning management system and/or the music teachers' access to the learning management system.
- How specific (or not) the administration is regarding how report card grades are calculated.
- Whether grades are presented as letters, numbers, or holistic comments.
- The inclusion of participation or behavior as part of the overall grade, as a separate grade, or the prohibition of its inclusion.

- The use and administrative intention of student growth objectives (SGOs).
- The current use or forthcoming implementation of "standards-based grading" in a school or district.
- The alignment (or not) of the general music class rotation schedule with the grade reporting schedule used by the school.

Administrative regulations cannot be ignored as they have a direct impact on how you shape your class and think about assessments. Music teachers must carefully balance their own beliefs about assessment and how they have structured their general music class with the grading, report card, and data transparency expectations of their school or district.

When in doubt, trust your expertise and consider the democratic principles laid out in this book. Possibilities for comprehensive and diverse musical experiences (democratic principle #5) and the associated formative and summative assessments have been presented throughout. As mentioned previously, the US National Core Arts Standards articulate the importance of progressively developing students' musical independence from fifth through eighth grade. Associated with the Standards are the Model Cornerstone Assessments (MCAs) for fifth and eighth grade which provide one set of benchmarks for the beginning and ending years of middle level general music. The MCAs are designed as *models* rather than standardized assessments dictating learning in middle level general music (Parkes, 2018). The MCAs may not work in your circumstance, but they might serve as tools or guides if you are struggling to develop your own assessments. Whether you choose an assessment tool featured in this book, the MCAs, or some other inspiration, I encourage you to modify your chosen resource to ensure it meets the needs of the young adolescents in your classroom. Regardless of the assessment choices you make, my argument is that assessments aligned with the Framework should be authentic and intentional, both formative and summative in nature, and involve all members of the classroom in the evaluation process.

Authentic and Intentional Assessments

Authentic and intentional assessments are an essential part of a well-planned curriculum. They are not an afterthought, but rather a "before"-thought. When assessments are planned in advance and aligned with the learning goal, administrative expectations can also be integrated as part of the planning.

Authentic assessments "engage students in real-world tasks and scenario-based problem solving" (Moon et al., 2005). Thus, authentic assessments are not focused on the ability to regurgitate facts or specific details, but rather on whether the learner can apply the knowledge and skills learned in the lesson to a new setting that represents how the knowledge or skill might be used beyond the classroom walls. Authentic assessments provide middle level general music students with musical experiences that simulate how people engage with music in the real-world. In the simplest terms, instead of having students complete a note or rhythm naming quiz (which can certainly be useful for practice), students can use their newly acquired note or rhythmic skills to improvise or compose something new or analyze or perform something unfamiliar (Burrack & Parkes, 2020). Thus, through the use of authentic assessments, a young adolescent might begin to see him/herself engaging in musical activities later in life, whether at home, at a concert hall, within an in-person or virtual music community, or in some other space waiting to be imagined.

Intentional assessments are those that explicitly align with the designated learning goal. Thus, teachers must identify the learning goal (standard and objective) before developing a corresponding assessment. For teachers who use the Understanding by Design approach to curriculum development, wherein teachers begin by identifying the learning goal and then determine the related formative and summative assessment measures prior to planning lesson activities, assessments are naturally aligned with learning goals (Wiggins & McTighe, 2005). Planning the perfect engaging lesson without knowing the assessment intent will result in a haphazard evaluation of student knowledge and a lack of direction in the curriculum. On the Framework, each assessment developed has a specific evaluative purpose in helping the teacher and the students understand progress toward or achievement of the learning goal. The alignment of assessment tools to the learning goal is what makes an assessment intentional.

Advanced planning of intentional and authentic assessments can serve to cultivate a positive classroom community. While perhaps not intended by the teacher, a lack of transparency regarding the learning goal perpetuates mystery around the learning process and can lead to unmotivated students who choose not to participate. To combat this, teachers who strive to create a responsive and motivating classroom community *share* the learning goal with the students and explain how the authentic and intentional assessments planned will help students demonstrate their understanding. In this way, music teachers provide young adolescents with autonomy to monitor their own progress toward the learning goal and encourage their competence as independent musical learners (see Chapter 3). In advocating that you share the learning goal with the students, I intend efforts by the teacher that move beyond writing the learning goal on the board. When teachers are intentional in their plans for assessing student learning and share those plans with young adolescents, students can more easily reflect on personal progress and consider whether they achieved success during a particular lesson. Young adolescents deserve this from their teachers. They have earned it, but they so often do not receive it.

Teacher Evaluation

Whatever intentional and authentic assessment choices you make as a teacher, your formative and summative assessments will play an important role in monitoring student growth and development. Teacher evaluation is essential in middle level general music both to ensure student progress toward the ultimate goal of independent engagement with music, but also to assess the success of the implemented curriculum and pedagogy. As teachers, we must continually reflect on whether our teaching is helping our students reach the learning goal. Formative and summative teacher evaluation that is authentic and intentional strives to achieve these goals.

Formative Assessment

When music teachers are purposeful in how they plan and implement their lessons, they include many forms of formative assessment—written, performed, spoken, sung, composed, and so on—to check students' understanding. Formative assessments are naturally embedded into any performance-focused activity because it is easy to hear and correct mistakes as they happen. However, not all activities in general music are performance-focused. Thus, it is important to design formative assessments for all forms of general music learning so that you can know whether students are progressing toward the specific learning goal and thus acquiring the knowledge and skills necessary to complete the planned summative assessment. Formative assessments to check for understanding can be as simple as thumbs-up/thumbs-down or as complex as a mini-composition project or other assignment that requires most of class or even several classes to complete. The Do-Nows shared in this book offer one possibility for daily formative assessments evaluated by the teacher that might also provide a teacher with a daily assessment grade if one is expected by administrators.

Abby describes her formative assessments:

> I do a lot more formative stuff than summative. And some of it, I record an actual grade and a portion of it is just for my knowledge to guide the direction of where we're going next. I do a lot with [mini] whiteboards in general music. If they can quickly name a [musical concept] and show it to me, I can take a [glance] at the class and go, okay, everybody knows what that is now. Those kinds of quick little formative things I think are really helpful.
>
> –Abby

Using her mini-whiteboards, Abby knows in a few seconds whether or not students comprehend the musical concept she is trying to teach. Likewise, when you learn that students are not making progress toward the specific learning goal, you have the ability to alter course, modify your lesson or unit, differentiate for some students, review and correct a misunderstanding, or make some other change to ensure student success. This freedom to respond to student needs is possible because the formative assessments were intentionally designed to provide the teacher and students with feedback on the path to achieving the learning goal.

Summative Assessment

All summative assessments, whether genre research projects, ukulele performance games, band compositions, a quiz or test, or some other form, should be designed authentically and intentionally and shared with students to guide their learning. Summative assessments are planned at important points throughout the middle level general music class, most commonly at the end of a unit or learning sequence. Jackie explains the importance and also the difficulty of planning summative assessments:

> It's difficult. You have to sit back and say, okay, what do I want them to understand and what do I want the final outcome to be? [In my computer-based general music class], the final outcome [is] can they use a computer correctly to create, on a fairly complex system, a minute and a half or two-minute song [with specific musical expectations]?
>
> –Jackie

In planning for summative assessment at the outset of the planning process, you know the end goal of the instructional activities and can thus plan activities that lead students toward an understanding of the selected standard and the associated objective. Thus, Jackie knows that through the process of preparing for and completing the computer composition projects (see Chapter 6), students will need to learn various compositional techniques as well as details about form and analysis. Thus, a clear and intentional summative assessment articulated in advance can help to guide the planning of specific lessons and activities to ensure student success on the final assessment.

In addition, when summative assessments are planned before instruction begins, they can be shared with students, as described in the Conceptual Framework document that supports the US National Core Arts Standards,

> [Assessments] should be presented at the *beginning* of a course or a unit of instruction to serve as meaningful and concrete learning targets for students. Such assessment transparency is needed if standards are going to be met. Students must know the tasks to be mastered well in advance, and have continued opportunities to work toward their accomplishment.
>
> (SEADAE, 2014b, p. 15)

When the end goal of a learning task is revealed to the students from the beginning, students understand the purpose of what the teacher is asking them to do. Thus, a lesson is not simply something to pass the time until the next period, but rather a purposeful and intentional process of learning whereby a student actively chooses to engage in learning and improve his/her knowledge and skills related to a specific goal.

Including Students in Evaluation

In the real-world, each audience member attending a concert has the freedom to provide his/her own personal critique of the performance, but in the classroom, students are often not provided space to critique a performance or evaluate their own success. This is a missed opportunity to cultivate educated audiences, future community music participators, and supporters of arts learning. While the music teacher will continue to play a major role in evaluating student work throughout the learning process, young adolescents are capable and should be included in this process. Including students as evaluators helps to develop each student's musical independence.

When students review their own work and the work of others, their own understanding of the learning goal improves. The importance of developing skills in evaluating self and peers is emphasized throughout the US National Core Arts Standards for general music, particularly at the fifth through eighth grade levels. The Standards ask students to evaluate their own compositions and provide rationales for changes (MU:CR3.1), evaluate when a piece is ready for performance (MU:PR5.1), and evaluate musical works or performances (MU:Re9.1). All peer or self-review requires a class review of the learning goal which strengthens students' understanding, provides them with a reminder of what they are working toward, and potentially enables them to see where their own work needs improvement. When students review the work of others, they often see where their own project is lacking or discover a good idea shared by their classmate which they are able to adopt as part of their own work. It is important to help students understand that getting ideas from peers is fine but that it is not acceptable to plagiarize their classmate's work. Helping students understand the difference can lead to conversations about copyright and respecting the work of others.

When students are involved in evaluating themselves and their peers, we must also teach them how to critique and provide useful and constructive feedback. We need to ensure that students know how to diplomatically phrase their feedback and to offer constructive suggestions to help each other improve. While many young adolescents may have participated in self-reflection or peer review in other courses, others may never have experienced this form of learning. It may help to begin this discussion by asking students what they already know about giving peer feedback and provide music-specific expectations. This will help to connect what happens in music to other subjects where peer review may also regularly occur. If students lack experience with reviewing themselves or others, modeling your expectations using example work may help guide students in initial peer or self-review efforts. In order for peer and self-evaluation to be successful, it is crucial that the positive and safe classroom environment discussed in Chapter 3 is maintained.

Formative Peer Review

Several of the teachers featured in this book use peer review at different times throughout their middle level general music courses. For example, Hannah has students create a listening map when they study Sonata Allegro Form as part of their Western music history unit. Once each student creates a map, they share their map with another student who is supposed to try to follow the listening map created by their peer. Hannah says,

> The partner has to follow the listening map. If it makes sense to the partner and they were able to follow it, they give [the map creator] a star or a smiley face. If they couldn't follow it, they [give] a frowning face.
>
> —Hannah

While Hannah uses the smiley or frowning face responses of peers to further evaluate the listening maps as a teacher and provide a grade, she could take this peer review one step further. If Hannah asked the peer reviewer to provide constructive feedback, whether written or verbal, to the listening map creator, and then required the creator to revise his/her listening map prior to submission for teacher evaluation, she would strengthen each student's understanding of the learning goal and inculcate the idea that learning is ongoing and never finished.

In the lesson plan sequence in Chapter 6, peer review is an explicit component of the digital technologies composition portfolio. However, other lesson sequences and activity ideas have also included ways in which peer review of ongoing work might serve to improve the work of all students in the classroom. When students are conducting peer review of work in progress, you may want to provide them with a graphic organizer or other tool to guide their peer review such as Teacher Resource 7.1. This simple tool might remind young adolescents of the learning goal and guide them in providing constructive peer review.

Teacher Resource 7.1

Peer Review Guide Sheet

Project Name:

Essential Question:

Standard(s):

Objective(s):

Your Name:	Name of Classmate Whose Work You Are Reviewing:

In 1-2 complete sentences, explain in your own words the expectations of the project:

In 1-2 complete sentences, describe the work your peer has created:

Doing Great	Needs Improvement
What are two things your peer did well? Be specific and give evidence or examples to support your positive feedback.	What are two specific things your peer could do to improve their work? Remember to provide a constructive example or suggestion so your peer can revise.

Group Work Peer Review

Another form of peer review that is important for young adolescents is peer review during and after group work. Learning to work collaboratively as a team is a difficult task for many young adolescents and thus it is important that they have the opportunity to critique the work of the peers with whom they work. Alexis uses this form of peer review to help her assess individual contributions to the final group product.

> I don't always do [peer review] with group assignments, I just kind of save it for when [issues arise in group work]. We'll do a group assessment at the end. [This way,] their teammates know that, yes, I saw [the issues], and yes you can write down [what happened].
>
> —Alexis

Similarly, when his eighth graders do their group song writing project, Eric asks them to complete weekly journals in order to provide him with formative evaluation of the group's progress:

> So, if a student is not working well or they're not being able to agree or they're stuck on a particular problem that they haven't been able to solve and for whatever reason haven't brought to my attention previously, I've learned about [the issue] through those weekly reflections that we do.
>
> —Eric

Eric uses weekly reflections as a standard part of the group songwriting project whereas Alexis has chosen to only use peer review when an intra-group issue has arisen. In my own classroom, integrating peer review and reflection as a regular part of group work has helped to perpetuate a positive classroom climate and aid students in successful collaboration.

Ideally, peer review of group work takes two forms, both formative and summative in nature. First, the teacher might request regular feedback about group collaboration through a simple exit ticket or student journal used regularly throughout a group project. Second, peer review of progress toward the learning goal might involve evaluation of their own group or the work of other groups. For example, midway through a project, two groups could be assigned to share their progress and provide peer review to one another. Likewise, at the end of the project, individual students might evaluate their group's progress toward the learning goal, or they might work as a group to evaluate all other groups when work is presented (see Lesson Sequence 1.1 & 5.1).

Summative Peer Review

Peer review of final products might take many forms and involve review of in-class presentations or those prepared for public presentation through Informances, School-Day Sharing

Events, or Service-Learning Performances. Peer review of final products is the approach taken by Jessica as part of her Coffee House performance (see Chapter 3):

> [At the Coffee House] they have to do peer critique and that's also part of their grade. So, [students] have to critique three peers. [They] have to use at least one music vocabulary term. And [they] have to say one thing that [they] think [their peer] did well and one thing that they can improve. So, they have to use a total of at least two vocabulary words [one for the positive and one for the critique in each review]. I go through all of them to make sure nothing is too mean, and [then] I give them back [to the person being reviewed].
>
> –Jessica

Jessica's approach to peer review during the Coffee House requires students to use musical vocabulary learned throughout the semester as part of their peer review. She also requires students to provide positive feedback and constructive critique, an important skill to cultivate in young adolescents. Critiquing final performances at the Coffee House requires students to synthesize their musical knowledge and apply it to a critique of a live performance presented by their peer. This authentic application of musical knowledge allows Jessica's students to become critical audience members, a skill they will use throughout their lives as they engage with music.

Formative Self-Reflection

Formative self-reflection is essential for young adolescents who are developing their independent musical identity. When young adolescents can judge for themselves where they have done well, where they ought to improve, and how to make improvements, they can begin to see that they do not need a teacher to be musical.

During his ukulele game-based unit (see Chapter 4), Eric has discovered that some students complete formative self-assessment independently when they try to begin learning a song that is too hard for their current ability.

> Usually [the students] discover on their own that they need to back things up and slow things down a bit more and go down to an easier [song] level. I think it's important for them to discover what they're capable of and also what they're not yet capable of. That also sets a [personal] goal for them if they want to get to the point of being able to play this particular [harder] song. I don't know offhand how many students do go back to those songs, but many of them do get to higher levels as the weeks go on.
>
> –Eric

The nature of Eric's game-based ukulele curriculum gives young adolescents a significant level of freedom to set their own learning goals and work to accomplish them. When students discover that they are not succeeding because a selection is too hard, they have the freedom to self-reflect, make a new choice, and strive for eventually learning to play their preferred song. This kind of formative self-assessment is key to developing young adolescents who are independent musical learners.

When I asked Lindsey, who is required to use standards-based grading, how she would prefer to grade her students if she were given ultimate freedom, she said:

> I really think that if I was completely able to be free [with my grading] I would like to have conferences with the students. [The conferences would focus] on self-reflecting [on] how they think they're doing, [and] setting a goal. [I would] not have any formal grades.
>
> —Lindsey

While Lindsey acknowledges that her imagined world of no formal grades is not realistic in most school communities, including her own, she has identified what she thinks would be ideal for her students in middle level general music: self-reflection through discussion and goal setting. Although Lindsey imagines a music learning environment focused on self-assessment absent of grades, formative and summative self-assessment can (and should) occur within the confines of a formal grading system.

Summative Self-Reflection

In addition, there are multiple ways in which self-reflection can be used as a summative assessment at the end of a performance, project, or the entire course. Katherine F. Thompson (2013) argues that an important component of any service-learning project is the reflection students do following the project. I extend this argument to include reflection on any public presentation of learning and the completion of projects not publicly shared. When you set a strong reflection prompt tied to the learning goal, students can connect their musical learning, feelings of musical competence, and developing autonomy as musicians to the public presentation of learning or the completion of a project, thus strengthening their understanding of how their work enabled them to grow over the course of the learning task. Both Robert and Eric have noticed that summative self-reflection reveals interesting things about their students.

> If I find that they're pretty hard on themselves. I'll take that as an opportunity to pull them aside and have a little conference and build them up a little bit. [I] let them know, what you're doing is pretty incredible stuff, and [that I'm] so proud of them. If they try really hard and they feel that they did not do as well as a colleague did or as they [personally] wanted to, that's an opportunity for coaching and people building.
>
> —Robert

> In sixth grade I've gotten some really interesting insight as to the way students view themselves before and after doing a project. A couple of years ago, when I started the cover song project, we did reflections on that [project] and [focused on] what did you learn from this [project]. [I got a lot of responses that said things like]: "I didn't think I'd be able to do this" or "I didn't realize how hard it was" or "I didn't realize how easy it was," depending on the student.
>
> —Eric

In both Eric's and Robert's cases, summative self-reflection helped them to get to know individual students better, develop stronger relationships with students, and understand students' experiences with a particular assignment. As another form of summative assessment, Robert asks each student in his class to write a letter to students who will take his class next year telling them how to succeed in the general music class. A final self-reflection at the end of your middle level general music class may serve to help young adolescents bring their learning experience to a close and reflect on how they might participate in music in the future. These summative self-reflections are essential for cultivating musical independence within each young adolescent who enrolls in middle level general music.

Joining Hands through Assessments

Hands-joined learning does not apply simply to in-classroom activities or to project-based learning activities. Joining hands and collaborating with students also applies to assessment. Just as students might participate in setting the parameters of a project, they might also join hands with their teacher in developing assessments, revising work to demonstrate growth, contributing to important data collection tasks, or furthering the positive learning environment.

Collaboratively Designed Assessments

One important way that young adolescents can contribute to their own learning and thus develop as independent learners is to collaborate with teachers in the development of assessments. Although Understanding by Design encourages the creation of assessments prior to any learning activities being developed, assessments or grading tools can also be designed collaboratively with students at the outset of a new unit of study and thus help the teacher shape the unit based on students' perspectives (democratic principle #2). When young adolescents collaborate with their teachers, their understanding of the learning objective and their personal progress toward the objective is increased.

Collaborating with students in the creation of either the assessment itself or the grading tool transforms class time from teacher-directed explanation of the assignment to hands-joined creation where young adolescents take ownership over the assessment. Yes, these collaborations take class time, but this is class time that strengthens student understanding. If you have never collaborated with students on an assessment, start small. Do not try to collaborate from start to finish on an assessment, but rather begin with an existing assignment or project for which the students already understand the guidelines. For example, the following steps outline one approach you might take to joining hands to create and edit a rubric as a class:

- Fill in the teacher portions of a three-level rubric template (such as Teacher Resource 7.2) and distribute it to the class.
- Lead a discussion about the assignment expectations and guide the class to articulate the highest-level expectations for each criteria.
- Divide the class into groups and assign each group to develop the statement for one remaining square of the rubric derived from the highest-level criteria established as a class (i.e., group 1, the lowest level of the second criteria; group 2, the second level of the first criteria).
- Collect each group's statement, review the statements (revise, if needed), and compile all statements into a finished rubric.
- Present the collective rubric to the class the next time you meet.

After presenting the completed rubric to the class, answer any questions the students have and modify the rubric, if needed. Assuming this first hands-joined rubric creation goes well, broaden the scope of the students' participation for the next assessment.

Teacher Resource 7.2

Collaboratively Created Rubric Template

Project Name:

Essential Question:

Standard(s):

Objective(s):

	With your group, create the rubric description for your assigned cell using the Level 3 descriptions as a guide.		*Write in the Level 3 descriptions that the whole class created.*
	Level 1 Needs Improvement	Level 2 Meets Most Expectations	Level 3 Meets or Exceeds All Expectations
Teacher Identified Criteria #1			
Teacher Identified Criteria #2			
Teacher Identified Criteria #3			

Repeating or Revising Assessments

Another developmentally appropriate way to join hands with students in authentic and intentional assessment is to allow them, where appropriate, to repeat assessments or to improve their work. Young adolescents need to understand that learning is ongoing and progressive. Repeating an assessment until they meet a certain threshold of proficiency enables young adolescents to advance their understanding of the musical content while revising their work emphasizes the importance of revision in the creative process.

Katie's focus is on student growth and development as a musician rather than the grade recorded in her gradebook. Thus, the opportunity to repeat an assessment allows her students to continue working to improve their skills and abilities and eventually meet her expectations of musical proficiency. Prior to her band project, Katie gives the students playing tests on each instrument (guitar, upright bass, piano, and drums) learned in class.

> You can take the test as many times as you want. It's mostly pass-fail. The purpose of the test is that you are able to have the basic skills to play the instrument, so I don't really care how long it takes you to get there, provided that you get there. I mean I guess I care in that eventually you're gonna be in the band [with your peers], so there is going to be a point where it will be awkward if you can't do [what I'm asking]. But, you know, if you can do that the third day versus the fourth day or even the fifth day, or if you have to come in after school and spend extra time on it, I don't think that should affect your grade.
>
> –Katie

Repeating assessments to demonstrate improvement, growth, and development as a musical learner will inculcate an understanding that the ability to independently improve and accomplish a musical goal lies within each young adolescent, not the teacher. This personal understanding is far more likely to cultivate an attitude of lifelong musical learning than one-time assessments and punitive grading.

A major component of the creative process, regardless of the artform, is revision. While students learn about revision in language arts, many young adolescents struggle with the critical thinking and attention to detail necessary to revise and resubmit their work. However, the revision process is essential to developing a musical phrase, thought, sketch, etc., into a more complete work. In Jackie's computer-based composition unit, she includes teacher feedback and opportunity for revision because students are allowed to self-pace their work throughout the unit.

> I had kids that finished up the assignment with, you know, three days to spare. [And they asked,] "what do I do now," and I said, "did you read over what I suggested for you to change?" For one student I wrote [something like], "well this is an interesting effect but it's a little boring and I think you can make this a lot better." He had turned the assignment in fairly early. He came back and sent me a different [composition]. So, I was able to bump his grade up. That's the nice thing about Google Classroom. [I] can actually give them feedback, and it's written out feedback, which I think is really important as a musician. You get a lot of oral feedback on things, but it's nice to get the written feedback.
>
> –Jackie

Both correcting work and repeating assessments allow students to better demonstrate their understanding, improve their abilities, or engage with the creative process. This hands-joined process has important implications for middle level general music.

Students' Contributions to Data Collection Tasks

If your school requires SGOs, I encourage you to reconsider the assessment tool(s) you use or develop for the required SGO documentation. Most music teachers are individually responsible for creating the tool used for SGO documentation; thus, this tool should work *for* you and support the kind of learning you want to facilitate in your classroom. Many teachers design their SGO assessment so that all students fail it at the beginning of the class and pass it at the end of the class. I recognize the administrative pressure many music teachers face to provide statistical data that demonstrates student growth. However, the student growth advocated for in this book reaches far beyond statistical representation on a single assessment measure.

In essence, the SGO assessment tool given to students at the beginning of the semester is a form of pre-assessment. Pre-assessments are designed to help teachers understand students' prior knowledge and learning needs on the broad topics likely covered in the class. Instead of thinking of the SGO assessment tool as simply a data collection mechanism, think of it as an authentic and intentional assessment that enables you to understand your students' learning needs and provides you with powerful information to shape each middle level general music class to meet the learning needs of the students enrolled. Imagine you are going to learn to about Balinese *gamelan* in your middle level general music class. What prerequisite knowledge do students need in order to be successful? Include this prerequisite knowledge on the SGO pre-assessment along with some questions about knowledge you intend to teach such as the pentatonic scale, physical playing techniques, ostinatos, aural musical cues, interlocking rhythms, etc. However, do not forget to also ask open-ended questions that will help you learn more about your students' musical interests and desires and then use this information to further refine your curriculum. If you choose to modify your SGO assessment in this way, I urge you to speak with your administration about how you intend to use SGO assessment data to improve teaching and how this moves beyond statistical data reporting. Your SGO assessment tool can be a powerful source of information to help you join hands with your students in developing a class that meets their music learning needs, but you need to help your administrators understand your reasoning.

Contributing to a Positive Learning Environment

In my discussions with the teachers, one topic that regularly reoccurred was the question of whether citizenship or participation should be included in the grading system devised for middle level general music. The teachers were divided on this topic and did not agree regarding whether daily participation grades contributed to a positive learning environment:

> The way I've always structured it, there's daily [participation] points allotted. I don't expect you to be an amazing guitarist the first time you pick it up, but if you're actively trying, and you're sticking with it, and you're asking questions, and you're working to improve, then [the participation points are] really your points to keep. [Participation] is very subjective, I realize, but it does cause [the students] to buy-in a little bit because they know that they can't just sit back and do nothing in this class, because it's a pretty big chunk of their grade.
>
> —Abby

> I don't feel like in general music, with the way that I do it, that [a participation grade is] necessary. If they're not going to do their listening log then that's a zero, so they obviously didn't participate on that. They either do their projects, or they don't do their projects. So, I don't do participation because their work is going to reflect that.
>
> –Alexis

As discussed in Chapter 3, a motivating classroom environment is cultivated through autonomy, relatedness, and competence. While I see the value in a daily participation as an external form of motivating students, my hope is that the classroom community developed in middle level general music cultivates internal learning motivation for young adolescents thus rendering the daily participation grade unnecessary. In this way, all students are internally motivated to help contribute to the positive learning environment because it was designed to meet their needs of autonomy, relatedness, and competence. Instead of daily participation grades, exit slips, self-reflections, and Do-Nows can provide formative assessment aligned with the learning goal that meets administrative requirements for each student to receive a daily grade.

Wrap-Up: Authentic and Intentional Assessment

The curricular freedom and flexibility available to those who teach middle level general music should be seen as a strength, particularly in relationship to assessment. However, administrative grading policies may appear to restrict this freedom and narrow the scope of assessment possibilities. I hope that you will endeavor to think creatively about how to incorporate authentic and intentional assessments as befits your local circumstances. Authentic and intentional assessment designed at the outset of a unit or in collaboration with students provides learning transparency, cultivates a purposeful and motivating classroom climate, and encourages young adolescents in their musical independence. When students receive formative and summative feedback from their teacher, their peers, and themselves, the transparency regarding their growth toward the learning goal gives young adolescents agency. In this way, assessments are no longer created to meet an administrative requirement dictating a particular number of grades per grading period, but rather intentionally and collaboratively designed to support and further student learning needs.

Although there is not a singular answer to questions of what and how to assess in middle level general music, I hope that you will be guided by the principles of the Fertile Ground Framework when designing assessments that meet your students where they are and guide them toward independence as musical learners. What are your students' needs and desires as music learners? How can you guide them toward musical independence by collaboratively developing authentic and intentional assessments? What administrative expectations do you feel are holding you back and how can you use those expectations to your advantage? How does the outer ring of the Fertile Ground Framework help to guide your thinking about collaborating with students, helping them make connections, or stretching their limits in middle level general music?

Conclusion

Promises of the Fertile Ground

> I love [my university], I loved the teachers that I had there, they're very skilled and they're great musicians, but we truly focused on teaching choir and teaching elementary music.... Absolutely nothing [about middle school]. Everything I learned about middle school I've learned through teaching middle school.
>
> –Nicole

> [The professor] I took middle school methods with was an excellent professor. I do think some of what he talked about developmentally I've used, like talking about respect and how to be hands-on. But I did not get much general music *at all* in undergrad. I think if anything, when I first started teaching, I tried to make general music performance based because that's what I knew. I think I try as hard as I can to fight that, to not make general music performance based, because that's not all that general music can be.
>
> –Lindsey

> I don't think I was prepared [to teach middle level general music] at *all* to be completely honest. I was definitely prepared to teach band and orchestra ... but general music, I was like, this is going to be a hot mess.
>
> –Jessica

We have all come to the task of teaching middle level general music at various points on our journey as music teachers. As Nicole, Lindsey, and Jessica all point out, preservice preparation programs in the United States typically prepare music educators for certification across all grade levels and all areas of music; thus, limited time and many competing factors often result in a minimal focus on middle level learning. While you may have first come to middle level general music unprepared, lacking in tools or resources, unfamiliar with young adolescence, or uncertain where to begin in designing your curriculum, I hope that you find comfort that you are not alone in these feelings. Each of the teachers in this book, along with countless other

DOI: 10.4324/9781003124245-9

unnamed music teachers, have faced the same challenges and have found ways to improve their practice, work with their students, and cultivate fertile ground.

Throughout this book, I have argued that middle level general music should be defined as developmentally appropriate music learning that inspires all young adolescents to continue learning both formally and informally in music. If we want young adolescents to continue learning music throughout their lives, we must model for them what it means to be lifelong learners. When we show students that we are willing to learn about what interests them, to try new things and potentially fail in front of them, and to integrate our new knowledge into the classroom (through various means), we begin to demonstrate how to be a lifelong learner in music. As we do so, we model to the young adolescents we teach that it is safe to make mistakes, learn from them, and develop ourselves more fully. We also implicitly send the message that we never stop learning as musicians and neither should they.

Assessing Ourselves as Reflective Practitioners

Reflection is key to fully embracing the Fertile Ground Framework and making change within your own practice. As reflective practitioners, we have a responsibility to both reflect-on our past practices and our new attempts at change, and to reflect-in the moment of teaching as we improvise with what our young adolescents bring with them to each class (Schön, 1983). My hope is that the Fertile Ground Framework will provide you with a new lens through which to review, reflect, and refine your own practices in middle level general music.

Here I share some overarching questions designed to catalyze your initial reflection-on your current practice:

- What is the story of your journey to middle level general music and how do you honestly feel about teaching middle level general music?
- How will you reshape your beliefs about teaching young adolescents and rethink possibilities for middle level general music?
- Will you reject deficit thinking and use inspiration found here to move toward fertile ground?
- Of the teachers featured throughout this book, whose choices or perspective resonates most with you and why?
- What parts of the Fertile Ground Framework are you doing well and where could you make improvements?
- What aspects of the Fertile Ground Framework challenge you to consider your own choices in the classroom in a new light?
- What short- and long-term goals would you like to set for yourself regarding your middle level general music class?
- What first, simple steps can you take to make one small change tomorrow?
- As you finish a rotation or semester, how do you assess yourself within the Fertile Ground Framework?

As reflective practitioners, we are tasked with questioning our practices and seeking self-improvement despite the reality that it is far easier to simply continue on the old path. But perhaps the act of thoughtfully considering the Fertile Ground Framework has left you feeling troubled or disoriented. In the quote that begins Chapter 1, music educators Margaret Barrett and Sandra Stauffer (2009) suggest that fertile ground begins with insight, but that insight often emerges from feeling troubled, challenged, or forced to see ourselves through a new lens. Sit with your disorientation and ask yourself why you feel this way and what you might do to change your feelings. As musicians we are enculturated at a young age toward perfection on our primary instrument. Thus, sitting with troubling feelings that stem from our own imperfections may be an uncomfortable endeavor. But, as Barrett and Stauffer suggest, these troubling feelings are common and may enable us to discover new insights in our own practice.

The lens of the Fertile Ground Framework may have raised questions that only you can answer about your practice, but I hope that it has also given you tools to conduct intentional and authentic assessment of yourself, your practices, and your beliefs as a middle level general music teacher. The Fertile Ground Framework will only work to reframe middle level general music if those who use it also turn the assessment on themselves as educators.

Imagining Possibilities for Middle Level General Music

As musicians and educators, we use our imaginations in many ways. Arts educator and aesthetic philosopher Maxine Greene described imagination as "the capacity to posit alternative realities," realities that move beyond the everyday experience (2001, p. 65). In our work as musicians and educators, we imagine the possible realities that might occur in the classroom or in performance as we prepare our daily responsibilities. Many teachers imagine possible student responses or reactions during lesson planning while others imagine engaging activities or class projects they hope to see to fruition. Imagination is part of envisioning a successful concert or creating long-term goals. Musical compositions cannot be realized without imagining music that has never before been heard.

Unfortunately, the realities of teaching day after day, year after year, sometimes impede imagination as we return to the "tried and true" lesson plans of the past, rather than imagining new possibilities. Greene says that "without the release of imagination, human beings may be trapped in literalism, in blind factuality" (2001, p. 65). Too often, literalism shapes middle level general music for many music teachers. Sometimes it is difficult to see anything beyond the world of our individual classrooms, our many responsibilities, and our isolation as the only music teacher (or one of only a few) in our school or district. Thus, we may fall into a trap whereby we are blinded by the realities, incapable of seeing beyond the challenges, and thus unable to imagine new possibilities for middle level general music. It is in this literalist trap, this reification of our experience within the walls of our classrooms, schools, or districts, that we find ourselves "resistant to reevaluation and change rather than [open] to imagination" (Greene, 1995, pp. 126–127).

Thus, we begin with self-reflection and thereby imagine other realities and possibilities. Enacting the Fertile Ground Framework requires an act of imagination, an ability to think beyond what currently exists. The Framework also requires a willingness to take a leap of faith into the unknown, trusting that the relationship you have cultivated with your students will enable successful, joyful, and creative music learning.

In my imagined reality, middle level general music is a class for everyone. It is filled with diverse and rich musical experiences, joyful, engaged, and active learners, and a teacher who breathes life into the learning by making learning relevant and connecting to the students as ever-changing whole individuals. I envision you accepting this challenge, striving to create a different kind of learning environment, and sharing the successes of that learning environment boldly with other music educators. I do not believe that this imagined possibility is far-fetched. In fact, as this book has shown, it is already occurring in many places and in many variations.

When I imagine this alternate reality for middle level general music, I do not imagine a specific curriculum being taught, but rather six democratic principles—educating the whole student, integrating students' perspectives, making connections, encouraging student growth, including comprehensive and diverse musical experiences, and teaching all students—implemented in order to achieve the classroom environment described throughout this book. There is no panacea for middle level general music. One unit of study may work with one group of students but not with another, whether in the same school or across the country. There are, however, many vast and varied curricular possibilities that may lead to the kind of learning environment I describe. For me, it is the learning environment cultivated by the music teacher—by joining hands, making connections, and stretching limits in a learning environment designed specifically for young adolescents—that facilitates a positive and motivating learning experience for the students and the teacher. It is through the establishment of this environment that my imagined possibility becomes reality; middle level general music becomes a fertile ground.

Validating the Fertile Ground Framework

If you have stuck with me thus far, I hope that you have found the Fertile Ground Framework useful to your own thinking. As I mentioned at the outset of this book, the Fertile Ground Framework is only one *possible* tool for improving middle level general music. I hope that what I have presented here inspires others to put forward different yet equally beneficial ideas about how to rethink middle level general music. The promises of the fertile ground are many and I hope that a chorus of voices are raised in offering many visions and versions of middle level general music (Eisner, 2002). Multiple voices joining the dialogue regarding middle level general music are welcomed as they strengthen the importance of cultivating young adolescents with dispositions toward lifelong musical learning.

As you use the Fertile Ground Framework to guide your general music instruction, I ask your help in validating, and if necessary, improving the Framework itself. As you rethink, redesign, and implement new strategies in your classroom aligned with the Fertile Ground Framework, what works and what does not work? Where do you need greater clarity about the Framework? How might I improve the Framework tool to better help other music educators succeed in middle level general music? While seemingly rhetorical questions, I hope that you will also reach out to share your stories of success and to provide constructive critiques so that the Fertile Ground Framework might evolve to better suit the teachers and learners in middle level general music. I hope that you as individual music teachers find fertile ground in your classroom by flexibly using the Fertile Ground Framework to best suit the young adolescents that you teach.

Appendix

Teacher Participants

Each teacher participant is briefly introduced in the Introduction. The descriptions here provide additional details regarding the teachers' school communities and the general music curricula taught at the time of the study.

Abby teaches middle school choir and general music at a 6-8 affluent suburban school in the Midwest. She has been a teacher for fourteen years, eight of which have been at the middle school level. During her early career she taught in a rural low-income school in the South. Her current general music curriculum consists of theory, guitar, piano, a dance unit, a music history project, and composition. Much of Abby's 2017-2018 teaching load was chorus with only a few sections of general music. Most recently, she has also added a self-contained special education general music class. For the past few years, the sixth grade general music curriculum has been a nine- or six-week class, but beginning in 2018-2019, the school moved to a semester schedule that essentially doubled the length of the curriculum. Although Abby thought she would be redesigning the general music curriculum for 2018-2019, she was reassigned to only choir due to increased enrollment.

Alexis teaches seventh and eighth grade general music, a high school music appreciation course, and non-auditioned middle school and high school choirs in a small Midwestern farming community in which grades K-12 are all housed under one roof. She has been a teacher for fifteen years and is certified in Kodály. The district divides the school into two sections: K-6 and 7-12. Although Alexis is considered a 7-12 teacher, her first year she also taught sixth grade general music. The largest minority demographic at her school is Latinx, but very few students have English language learning needs. The general music classes are typically a semester long and meet every day for about 50 minutes. Some years Alexis has a seventh grade and an eighth grade class, but other years the grade levels are combined. Students are not required to take general music but can take general music and still participate in ensembles. She has two different general music curricula: one for even numbered years, which focuses on famous composers and instruments of the orchestra, and one for odd numbered years where she has tried numerous things including Garage Band and world music.

Danielle teaches general music along with choral and instrumental ensembles at a K-8 charter school in the Northeast. She has over 25 years of experience and is an alternate route certified teacher with a degree in piano performance. Her early career experiences include high school choir and musical theatre and middle school general music and choir, along with various community-related accompanying and performance experiences. Danielle began working at the charter school during its second year of existence and for the past 21 years has continued to build its music program. At her school, general music is required for students through sixth grade and is then an elective option for seventh and eighth grade. The K-8 general music program has a strong vocal focus and includes an interactive study of opera and symphonic repertoire.

Eric teaches general music at a 5–8 school in a small suburban district in the Northeast while concurrently pursuing his doctorate. He has worked at his current school for five years, but also has experience teaching K-8 general music part-time as well as collegiate level teaching. The general music curriculum has a ukulele, technology, and composition focus and Eric primarily focuses on sixth and eighth grade, although he previously taught the other grades and band pull-out lessons. All students in the school take general music for a quarter of the school year, every day for 42 minutes. In addition, his school is one of several buildings that provides services for middle level aged students with disabilities in the county, all of whom are integrated into the general music class with their peers.

Hannah teaches general music, choir, and a musical theatre class at a 7–9 school in an affluent school district, the largest in her Western state. She has been teaching middle level for ten of her eleven years teaching. She is certified in all three levels of Kodály and her general music curriculum is singing focused with explorations into music theory, music history, world music, and composition. At the school, general music is one of the arts rotation classes offered to students and is most often taken by seventh graders. Students who take general music are typically those not enrolled in an ensemble. Hannah's musical theatre class is an auditioned course taught in the spring for students wanting to participate in the musical. In 2018–2019, all of Hannah's general music classes were rescheduled as beginning choir.

Holly teaches seventh grade general music and a before-school choir at both of the 7–8 schools in a medium-sized district in the Midwest. She is an 18-year veteran who worked several positions prior to her current one, most recently K-8 general music at small rural public school. In her current position, the before-school choir combines students from both schools while her school day consists of six general music periods divided between the two schools. All seventh grade students take general music every day for one quarter of the school year and her general music curriculum focuses on the history of rock and roll.

Jackie teaches general music and band while serving as the fine arts coordinator for a small suburban K-8 school district in the Southwest. Her K-8 school is designated as an open enrollment arts academy and is also a Title 1 school with a significant English Language Learner population. During her 10-year teaching career, she has taught at three different schools and in her current district for 7 years. She has taught various grade configurations kindergarten through eighth grade. Teaching is her second career and she has earned the first level of Kodály certification. Currently all 6th-8th graders take general music as part of a related arts wheel where they attend music for about three weeks, then rotate to other classes, eventually rotating back to music three total times during the school year. In sixth grade, the general music class focuses on piano keyboard skills while in seventh and eighth grade the focus is on music technology.

Jessica is a sixth year teacher who teaches general music and orchestra in a large, diverse, suburban district in a mid-Atlantic urban center. In the summer of 2018, she was transitioning to a new school within the same district. In her 2017–2018 position there was no course specifically called general music, but the school offered a full-year guitar course and a semester-long digital music elective. Jessica was instrumental in creating the guitar class, which surveys various musical styles including mariachi, flamenco, Irish folk, American folk, and pop. During 2018–2019, Jessica taught band and orchestra as well as a quarterly rotation general music elective.

Katie teaches general music, drama, and choir at a large suburban school district in New England. At her Title 1 6–8 school, there is wide economic disparity based on student home neighborhood. She is in her thirteenth year as a teacher and holds a master's, rather than a bachelor's degree in music education. General music is taken for a quarter of the year by all students in the school for four days of a six-day schedule, typically 25 days total. The general music curriculum focuses on developing various musical skills through instruments and composition. While she has taught all general music courses offered at her school, Katie primarily teaches the popular music instruments and composition-focused 8th grade general music course.

Lindsey teaches choir and sixth through eighth grade general music at a 6–8 school in a small preK-8 suburban district outside a major urban center in the Midwest. She has been a teacher for twelve years, nearly all of them at her current school. Her school has a high first- and second-generation immigrant population and a high poverty rate. At her school, general music is taught on a rotation with other elective courses: sixth graders receive 12 weeks while seventh and eighth graders receive 6 weeks. All classes are 45 minutes in length, and she teaches all students in the school each year. In sixth grade, the curriculum is a survey of topics including composition, jazz, and musicals, seventh grade focuses on world music drumming, while eighth grade focuses on guitar and cover songs. During 2017–2018, she piloted a new project with the STEM teacher where seventh grade students built ukuleles using found objects.

Nicole teaches sixth through eighth grade general music and choir in a small rural district in a Mid-Atlantic state. Her school recently added fifth grade to the sixth through eighth grade building and the student population is predominantly white. She is in her fifth year teaching middle level general music. In her 11-year career, she taught high school music, elementary general music, and instrumental music in various configurations. Her current general music classes are taught on a related arts wheel rotation format of 75-minute periods for 20 days. In sixth grade, the curriculum surveys musical cultures around the world through instruments, in seventh grade students learn basic piano and ukulele skills, and in eighth grade the curriculum focuses on guitar.

Robert teaches a combined 7th and 8th grade general music class along with band, orchestra, and choir at a 6–8 arts-focused school in a college town in a Western state. He is a 20-year veteran teacher who completed his master's degree before he started teaching. Robert took this position because he was interested in developing the general music curriculum from the ground up; he has worked his entire career at his current school. The school district serves a diverse population and has open-enrollment, but the students do not apply to attend the arts-focused middle school. Students self-select general music, called "Music Focus," as a music elective in addition to their ensemble participation. The curriculum focuses on ethnomusicology and a project-based approach to music composition. Robert sees his general music class for one class period every day for the entire school year. Many of the students enrolled in Robert's general music class are students designated as gifted and talented.

Tyler teaches second through eighth grade general music as well as band and choir at a preK-8 Catholic academy. His school, in a Mid-Atlantic urban center, serves a primarily minority immigrant population. Tyler is a second career teacher who recently completed alternate route certification through a master's degree program. His previous careers included working as a performing rock musician and curriculum designer for an educational publisher. After working at a Montessori school, he joined the faculty of his current school five years ago in part to pursue licensure. He recently completed level two of the Kodály certification. His performing career heavily influences his middle level general music (5–8), which focuses on composition, guitar, piano, and singing. Beginning in fifth grade, students are required to take general music two times per week for one trimester.

References

Abrahams, F. (2005). Singing in middle school general music classes. In S. L. Burton (Ed.), *Engaging musical practices: A sourcebook for middle school general music* (pp. 31–47). Lanham, MD: Rowman & Littlefield Publishers.

Abril, C. R. (2016). Untangling general music education: Concept, aims, and practice. In C. R. Abril & B. M. Gault (Eds.), *Teaching general music: Approaches, issues, and viewpoints* (pp. 5–22). New York, NY: Oxford University Press.

Akos, P., Charles, P., Orthner, D., & Cooley, V. (2011). Teacher perspectives on career-relevant curriculum in middle school. *RMLE Online: Research in Middle Level Education Online, 34*(5), 1–9.

Allsup, R. E. (2016). *Remixing the classroom: Toward an open philosophy of music education*. Bloomington, IN: Indiana University Press.

Arhar, J. M. (2013). Interdisciplinary teaming: A context for learning. In P. G. Andrews (Ed.), *Research to guide practice in middle grades education* (pp. 615–632). Westerville, OH: Association for Middle Level Education.

Armstrong, T. (2010). *Neurodiversity: Discovering the extraordinary gifts of autism, ADHD, dyslexia, and other brain differences*. Cambridge, MA: DaCapo Press.

Barrett, J. R. (2016). Adopting an interdisciplinary approach to general music. In C. R. Abril & B. M. Gault (Eds.), *Teaching general music: Approaches, issues, and viewpoints* (pp. 168–182). New York, NY: Oxford University Press.

Barrett, J. R., McCoy, C. W., & Veblen, K. K. (1997). *Sound ways of knowing: Music in the interdisciplinary curriculum*. New York, NY: Schirmer Books.

Barrett, M. S., & Stauffer, S. L. (2009). Introduction. In M. S. Barrett & S. L. Stauffer (Eds.), *Narrative inquiry in music education: Troubling Certainty* (pp. 1–4). New York, NY: Springer.

Barrett, M. S., & Stauffer, S. L. (2012). Resonant work: Toward an ethic of narrative research. In M. S. Barret & S. L. Stauffer (Eds.), *Narrative soundings: An anthology of narrative inquiry in music education* (pp. 1–17). New York, NY: Springer.

Beane, J. A. (1993). *A middle school curriculum: From rhetoric to reality* (2nd ed.). Columbus, OH: National Middle School Association.

Bell, A. P. (2014). Guitars have disabilities: Exploring guitar adaptations for an adolescent with Down syndrome. *British Journal of Music Education, 31*(3), 343–357.

Bergonzi, L. S. (2015). Gender and sexual diversity challenges (for socially just) music education. In C. Benedict, P. Schmidt, G. Spruce, & Paul Woodford (Eds.), *The Oxford handbook of social justice in music education* (pp. 221–237). New York, NY: Oxford University Press.

Bishop, P. A., & Downes, J. M. (2013). Technology in the middle grades classroom. In P. G. Andrews (Ed.), *Research to guide practice in middle grades education* (pp. 267–302). Westerville, OH: Association for Middle Level Education.

Bishop, P., Falk-Ross, F., Andrews, G., Cronenberg, S., Moran, C., & Weiler, C. (2018). Digital technologies literature review. In S. B. Mertens & M. M. Caskey (Eds.), *Literature reviews in support of the middle level education research agenda* (pp. 175–200). Charlotte, NC: Information Age Publishing.

Bishop, P. A., & Harrison, L. M. (2021). *The successful middle school: This we believe*. Columbus, OH: Association for Middle Level Education (AMLE).

Bradley, D. (2015). Hidden in plain sight: Race and racism in music education. In C. Benedict, P. Schmidt, G. Spruce, & P. Woodford (Eds.), *The Oxford handbook of social justice in music education* (pp. 190–203). New York, NY: Oxford University Press.

Brazee, E. N. (2005). The middle school concept. In V. A. Anfara, Jr., G. Andrews, & S. B. Mertens (Eds.), *The encyclopedia of middle grades education* (pp. 283-286). Columbus, OH: National Middle School Association.

Brinthaupt, T. M., Haupt, S. B., Lipka, R., Robison, J. A. (2020). Middle level teachers' education technology use: Challenges, barriers, and successes. In S. L. Stacki, M. M. Caskey, & S. B. Mertens (Eds.), *Curriculum, instruction, and assessment: Intersecting new needs and new approaches* (pp. 223-245). Charlotte, NC: Information Age Publishing.

Bruner, J. (1960). *The process of education*. Cambridge, MA: Harvard University Press.

Burrak, F., & Parkes, K. A. (2020). Assessment across a K-12 school music program. In Parkes, K. A. & F. Burrack (Eds.), *Developing and applying assessments in the music classroom* (pp. 27-44). New York, NY: Routledge.

Burton, S. L. (Ed.), (2012). *Engaging musical practices: A sourcebook for middle school general music*. Lanham, MD: Rowman & Littlefield Education.

Bush, J. M. (2017). *The relationship between active and passive music activities and students' on-task behaviors in fifth-grade general music class (Doctoral dissertation)*. Retrieved from ProQuest Dissertations and Theses database (UMI No. 10702622).

Campbell, D. L. (2009). *Relationships among middle school students' music possible self beliefs and their music participation* (Doctoral dissertation). Retrieved from ProQuest Dissertations and Theses database (UMI No. 3380884).

Campbell, P. S. (2004). *Teaching music globally*. New York, NY: Oxford University Press.

Campbell, P. S. (2005). Deep listening to the musical world. *Music Educators Journal, 92*(1), 30-36.

Campbell, P. S. (2016). World music pedagogy: Where music meets culture in classroom practice. In C. R. Abril, & B. M. Gault (Eds.), *Teaching general music: Approaches, issues, and viewpoints* (pp. 89-111). New York, NY: Oxford University Press.

Carolan, B. V., & Chesky, N. Z. (2012). The relationship among grade configuration, school attachment, and achievement. *Middle School Journal, 43*(4), 32-39.

CAST. (2018). Universal Design for Learning Guidelines version 2.2. Retrieved from http://udlguidelines.cast.org

Claravall, E. B., & Irey, R. (2020). Historical thinking in the middle school classroom: Integration of authentic curriculum, instruction, and assessment. In S. L. Stackie, M. M. Caskey, & S. B. Mertens (Eds.), *Curriculum, instruction, and assessment: Intersecting new needs and new approaches* (pp. 31-53). Charlotte, NC: Information Age Publishing.

Cronenberg, S. (2016). *Music at the middle: Principles that guide middle level general music teachers* (Doctoral dissertation). Retrieved from ProQuest Dissertations & Theses Global (UMI No. 1857495335).

Cronenberg, S. (2020a). Music teachers' perceptions of general music as a required middle level course. *RMLE Online: Research in Middle Level Online, 43*(9), 1-24.

Cronenberg, S. (2020b). Rethinking middle level general music: Five democratic principles to enhance student engagement. *Tempo, 74*(3), 28-31.

Cushman, K., & Rogers, L. (2008). *Fires in the middle school bathroom: Advice for teachers from middle schoolers*. New York, NY: The New Press.

Daniels, E. (2010). Creating motivating learning environments: What we can learn from researchers and students. *The English Journal, 100*(1), 25-29.

Davis, V. W. (2011). What middle school students need from their general music class (and how we can help). *General Music Today, 24*(3), 17-22.

Deci, E. L., & Ryan, R. M. (1985). *Intrinsic motivation and self-determination in human behavior*. New York, NY: Plenum.

DeLorenzo, L. C. (2016). Introduction. In L. S. DeLorenzo (Ed.), *Giving voice to democracy in music education: Diversity and social justice* (pp. 1-9). New York, NY: Routledge.

Delpit, L. (1995). *Other people's children: Cultural conflict in the classroom*. New York, NY: The New Press.

DeMink-Carthew, J., & DeMink, J. (2016). "Hands-joined" projects: A framework for co-developing projects with teachers and students. *AMLE Magazine, 4*(3), 34-38.

DeMink-Carthew, J., & Olofson, M. W. (2020). Hands-joined learning as a framework for personalizing project-based learning in a middle grades classroom: An exploratory study. *RMLE Online: Research in Middle Level Education, 43*(2), 1-17.

Dewey, J. (1916). *Democracy and education: An introduction to the philosophy of education*. New York, NY: Macmillan Publishers.

Dewey, J. (1938/1998). *Experience and education*. New York, NY: The MacMillan Company.

Dunbar-Hall, P., & Wemyss, K. (2000). The effects of the study of popular music on music education. *International Journal of Music Education, 36*(1), 23-34.

Eisner, E. W. (2002). *The arts and the creation of mind*. New Haven, CT: Yale University Press.

Elliott, D. J. (2016). Artistic citizenship, personhood, and music education. In L. S. DeLorenzo (Ed.), *Giving voice to democracy in music education: Diversity and social justice* (pp. 13-35). New York, NY: Routledge.

Elliott, D. J., & Silverman, M. (2015). *Music matters: A philosophy of music education* (2nd ed.). New York, NY: Oxford University Press.

Erion, C. (n.d.). *Humming and Whooping* [Vocal Score] (self-published). Retrieved from the University of Missouri, Kansas City library.

Gadamer, H. G., Weinsheimer, J. & Marshall, D. G. (2004). *Truth and method*. London, England: Continuum International.

Gay, G. (1994). Coming of age ethnically: Teaching young adolescents of color. *Theory into practice*, *33*(3), 149-155.

Giebelhausen, R. (2015). In the beginning of the middle: Curriculum considerations for middle school general music. *General Music Today*, *29*(1), 41-45.

Glover, E. A., & Zwemke, B. D. (2016). Interdisciplinary team organization. In S. B. Mertens, M. M. Caskey, & N. Flowers (Eds.), *The encyclopedia of middle grades education* (2nd ed.). Charlotte, NC: Information Age Publishing.

Grant, M. M., & Branch, R. M. (2005). Project-based learning in a middle school: Tracing abilities through the artifacts of learning. *Journal of Research on Technology in Education*, *38*(1), 65-98.

Green, L. (2002). *How popular musicians learn*. Aldershot: Ashgate Publishing.

Green, L. (2006). Popular music education in and for itself, and for 'other' music: Current research in the classroom. *International Journal of Music Education*, *24*(2), 101-118.

Green, L. (2008). *Music, informal learning and the school: A new classroom pedagogy*. Surrey: Ashgate Publishing.

Greene, M. (1995). *Releasing the imagination: Essays on education, the arts, and social change*. San Francisco, CA: Jossey-Bass.

Greene, M. (2001). *Variations on a blue guitar: The Lincoln Center Institute lectures on aesthetic education*. New York, NY: Teachers College Press.

Haldeman, E. (1988). General music–What is it? In MENC (Ed.), *Readings in general music: Selected reprints from Soundings, a publication of the Society for General Music, 1982-1987* (pp. 2-4). Reston, VA: MENC, Music Educators National Conference.

Hamann, K. L. (2007). Influence on the curriculum choices of middle school choir teachers. *Update: Applications of Research in Music Education*, *26*(1), 64-74.

Harrison, L. M., Hurd, E., & Brinegar, K. M. (2019). Exploring the convergence of developmentalism and cultural responsiveness. In K. Brinegar, L. Harrison, & E. Hurd (Eds.), *Equity & cultural responsiveness in the middle grades* (pp. 3-21). Charlotte, NC: Information Age Publishing, Inc.

Hedden, D. G. (2002). A philosophy of general music. *General Music Today*, *16*(1), 1-5.

Hickey, M. (2012). *Music outside the lines: Ideas for composing in K-12 music classrooms*. New York, NY: Oxford University Press.

Hinckley, J. M., & Shull, S. M. (Eds.). (1996). *Strategies for teaching middle-level general music*. Reston, VA: MENC, The National Association for Music Education.

Hoffman, M. E. (1981). The heart of the school music program. *Music Educators Journal*, *68*(1), 42-43.

Individuals with Disabilities Education Act (IDEA). (2004). https://sites.ed.gov/idea/statuteregulations/

Isbell, D. (2007). Popular music and the public school curriculum. *Update: Applications of Research in Music Education*, *26*(1), 53-63.

Jagla, V. M. (2016). Service learning. In S. B. Mertens, M. M. Caskey, & N. Flowers (Eds.), *The encyclopedia of middle grades education* (2nd ed., pp. 346-349). Charlotte, NC: Information Age Publishing.

Kennedy, M. A. (2002). Listening to the music: Compositional processes of high school composers. *Journal of Research in Music Education*, *50*(2), 94-110.

Kilpatrick, W. H. (1936). *Remaking the curriculum*. New York, NY: Newson & Company.

Kruse, A. J. (2016). Being hip-hop: Beyond skills and songs. *General Music Today*, *30*(1), 53-58.

Kuhn, D. (2009). Adolescent thinking. In R. M. Lerner, & L. D. Steinberg (Eds.), *Handbook of adolescent psychology* (3rd ed., volume 1, pp. 152-186). Hoboken, NJ: John Wiley & Sons.

Ladson-Billings, G. (1995). But that's just good teaching! The case for culturally relevant pedagogy. *Theory into Practice*, *34*(3), 159-165.

Lenhart, A. (2015). *Teens, social media, and technology overview 2015: Smartphones facilitate shifts in communication landscape for teens*. Pew Research Center. Retrieved from https://www.pewresearch.org/internet/2015/04/09/introduction-teens-tech/

Louk, D. P. (2002). *National standards for music education: General music teachers' attitudes and practices* (Doctoral dissertation). Retrieved from ProQuest Dissertations & Theses Global (UMI No. 3042585).

Lounsbury, J. H. (2009). Deferred but not deterred: A middle school manifesto. *Middle School Journal, 40*(5), 31-36.

Lucas, M. (2011). Adolescent male attitudes about singing in choir. *Update: Applications of Research in Music Education, 30*(1), 46-53.

McAnally, E. A. (2016). *Middle school general music: The best part of your day* (2nd ed.). Lanham, MD: Rowman & Littlefield Publishing.

McDowell, C. (2010). An adaptation tool kit for teaching music. *Teaching Exceptional Children Plus, 6*(3), 2-20.

McEwin, C. K., & Greene, M. W. (2011). *The status of programs and practices in America's middle schools: Results from two national studies*. Westerville, OH: Association for Middle Level Education.

Mee, M., & Haverback, H. R. (2016). Young adolescent development. In S. B. Mertens, M. M. Caskey, & N. Flowers (Eds.), *The encyclopedia of middle grades education* (2nd ed., pp. 437-440). Charlotte, NC: Information Age Publishing.

Menard, E. (2013). Creative thinking in music: Developing a model for meaningful learning middle school general music. *Music Educators Journal, 100*(2), 61-67.

Menard, E. A. & Rosen, R. (2016). Preservice music teacher perceptions of mentoring young composers: An exploratory case study. *Journal of Music Teacher Education, 25*(2), 66-80.

MENC. (1994). *National standards for arts education: What every young American should know and be able to do in the arts*. Lanham, MD: Rowman & Littlefield Education.

Michelli, N. M., & Jacobowitz, T. (2016). Why do we educate in a democracy?: Implications for music education. In L. S. DeLorenzo (Ed.), *Giving voice to democracy in music education: Diversity and social justice* (pp. 36-50). New York, NY: Routledge.

Milner, H.R. IV., Cunningham, H. B., Delale-O'Connor, L., & Kestenberg, E.G. (2019). *"These kids are out of control": Why we must reimagine "classroom management" for equity*. Thousand Oaks, CA: Corwin.

Moon, T. R., Brighton, C. M., Callahan, C. M., & Robinson, A. (2005). Development of authentic assessments for the middle school classroom. *The Journal of Secondary Gifted Education, 16*(2/3), 119-133.

Morris, R. (2009). *Managing sound sensitivity in Autism Spectrum Disorder: New technologies for customized intervention* [Unpublished master's thesis]. Massachusetts Institute of Technology.

Nakkula, M. J., & Toshalis, E. (2006). *Understanding youth: Adolescent development for educators*. Cambridge, MA: Harvard Education Press.

National Middle School Association (NMSA). (2010). *This we believe: Keys to educating young adolescents*. Westerville, OH: NMSA.

O'Neill, M. (1990). *Hailstones and halibut bones*. New York, NY: Delacorte Press.

Parkes, K. A. (2018). Model cornerstone assessments. In F. Burrack, & K. A. Parkes (Eds.), *Applying model cornerstone assessments in K-12 music: A research-supported approach* (pp. 1-7). Lanham, MD: Rowman & Littlefield.

Pautz, M. (2010). Both performance and informance: Not "either-or" in elementary general music. *General Music Today, 23*(3), 20-26.

Regelski, T. A. (2004). *Teaching general music in grades 4-8: A musicianship approach*. New York, NY: Oxford University Press.

Rockoff, J. E., & Lockwood, B. B. (2010). Stuck in the middle: How and why middle schools harm student achievement. *Education Next, 10*(4), 68-75.

Roney, K. (2005). Young adolescent development. In V. A. Anfara, Jr., G. Andrews, & S. B. Mertens (Eds.) *The encyclopedia of middle grades education* (pp. 397-401). Westerville, OH: National Middle School Association.

Saunders, J. A. (2010). Identity in music: Adolescents in the music classroom. *Action, Criticism, and Theory for Music Education, 9*(2), 70-78.

Schaefer, M. B., & Rivera, L. M. (2016). College and career readiness. In S. B. Mertens, M. M. Caskey, & N. Flowers (Eds.), *The encyclopedia of middle grades education* (2nd ed., pp. 94-97). Charlotte, NC: Information Age Publishing.

Schön, D. A. (1983). *The reflective practitioner: How professionals think in action*. New York, NY: Basic Books.

Scott, S. (2011). Contemplating a constructivist stance for active learning within music education. *Arts Education Policy Review, 112*(4), 191-198.

Seidman, I. (2013). *Interviewing as qualitative research: A guide for researchers in education and the social sciences* (4th ed.). New York, NY: Teachers College Press.

Shabani, K., Khatib, M., & Ebadi, S. (2010). Vygotsky's Zone of Proximal Development: Instructional implications and teachers' professional development. *English Language Teaching, 3*(4), 237-248.

Shuler, S. C., Norgaard, M., & Blakeslee, M. J. (2014). The new national standards for music educators. *Music Educators Journal, 101*(1), 41-49.

Silverstein, L. B., & Layne, S. (2010). *Defining arts integration*. The Kennedy Center ArtsEdge. Retrieved from https://www.kennedy-center.org/education/resources-for-educators/classroom-resources/articles-and-hot-tos/articles/collections/arts-integration-resources/what-is-arts-integration/

Silvestri, J., Ehrenberg, H., Dick, L., & Shim, P. (2018). Universal design for music: Exploring the intersection of deaf education and music education. *Journal of American Sign Languages & Literatures*. Retrieved August 7, 2020, from https://journalofasl.com/universal-design/

State Education Agency Directors of Arts Education (SEADAE). (2014a). *National Core Arts Standards*. Dover, DE: SEADAE. Retrieved from https://www.nationalartsstandards.org/

State Education Agency Directors of Arts Education (SEADAE). (2014b). National Core Arts Standards: A Conceptual Framework [PDF file]. Dover, DE: SEADAE. Retrieved from https://www.nationalartsstandards.org/content/national-core-arts-standards

State Education Agency Directors of Arts Education (SEADAE). (2014c). National Core Arts Standards: Music [PDF file]. Dover, DE: SEADAE. Retrieved from http://www.nationalartsstandards.org/sites/default/files/Music%20at%20a%20Glance%20rev%2012-1-16.pdf

Stauffer, S. L., & Saunders, T. C. (1992). The middle school model and general music. *General Music Today, 6*(1), 6-10.

Stevenson, C. (2002). *Teaching ten to fourteen year olds* (3rd ed.). Boston, MA: Allyn & Bacon.

Strand, K. (2006). Survey of Indiana music teachers on using composition in the classroom. *Journal of Research in Music Education, 54*(2), 154-167.

Sweet, B. (2010). A case study: Middle school boys' perceptions of singing and participation in choir. *Update: Applications of Research in Music Education, 28*(2), 5-12.

Sweet, B. (2016). *Growing musicians: Teaching music in middle school & beyond*. New York, NY: Oxford University Press.

Sweet, B. (2020). *Thinking outside the voice box: Adolescent voice change in music education*. New York, NY: Oxford University Press.

Thompson, D. E. (2011). Speaking their language: Guitar tablature in the middle school classroom. *General Music Today, 24*(3), 53-57.

Thompson, K. F. (2013). Service learning: connecting curriculum to community. In P. G. Andrews (Ed.), *Research to guide practice in middle grades education* (pp. 247-265). Westerville, OH: Association for Middle Level Education.

Tomlinson, C. A. (2013). Differentiating instruction as a response to academic diversity. In P. G. Andrews (Ed.), *Research to guide practice in middle grades education* (pp. 217-246). Westerville, OH: Association for Middle Level Education.

Vagle, M. D., & Hamel, T. M. (2019). Missed opportunities, no more. In K. Brinegar, L. Harrison, & E. Hurd (Eds.), *Equity & cultural responsiveness in the middle grades* (pp. 23-43). Charlotte, NC: Information Age Publishing, Inc.

Valencia, R. R. (1997). *The evolution of deficit thinking: Educational thought and practice*. Washington, DC: Falmer Press.

Valentine, J. W., Clark, D. C., & Clark, S. N. (2016). Middle level education: Origin of the term. In S. B. Mertens, M. M. Caskey, & N. Flowers (Eds.), *The encyclopedia of middle grades education* (2nd ed., pp. 254-256). Charlotte, NC: Information Age Publishing.

Vygotsky, L. S. (1978). *Mind in society: The development of higher psychological processes*. Cambridge, MA: Harvard University Press.

Wall, M. P., & Wall, J. K. (2016). Artistic citizenship, personhood, and music education. In L. S. DeLorenzo (Ed.), *Giving voice to democracy in music education: Diversity and social justice* (pp. 123-137). New York, NY: Routledge.

Waring, S. M., & Robinson, K. S. (2010). Developing critical and historical thinking skills in middle grades social studies. *Middle School Journal, 42*(1), 22-28.

Wiggins, G., & McTighe, J. (2005). *Understanding by design* (2nd ed.). Alexandria, VA: Association for Supervision and Curriculum Development.

Wiggins, J. (2007). Compositional process in music. In L. Bresler (Ed.), *International handbook of research in arts education* (pp. 453-470). Dordrecht, Netherlands: Springer.

Wiggins, J. (2015). *Teaching for musical understanding* (3rd ed.). New York, NY: Oxford University Press.

Wiggins, J. (2016). Teaching music with a social constructivist vision of learning. In C. R. Abril & B. M. Gault (Eds.), *Teaching general music: Approaches, issues, and viewpoints*. New York, NY: Oxford University Press.

Wineburg, S. (2001). *Historical thinking and other unnatural acts: Charting the future of teaching the past*. Philadelphia, PA: Temple University Press.

Wineburg. S. (2007). Unnatural and essential: The nature of historical thinking. *Teaching History, 129*, 6-11.

Woodford, P. G. (2005). *Democracy and music education: Liberalism, ethics, and the politics of practice.* Bloomington, IN: Indiana University Press.

Yoon, B., & Uliassi, C. (2019). Educators' practice for English language learners' critical consciousness: From marginalized identities to active agents. In K. Brinegar, L. Harrison, & E. Hurd (Eds.), *Equity & cultural responsiveness in the middle grades* (pp. 239-253). Charlotte, NC: Information Age Publishing, Inc.

Zaffini, E. D. (2015). Using "informances" in general music. *General Music Today, 28*(2), 13-17.

Zaffini, E. D. (2018). A deeper glimpse into the national core arts standards for general music. *General Music Today, 31*(3), 57-60.

About the Author

Stephanie Cronenberg is Assistant Professor of Music and Director of Clinical Experience and Practice at Mason Gross School of the Arts at Rutgers, The State University of New Jersey, where she teaches undergraduate courses in music education and graduate courses in research and pedagogy. Stephanie earned her PhD in Curriculum and Instruction from the University of Illinois at Urbana-Champaign. She previously taught 4th–8th grade general music in Maryland and Illinois and served as the Director of Education and Community Programs for The Choral Arts Society of Washington in DC. Her research interests include middle level general music, teacher experiences of practice, narrative and mixed methods research methods, and preservice music teacher education.

Index

Note: Page numbers in *italics* refer to figures. Page numbers followed by "n" refer to notes. Music teacher-participants are indexed under their first name pseudonym to reflect the way they are referred to throughout the text.

9780367643775